BREAKTHROUGH PRINCIPALS

Jean Desravines
Jaime Aquino
Benjamin Fenton
with Lori Taliaferro Riddick and Jill Grossman

BREAKTHROUGH PRINCIPALS

A Step-by-Step Guide to Building Stronger Schools

A Wiley Brand

Published by Jossey-Bass

A Wiley Brand

One Montgomery Street, Suite 1000, San Francisco, CA 94104-4594 — www.josseybass.com

Jossey-Bass books and products are available through most bookstores. To contact Jossey-Bass directly call our Customer Care Department within the U.S. at 800-956-7739, outside the U.S. at 317-572-3986, or fax 317-572-4002.

Wiley publishes in a variety of print and electronic formats and by print-on-demand. Some material included with standard print versions of this book may not be included in e-books or in print-on-demand. If this book refers to media such as a CD or DVD that is not included in the version you purchased, you may download this material at http://booksupport.wiley.com. For more information about Wiley products, visit **www.wiley.com**.

Library of Congress Cataloging-in-Publication Data Available at:

ISBN 978-1-118-80117-8 (Paperback)
ISBN 978-1-118-80097-3 (ePDF)
ISBN 9781-1-188-0100-0 (ePUB)

Cover design: Wiley

Cover image: © Kadir Barcin/Getty Images, Inc.

Printed in the United States of America

FIRST EDITION

PB Printing SKY10031306_110821

CONTENTS

For all the transformational school leaders with whom we have worked, who have inspired and informed us about what is truly possible for all children

ABOUT THE AUTHORS

Jean Desravines serves as chief executive officer of New Leaders, an innovative school reform organization that develops and supports highly effective leaders to turn around the nation's high-need public schools. He has more than fifteen years of leadership experience in education and community development, with a primary focus on improving outcomes for students in underserved communities. Before joining New Leaders, Jean served as senior counselor to the chancellor of New York City's public school system, the executive director for the Office of Parent and Community Engagement, chief of staff to the senior counselor for Education Policy, and director for Community Relations at the New York City Department of Education.

Jean serves as a board member for 100Kin10; America Achieves; his alma mater, St. Francis College; and St. Benedict's College Prep in Newark, New Jersey. He served on Governor Andrew M. Cuomo's Education Reform Commission and was been named to Forbes's Impact 30, recognizing the world's leading social entrepreneurs. Jean received a BA in history from St. Francis College and a Master's degree in Public Administration from New York University.

Jaime Aquino is the chief program officer for New Leaders. In this role, he oversees the design, development, and delivery for the organization's core programs, ensuring that participants acquire the essential leadership skills needed to build vibrant schools and advance student achievement. Prior to joining New Leaders, he held leadership positions in several major school districts, including deputy executive director for the Division of Instructional Support and local instructional superintendent for New York City, deputy superintendent of instruction for Los Angeles Unified School District, chief academic officer in Denver, and deputy superintendent in Hartford, Connecticut.

Jaime holds a PhD in curriculum and teaching from Fordham University. In 1990 he was named New York State Bilingual Teacher of the Year. In addition, he was featured in the videotape series Approaching the Vision of the National Council of Teachers of Mathematics (NCTM) Standards: A Videotape Series for Teacher Development.

Benjamin Fenton is cofounder and chief strategy officer at New Leaders. A recognized expert on the quality of principals, Ben leads New Leaders' human capital consulting initiatives, helping states and districts develop new policies and practices for principal evaluation and effectiveness. He is also responsible for the ongoing implementation of the New Leaders research agenda and programmatic evaluation. He co-led the development of New Leaders' Transformational Leadership Framework, identifying the school practices and principal actions found in high-gaining, high-poverty public schools.

Ben was a founding board member of Teach Plus, a nonprofit dedicated to retaining and developing great teachers who improve student achievement. He formerly worked as a consultant at McKinsey & Company, focusing on marketing and operational efficiency. Ben is a graduate of Harvard College and the Harvard Business School, where he received the Fiske award for excellence in teaching in the Economics Department.

Lori Taliaferro Riddick is executive director of leadership development for Cleveland Metropolitan School District (CMSD). In this role, she supports academic superintendents and aspiring academic superintendents by building individual and team capacity, facilitating successful implementation of the network and investment school strategy, and assessing the effectiveness and impact of each principal supervisor's work.

Prior to her work with CMSD, Lori was the executive director of policy and practice services at New Leaders. In that role, she managed the qualitative research project to identify the principal actions and school practices in schools that were realizing dramatic achievement gains, resulting in the Transformational Leadership Framework. Lori also developed and implemented evaluation tools for new principals and systems for multiple school districts, including the New Orleans Recovery School District and Newark Public Schools, and states, including Illinois and Louisiana. Based on these experiences, Lori created the New Leaders principal evaluation rubric as an example for other states and districts to use or adapt.

Lori received a BA in urban studies and an MS in education from the University of Pennsylvania.

Jill Grossman is a writer and researcher for New Leaders. She has conducted research for school districts and nonprofit organizations on principal training programs, school autonomy, and teacher teams. Before working in education policy, Jill spent fifteen years as an editor and writer for New York City news outlets, including *City Limits* magazine, insideschools.org, and a number of community newspapers. Her work examined the challenges and achievements that urban communities experience, particularly around housing, homelessness, schools, and politics.

Jill has taught graduate and undergraduate courses in journalism at New York University and Columbia University. As a GED teacher at community-based organizations and colleges, she created curricula that pushed her students to think, read, and write critically, and this curricular work was featured in the *New York Times*. She also served as president of the board of directors of a Montessori preschool in Brooklyn. Jill holds a master's degree in education policy from Teachers College, Columbia University, and a BA from Vassar College.

ABOUT NEW LEADERS

New Leaders ↗ Founded in 2000 by a team of social entrepreneurs, New Leaders is a national nonprofit that develops transformational school leaders and designs effective leadership policies and practices for school systems across the country. Research shows, and our experience confirms, that strong school leaders have a powerful multiplier effect, dramatically improving the quality of teaching and raising student achievement in a school. We have trained more than sixteen hundred leaders nationwide and have affected over 350,000 students. Students in New Leaders schools consistently achieve at higher levels than their peers, have higher high school graduation rates, and are making progress in closing the achievement gap. As New Leaders enters its second decade, we are broadening our work in order to reach more students with greater impact. Beyond training new principals, we are now developing transformative leaders throughout schools and school systems—from teacher leaders and assistant principals to veteran principals and district supervisors. We are also working with school systems to build the kinds of policies and practices that allow strong leaders to succeed in driving academic excellence for students.

PART ONE
DIAGNOSING YOUR SCHOOL'S STAGES OF DEVELOPMENT

Introduction

Chapter One
The Stages of School Development

Chapter Two
Diagnosis and Action Planning

INTRODUCTION

AS A RECENT GRADUATE OF THE NEW LEADERS PRINCIPAL TRAINING PROGRAM, Janeece Docal was excited about her next step as the new principal of Powell Elementary School in Washington, DC. Thrilled to be working in a community where she had previously taught—some of the elementary school parents had been her students when they were in high school—Docal also had real trepidation given what she knew about the school. Powell had been labeled as "failing" for more than two years and had recently cycled through a number of principals. Parents were concerned about whether the school was meeting the needs of their children, almost all of them first-generation Americans. Before Docal started, they protested a district proposal to close the school; they wanted a good neighborhood school where they could be actively engaged and know that the many Spanish speakers in their ranks would be supported. They wanted a community school that worked.

Docal knew she needed to lead a dramatic transformation so that the school could deliver the outstanding education its students deserved. The big question was where to begin. She could focus on only a few priorities at once, but everything was essential. She knew she needed to first focus on areas that would deliver the greatest benefit for the students.

To find her answers, she spoke with staff, parents, and community members, asking what they hoped for the school's future, what was working well at Powell, and what needed to change. She and her staff also examined a variety of data, asking themselves: "What does a scholar leaving Powell need to know and be able to do?" The answers formed the basis for a shared vision for the school's future. Working backward from that vision, Docal's team looked at what practices the school already had in place that would advance that vision and what high-impact actions they could take to help the school improve in areas where it was falling short.

They created a school improvement plan centered on three priorities: increasing the rigor of curriculum and assessments, improving family engagement, and setting up students for social-emotional success. Docal developed a program that welcomed families into the school and increased parent involvement both inside and outside classrooms.

She and her staff designed an instructional program centered on project-based learning that aligned with local learning standards but also engaged students in ways that inspired their curiosity and pushed them to study topics in depth and from interdisciplinary perspectives. She also built time into the schedule for teachers to regularly collaborate on refining lessons and curriculum based on how students were doing and where they needed extra support.

Underlying all of this work was Docal's deep conviction that all students could perform at high levels if they were given the right supports and if the school fostered a culture of continuous improvement for children and adults alike.

These changes bore fruit almost immediately. Powell experienced dramatic student achievement gains, including a 14 percent increase in reading scores in her first year and a 16 percent increase in math scores in her second. The school's halls are clean, bright, and lined with dynamic classrooms. It is not unusual to see parents in the building, and Docal even initiated staff visits to student homes, a strategy that effectively eliminated chronic truancy at the school.

With those changes in place, both teachers and parents came to trust Docal and were inspired by the promise of the school's future. Said one parent, "She looked at the school not just from an academic standpoint, but very much as a whole community [with a focus on] involving teachers, students and parents."[1] Docal continued to make improvements in her initial priority areas while adding new initiatives such as a student leadership program.

By taking this systematic approach to school improvement, Docal and her staff transformed Powell from a school that many local families avoided to a model of what an excellent neighborhood school should look like, with an award-winning bilingual program. The student body has more than doubled in size from 200 to 450 students, and Powell now has a waiting list of families eager to enroll. Student proficiency in reading and writing nearly doubled, and math proficiency rose by one-third. Docal's transformative leadership was recognized when she was honored as the District of Columbia Public Schools Principal of the Year in 2014.

THE TRANSFORMATIONAL LEADERSHIP FRAMEWORK IN ACTION

In making these substantial improvements at Powell, Docal was bringing the Transformational Leadership Framework (TLF) to life. That framework, the focus of this book and published in full in our earlier book, *The School Leadership Playbook*, outlines a set of high-leverage actions great principals like Docal have taken to improve their schools. By breaking down these actions, the TLF provides a road map for leaders seeking to build vibrant schools where teachers and students work together to continuously improve their schools.

Principals can directly influence student achievement, but their greatest impact comes through establishing effective school practices and building a strong instructional culture. The TLF outlines the ideal sequence for implementing these proven practices, helping leaders understand what important steps to take first during the journey to sustained school improvement.

The TLF will help you assess the current state of your school and identify priority areas for improvement. By using this framework as part of your annual planning and improvement process, you can design a plan that builds on the school's distinctive strengths while also identifying and addressing its high-priority growth areas. After implementing that plan, you can use the TLF regularly to evaluate your plan's effectiveness, make adjustments, and begin the process anew. This is by no means a linear process, and it requires a balancing act of choosing and focusing on priority areas while maintaining all the other areas of your school. But by repeating this cycle, leaders can readily recalibrate priorities, looking to the TLF at every stage as they respond to their school's most pressing needs.

This is the approach Docal followed when she took the helm at Powell Elementary. She knew that the diagnosis she made using the TLF was not a judgment on her or her staff, but an opportunity to identify and enact the changes needed to better support students' learning. A national nonprofit that develops transformational school leaders and designs effective leadership policies and practices for school systems across the country, New Leaders prepares all of our principals to continuously assess and improve the schools they lead. Our principals work in diverse schools, large and small, charter and district, across all grade levels and in different areas of the country. No two schools are identical, but New Leaders encourages every school leader to regularly analyze where she or he needs to take the school next.

For the first time, *Breakthrough Principals* shares the strategies and actions that have enabled New Leaders' principals to deliver outsize gains for students with education leaders outside its own programs.[2] By providing tools that New Leaders–trained principals use, this book walks you through how to identify your school's needs, how to determine the most efficient and essential actions you and your staff can take to improve student learning at your school, and how you can best put those practices in place.

You probably already spend time reflecting on your school's strengths and weaknesses and making changes based on those reflections. However, the practices that will truly accelerate school improvement are not necessarily intuitive. In fact, the differences between what works and what doesn't were not always obvious to us. A few years into our work training principals and researching school leader practices, we noticed that school leaders with similar training, values, and approaches to leadership were delivering vastly different student outcomes. We wondered what principals whose schools were seeing sustained improvement were doing differently from their counterparts at schools achieving only incremental progress. We set out to answer this question, researching and documenting the high-leverage actions top principals were using to achieve consistent gains.

Through this research, we identified a set of common practices top principals put in place to improve their schools, regardless of school size, location, and student demographics. These actions enabled other members of their school communities to modify their own practices in ways that bolstered student learning. We have organized these actions taken by principals and other school stakeholders into five key categories: learning and teaching, school culture, talent management, planning and operations, and personal leadership. Together, they comprise the TLF as outlined in this book.

Presenting you with a framework of actions and wishing you well would not be the most effective way to share our learning. This book therefore provides concrete guidance for *how* to take these practices off the page and put them into action.

Breakthrough Principals includes a detailed set of tools and resources to support you as you use the framework to diagnose your school's needs and develop specific plans to address them. We also present vignettes to illustrate what these actions look like in an actual school setting. For example, we introduce you to an elementary school leader in Chicago who, after revamping his school's budgeting process, has enjoyed large annual surpluses that he has rededicated to implement structural and programmatic school improvements. You will meet a high school principal in Hayward, California, who, with his teachers, created a goal-setting system that has challenged students to learn at much higher levels, contributing to dramatically improved student achievement, college attendance, and college completion rates.

Our hope is that this book will help you to answer several important questions:

- How do I assess which of the framework's practices are already in place at my school?

- What leadership practices do I have in place to support all of my staff's efforts around improving student learning, and what leadership actions do I need to take to be better able to improve all aspects of my school?

- How do I identify which key actions to enact first?

- Once I have prioritized a few key actions to take, how do I do so most effectively?

- How do I determine which members of my staff can help me implement and monitor these practices?

- How can I support staff so that they are able to successfully monitor implementation of these practices and assess their effect on student learning?

- How do we determine when we are ready to put the next stage of practices in place to improve student learning even more?

Our goal is for the TLF to make your job more manageable and ensure that your school improvement strategy yields the results we all seek for our students: a robust and engaging education that prepares them for success in college, careers, and life.

WHY FOCUS ON THE WORK OF THE PRINCIPAL?

New Leaders was founded on the premise that schools will not be great without great leaders. Our work therefore focuses on developing and advocating for strong school leaders because we have seen firsthand that high-performing schools have a few things in common: strong core values, a clear mission, high expectations for staff and students, and an outstanding principal capable of advancing that vision. You probably wouldn't be reading this book if you didn't also believe in the central role principals can play in schools.

If you, as a leader, ever doubt the impact you can have on each student in your school, plenty of research confirms that great principals play an instrumental role in student success.[3] On average, a principal accounts for 25 percent of a school's total impact on student achievement,[4] second only to classroom teaching.[5] In fact, student achievement in schools led by principals with highly effective leadership practices can be as much as twenty points higher than at schools run by average-performing principals.[6] Strong leaders are even more essential when it comes to turning around persistently struggling schools: research shows that schools cannot reverse a long-standing pattern of poor performance without effective leadership in place.[7]

As principal, you are in a unique position to ensure that your school has a productive culture, rigorous instruction, and the right staff to enable students to excel. Some 97 percent of teachers have said that supportive leadership is essential for keeping good teachers in their school.[8]

Your leadership can inspire both students and educators to believe that every child can succeed with the right support and through hard work. You can accomplish this by establishing and maintaining systems that enable teachers to continuously improve their instruction, such as creating teacher teams and building regular time into the schedule for them to meet, collaborate, and innovate. You can cultivate other school leaders to support and reinforce your efforts to guide colleagues toward classroom excellence. And you can create a school climate that attracts, develops, and retains great teachers by giving them meaningful feedback and support to grow as educators and professionals.

New Leaders has spent the past fifteen years designing, implementing, and refining training to develop transformational leaders who apply these approaches to get results for students. This book shares the lessons we have learned to help educators across the field achieve similar success.

WHAT IS THE TRANSFORMATIONAL LEADERSHIP FRAMEWORK?

New Leaders developed the TLF to pinpoint the practices commonly found in schools that were significantly advancing student achievement and in what sequence principals and their teams implemented those practices to deliver consistently great outcomes for students. To develop the TLF, we conducted an extensive review of the research on the practices of effective schools, turnaround schools, secondary schools, and leadership. We found descriptions of excellence in high-poverty schools, but fewer data about how leaders transformed those schools over time into centers of excellence. We then visited more than one hundred schools across the country that had achieved rapid gains in student achievement (we refer to the principals at these schools as "effective" throughout the book) to determine what practices distinguished those schools from similar ones that were seeing only incremental gains. We looked at schools run by principals who had been trained by New Leaders, as well as a broader group of principals identified through the Effective Practice Incentive Community (EPIC) program, a grant-based research program intended to identify and share effective leadership practices in urban schools across the country.

We sought to answer a few key questions:

1.   What specific actions do principals of high-gaining schools take to improve student achievement?
2.   What specific actions do principals of high-gaining schools take to improve teacher effectiveness?
3.   What distinguishes principals of high-gaining schools from other principals?
4.   What school practices are evident in high-gaining schools?

Patterns quickly emerged, and it became clear what principals in high-gaining schools were doing to dramatically increase student achievement. As we have had other researchers study the framework, they have also found the TLF can help both new and experienced leaders develop schools centered on improving student achievement.

The TLF does this, researchers said, by giving a comprehensive overview of school leadership, looking not only at instructional practices but at some of the underlying conditions that affect student learning, particularly school culture and teacher collaboration.[9] The resulting framework presents a comprehensive overview of these actions.

Because New Leaders is an organization dedicated to serving schools with high percentages of low-income and minority students, two populations that have historically been ill served by public education, many of the example schools in this book were initially in significant need of improvement. A few were even designated as turnaround schools by their state or district at the time the principal came to the school. But we believe any principal at any school can use this book; even a thriving school can grow and improve. This is especially true in an era of rising expectations, where principals are charged with closing achievement gaps and meeting higher academic standards that prepare all students for college and careers. This book and the framework it presents will help you identify the few new practices that are likely to have the greatest impact in improving your school and ensuring that all students get what they need to succeed.

One point is important to keep in mind as you read. While we wanted to make sure that the schools we highlight in this book experienced tremendous success, the principals we highlight did a lot of things to improve student learning at their schools. In most vignettes, we focus on one particular practice that the principal put in place. However, when we give student achievement data to show how a school improved over time, we do not intend to suggest that any single practice yielded increased achievement. To deliver sustained improvement, each principal put multiple effective practices in place.

THE STRUCTURE OF THE TRANSFORMATIONAL LEADERSHIP FRAMEWORK

The TLF centers around five categories that effective schools focus on to achieve sustained school improvement:

- Learning and teaching
- School culture
- Talent management
- Planning and operations
- Personal leadership

In schools in which students achieve consistent academic growth, the categories do not stand alone; they function interdependently. The first two categories represent the two primary drivers of student achievement: rigorous goal- and data-driven learning and teaching and school culture organized around high expectations for staff and students alike. The learning and teaching category outlines content and instructional strategies to improve academic offerings and performance. The school culture category describes the values, expectations, and supports that allow students to develop confidence in their academic potential and achieve at a high level.

Two additional categories of a principal's work are essential to supporting this work. Talent management recognizes the essential role each staff member plays in creating and sustaining schoolwide change, and the planning and operations category comprises the logistical structures that advance the principal's vision and priorities.

Undergirding the success of the work in all of these categories are the practices that make up personal leadership. This category encompasses everything a successful principal does to set the tone for all student and adult relationships and practices in the school. Although it appears as the next-to-last chapter in this book, we cannot emphasize enough the importance of measuring your own actions as a leader against this outline of leadership practices. Effective leadership cannot be reduced to a single style or personality type, and the leadership skills we outline are not fixed but can be developed over time. The strongest principals we have met have many of these personal leadership practices in place. Their work around school culture, learning and teaching, talent management, and planning and operations are all bolstered by their unwavering belief in every student's ability to succeed and their capacity to inspire everyone else in the school building to share that belief. They also share a willingness to face challenges head-on, along with a commitment to continuously assessing and refining their school improvement strategy.

Moving your school forward requires regular reflection on your own work and giving honest but respectful feedback and support to your teachers, even when this involves difficult conversations. The personal leadership practices we outline in chapter 7 can guide you in considering your strengths, the challenges you expect to encounter at your school over the coming year, and the ways in which you can address those challenges with greatest success.

Each of the five categories is described from the broadest view of a leader's efforts, which we call *levers*, down to the specific *actions* that principals and school teams implement to improve student performance, illustrated in figure I.1. Each action is divided into *principal actions* that principals and leadership team members must take and *school actions* that flow from those practices. School actions are the consistent and observable activities of staff, students, and families within the school community that lead to improvements in student outcomes.

Together these pieces describe transformative school leadership and the school practices that flow from it. In this way, the TLF offers new and practical research to the field

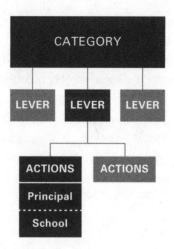

Figure I.1 Structure of the TLF.

of school leadership. Where existing studies have identified principals' actions that foster achievement growth and separate research has examined effective actions taken by school communities, the TLF brings both principal and school actions together. Our framework shows how specific school leader actions have influenced and enabled schoolwide practices that have collectively yielded sustained improvements in student achievement.

STAGES OF SCHOOL DEVELOPMENT

If you think of the development of a child, you can outline stages of development fairly easily. You know, for example, that before a baby can run, she first must learn to roll over, push herself up, stand, cruise, and walk. In our research, we found that schools and principals that were able to accelerate student learning and achieve sustained growth all implemented a similar set of actions over time and in a particular sequence. For example, among schools needing significant improvements in instruction, we found that they first established a small number of consistent instructional routines and instructional strategies across all classrooms and staff (what we call a stage 1 action) before deepening their professional development and focus on classroom differentiation and individual student supports (stage 2 and 3 actions). In the TLF, we describe these patterns and sequence of school actions as stages of school development, or *stages*.

Knowing what stage your school is in in its growth toward your goals will enable you to take powerful actions to move your school forward. These three stages guide principals in determining which high-leverage actions are already in place at their schools across all five categories and what actions they should take to improve their school.

(Although it is not part of the framework, in this book we also refer to a stage 0 when we describe the work of schools that are not yet implementing any of the actions outlined in a particular lever of the framework.) You will find detailed outlines of the characteristics of each stage in the next chapter, along with guidance on assessing where your school stands.

Our studies showed that as schools successfully implemented most of the school actions in a particular stage of the TLF, they made significant gains in student outcomes. In the learning and teaching category, for instance, we looked at schools initially lacking consistent classroom procedures to support student learning. Introducing certain stage 1 practices yielded initial improvements in student achievement, but those gains plateaued if schools failed to build on that foundation by implementing stage 2 actions. This explained a consistent finding of research on high-poverty schools: that these schools often make rapid improvements in student outcomes, but then struggle to sustain those outcomes or accelerate the pace of improvement over the long term.

This concept of stages of development has provided significant and much-needed guidance for leaders entering schools needing improvement. Although these leaders are often familiar with the research around high-performing schools, including high-performing, high-poverty schools, the gap between those research-based practices and the challenging realities facing their own schools can sometimes feel impossible to overcome. The TLF provides a clear road map for school improvement and serves as an ongoing guide to leaders in regularly assessing conditions in their schools and continually moving students toward high and sustained academic achievement.

HOW TO USE THIS BOOK

This book shares our learning with educators like you who are striving to improve educational outcomes for all the children in your school. *Breakthrough Principals* shows you how to put the TLF to work in your schools. For each category in the framework, we provide sample tools that successful principals use, such as schedules, protocols, and hiring tools, as well as activities you can do on your own and with your staff to begin to make changes that are right for your school. (Each Principal's Tool referred to within the chapters can be found in the Principal's Tool Kit in the appendix at the back of this book.) To illustrate how the framework and our diagnosis process work in practice, we include vignettes and case studies of principals from around the country in both district and charter schools who have successfully implemented the practices outlined in the framework.

Begin by reading the next two chapters, which provide more detail about the concept of stages of development and recommendations on how to use the TLF to diagnose the stage of your school. Once you do that, you can begin to familiarize yourself with the framework as a whole. You can access the entire framework on our companion website at www.wiley.com/go/newleaders. From there, you can read through each of the key levers and examine the tools we offer to help you use the framework. We expect different readers will use the book differently, depending on the needs of their school and comfort with the diagnostic tools. You might want to read the book all the way through initially to get detail about each category. Or if you feel ready to dive into your diagnosis process using the framework, you should begin that work, referring occasionally to category chapters as questions arise.

If there are particular sections of the framework for which you have questions about the stage of your school, you can refer to the tools and reflection questions in the Principal's Tool Kit in the appendix.

Once you've diagnosed your school's current state across each of the key levers, described in chapter 2, you can begin the work of selecting a few key areas for improvement and specific actions that you want to implement at the school level. With your priorities chosen, you can also return to the category chapters for much more detail on specific practices, tools, and detailed case studies of principals successfully implementing those practices. As you continue your improvement work over time, you can return to the TLF to conduct annual diagnostic checks as part of your school planning process to monitor your progress and identify any new areas for improvement.

Because we have seen that principals are most successful in this work when they partner with a team of leaders in their building, we encourage you to introduce this book to your leadership team and to read, discuss, and apply the tools together. We hope this book will be a professional development tool for you and your staff to build a shared vision of the priority actions for school improvement and the sequence of those actions. For example, you might have different leadership team members focus on different priority categories, using the tools and stories to begin developing an action plan for addressing those needs and monitoring the school's progress toward goals. To make these tools easier to use, we offer them to you on our website, at www.wiley.com/go/newleaders.

Although we address personal leadership toward the end of the book, we find that principals are best able to do the work of transformational leaders when they start by giving deep consideration to who they are as a leader. Chapter 7 on personal leadership offers assessment tools to help you identify your own strengths and growth areas when it comes to leadership skills and actions. We encourage you to use that chapter to set your own personal leadership goals, look at your strengths and areas in need of improvement, and consider what challenges you might encounter at your school this year. What skills can you already rely on to handle those challenges, and which skills do you want to develop? Given that an important part of being a leader is accepting and using input from colleagues, you will also get tremendous benefit from sharing that chapter with a coach, a mentor, and members of your team and getting their perspective on your leadership practice strengths and areas in need of improvement.

Finally, while most of this book is targeted to principals and school leadership teams, we end with a chapter for principal supervisors exploring how they can support school leaders in using the TLF. School leaders can also use this chapter to determine the best ways to work with district staff and their supervisors. And principal supervisors can use the case studies and tools to improve their own work in supporting school leaders.

We hope this book will become an active part of your library, that you will return to it as you do your annual planning and prepare to approach any problem at your school that you are unsure how to solve. We believe that implementing these actions will help you build a thriving school where great teachers love to work and students get a world-class education that prepares them to excel in school and beyond.

The Stages of School Development

AS WE BEGAN RESEARCHING SCHOOLS THAT WERE MAKING SIGNIFICANT improvements in student achievement, we spent months talking to principals, teachers, parents, and students about their practices. We visited classrooms, teacher team meetings, community forums, and student assemblies. Our plan was to focus on current practices at each school, looking for effective strategies in use that we could recommend to all our principals. We also asked a lot of questions about their history. What was the school like when you first arrived? What were the first changes you made? What worked and what didn't work? From these questions we built case studies of a number of schools, summarizing their improvement stories, with the assumption that these would be an effective teaching tool for our aspiring principals.

As we began to review the cases as a group, we realized to our surprise that there were consistent patterns these principals and schools had experienced in their improvement journeys. Although no two schools were exactly alike in their progression over time, the sequence of action steps and improvements each school took was much more consistent across successful schools than we had expected. This insight led us to recognize the importance of thinking about school improvement in terms of stages of school development. Just as a child learning to read must be taught skills sequentially and in predictable stages, school development requires multiple, predictable steps enacted in a particular sequence. By tackling school priorities sequentially, these highly effective principals were able to deliver continuous, measurable improvements in student learning.

At the same time, just as a child will struggle if asked to read *Goodnight Moon* before understanding the relationships between letters and sounds, schools struggle if leaders jump ahead to implement higher-order practices before foundational stage practices have been established. As one example, we visited one struggling school and sat in on an intensive professional development session focused on student differentiation in the classroom. Differentiation was a key priority for the school district, and the school leadership team had decided to invest significant dollars in a set of professional development sessions on the topic. However, as we observed multiple classrooms that day, we noted that many teachers lacked the core practices of effective lesson planning and there was no existing base of consistent and well-implemented instructional strategies for math or literacy instruction. These teachers didn't yet have solid content to differentiate their lessons around. They needed real help in developing stage 1 practices around instructional strategies as a first step to start their improvement journey.

Experiences like this made it clear that paying attention to the school's developmental stage is critical. Without a strategic focus on stages and sequence, principals and schools can feel as if they are on a treadmill, working hard but not seeing much progress. By contrast, implementing school actions in a developmentally logical sequence ensures key conditions are in place to allow you to continuously build on your progress. By getting results that are visible to both students and teachers, members of your school community will be inspired to keep striving to do better.

This chapter provides an overview of what each stage of the Transformational Leadership Framework (TLF) looks like in practice. In the next chapter, we show you how to use the TLF to diagnose your school's current developmental stages by examining what framework actions your school is implementing consistently. The rest of the book then helps you learn more about how to do this work within each category.

OVERVIEW OF STAGES

The TLF provides a clear starting point and helps you map the trajectory of change in your school by breaking each action in the TLF into stages of development. In this way the TLF can serve as an ongoing guide to help you diagnose the current state of your school and continually make improvements that lead to reaching and sustaining high levels of student achievement.

Before we explain how to use the TLF to improve your school, we introduce you to the structure of the framework and explain how to read the pieces of the TLF that you will encounter throughout the book. Table 1.1 offers a sample TLF table for planning and operations. This table breaks down a set of actions within one broader principal practice, or lever.

Table 1.1 Sample TLF Table for Planning and Operations for Lever 3, Budget, and Action 1, Budget and Resources

	PRINCIPAL ACTIONS	SCHOOL ACTION
Stage 1	Conduct a comprehensive review of all current resources (financial, staff, in-kind, supplemental, external partners/programs/resources) and, wherever possible, shift existing resources to align to strategic priorities. Identify key partners in the school and the system to support the budgeting process.	School resources are reallocated to support strategic priorities.
Stage 2	Forecast new resources and materials needed two to three years out based on the strategic plan (e.g., robust classroom libraries to increase literacy skills of students) and begin purchasing and planning for these needs.	Staff forecast resources they will need, accounting for materials they can reuse, to support strategic priorities.
Stage 3	Effectively leverage all potential resource sources through an ongoing, active approach to budget and resource management.	New resources and external partnerships are adequate to fund professional development and student intervention time and skills.

As you can see from table 1.1, within each category and lever of the TLF, each major action is divided into three stages: 1, 2 and 3. Stage 1 actions are the initial practices that schools put in place to jump-start improvements, stage 2 actions enable schools to address the needs of different groups of students, and stage 3 actions are higher-order practices that we found in consistently high-performing schools.

We've identified two component parts in each stage:

- Principal actions: Steps the principal can take to drive consistent implementation of changes in the school
- School actions: Consistent and observable behaviors of staff and students

The principal actions provide the support that the wider staff community needs to put the school actions in place, leading in turn to improved student performance. In other words, if you find that your school is demonstrating stage 2 school actions in a particular lever and you want to focus on implementing stage 3 school actions as your next priority, you would look to the stage 3 principal actions as your guide for specific steps you can take that will provide a foundation for successful implementation of stage 3 school actions.

It is important to keep in mind that a good diagnosis of school actions will likely reveal variation within categories. For example, within the category of learning and teaching, you might find your practices around the "using data" lever are currently in stage 2, but you might still be at stage 1 when it comes to creating a pyramid of academic interventions. You and your staff will find your unique path through the TLF based on the distinctive needs of your school. The TLF does not prescribe the same path and actions in the same sequence to every school; rather, it offers a process to guide you through the work of improving your school.

How the Stages of the TLF Work

In this section, we provide general definitions of each stage of development within the TLF, as found within the school culture, learning and teaching, talent management, and planning and operations categories, along with the key levers within each of those categories. (Personal leadership is not broken into stages because effective leaders demonstrate these actions regardless of the current state of their school.) You will not find stage 0 actions described in the TLF, but we use the term *stage 0* to describe the absence of any of the actions present in the other stages. Schools without any stage 1, 2, or 3 actions tend to be very low-performing schools that have often experienced multiple changes in leadership in a short period, leading to instability in implementation of school actions and the absence of consistent schoolwide systems and structures.

Stage 1

In schools in stage 1 for any particular lever, principals develop and introduce basic systems and structures to support school improvement goals and spend significant time monitoring and reinforcing the transition to these systems. These foundational systems and structures enable the school to move from being unfocused and even chaotic to having clear expectations and staff practices across the school. Here are examples of stage 1 principal actions from each category:

- *Learning and teaching*: Model effective approaches to unit planning and regularly review unit plans to provide teacher teams with feedback on their plans.
- *School culture*: Work collaboratively with staff to develop a short list of student behavioral expectations and staff responses that staff members implement consistently.
- *Talent management*: Define the roles and responsibilities for the instructional leadership team, including supporting and leading teacher team meetings, leading data-driven instruction cycles, conducting teacher observations, providing feedback, and completing final evaluations.

- *Planning and operations*: Conduct a comprehensive review of all current resources (financial, staff, external partnerships, use of time) and shift existing resources to align with strategic priorities.

Stage 2

In stage 2, the school leader develops staff capacity to take on leadership roles across the TLF categories, building a high-functioning instructional leadership team with strong teacher leaders. Stage 2 actions meet the needs of individual students more effectively than stage 1 practices do. These sample principal actions illustrate what the practices listed under stage 1 above look like when they advance to stage 2:

- *Learning and teaching*: Develop the capacity of the instructional leadership team to review unit and lesson plans to ensure alignment and rigor.
- *School culture*: Establish age- and developmentally appropriate behavioral expectations, and create structures to implement frequent teaching and reinforcement of those behaviors.
- *Talent management*: Design year-long professional learning for the instructional leadership team members to ensure consistency in their assessment of teacher practice and build the capacity of instructional leadership team members to conduct observations and provide effective feedback.
- *Planning and operations*: Forecast new resources and materials needed two to three years in the future based on the strategic plan, and begin purchasing and planning for those needs.

Stage 3

In stage 3, the principal has developed systems that foster a deep sense of ownership for key actions across staff, students, and families. Because nearly every member of the school community is invested in these practices and has the capacity to implement them consistently, the school is able to sustain high levels of student outcomes even during staff or leadership transitions. The school has a clear pipeline denoting which staff members will take on future tasks and who, outside of the principal, will take on leadership roles. These sample principal actions show what the practices listed under stage 2 look like when they move to stage 3:

- *Learning and teaching*: Lead the annual review process in which staff collaborate to assess the alignment and quality of curriculum plans and materials.
- *School culture*: Build student capacity to teach school values and behaviors to peers and hold each other accountable for living them.

- *Talent management*: Build systems for distributed leadership through which members of the instructional leadership team manage specific initiatives and grade-level teams or departments.
- *Planning and operations*: Effectively leverage all potential resource sources through an ongoing, active approach to budget and resource management.

Moving through the Stages

To illustrate how a school moves through the stages of a particular action within the TLF, we give you the story of one school whose staff made sequential changes to their practices around behavioral expectations, following the stages of the framework, and, over time, saw improvement in student behavior and academic performance. We provide vignettes like this one throughout the book.

CREATING A CULTURE OF LEARNING: MOVING FROM STAGE 1 TO STAGE 3 FOR BEHAVIORAL EXPECTATIONS

Leadership Public Schools, Richmond, California

When Shawn Benjamin became principal of LPS Richmond, she faced a daunting challenge. A charter network high school located in the high-poverty city of Richmond in Northern California, LPS was surrounded by a neighborhood where violence was endemic and drive-by shootings were all too common.

Benjamin arrived to find that the culture of the neighborhood carried into the school itself, with few systems in place to support student safety or learning. The school had had five principals in four years, leaving parents angry about the instability and poor educational quality their children were experiencing. At the time, only 21 percent of students met proficiency benchmarks in English, and math results were even more abysmal, with just 5 percent of students performing at grade level. About one-third of the students arrived late to school each day.

"In the beginning, we tried so many different things," Benjamin said. "I would hand out hot chocolate to kids who came on time; we held raffles for those kids.... That was my job eight years ago." As she has led her school through the stages of development around behavioral expectations, however, her job has transformed. "Now I am developing a culture of learning," she said. "Rather than telling kids, 'Don't fight in class,' now we are saying, 'If you are struggling with an issue, if you are confused in class, you need to take action, to make an appointment to see your teacher.' We are connecting everything to what it means to be ready for college. My work is about what are the specific behaviors students are going to need in college and how do we create that environment."

How did Benjamin and her staff get to the place they are in today? During her first year at Richmond, as she reviewed school conditions to identify her top priorities for changes that year, Benjamin saw that the school lacked a clear and consistent system for managing behavioral expectations across the school. She knew from her New Leaders training that establishing those expectations was a precondition to academic success; without them, behavior issues would continue to disrupt teaching and learning. She knew that this issue needed to be addressed immediately so that teachers and students could focus on academic priorities.

Benjamin developed a plan to establish consistently high behavioral expectations for students. Since this was a major culture shift for the school, she and her team tackled the work in a disciplined way, working step-by-step and building on a foundation of strong practices as she moved through the key development stages outlined in table 1.2.

Benjamin and the school's dean of students began by creating a comprehensive schoolwide discipline system that set clear expectations for student and staff behavior on attendance, tardiness, school cleanliness, and classroom performance, a stage 1 action for behavioral expectations. As part of that system, she looked at the way the physical space was organized (a stage 2 action in the lever on facilities in planning and operations) and discovered areas of the school that were unsupervised where students frequently had altercations. So she changed the ways students moved through the building, making sure that adults were on site or within earshot anywhere students passed through the halls.

She and her staff designed a tiered behavior support plan that addressed rule violations and had four levels of intervention involving teachers, advisors, family members, and, for the final tier, the principal. Like many behavior systems found in high schools, Benjamin's approach had staff members problem solving with students, working together to correct inappropriate behavior, creating contracts and time lines for addressing challenges, and establishing regular check-ins to ensure things remained on track. That first year, they also created rewards for good behavior. If Benjamin and the dean found that students behaved well over the course of each week, they would give students a dress-code-free Friday.

Benjamin made it clear to students and families that she and the staff took the new discipline program seriously. In her first year as principal, 25 percent of students were suspended, up from 5 percent the year before. After that,

Table 1.2 Behavioral Expectations

	PRINCIPAL ACTIONS	SCHOOL ACTIONS
Stage 1	Describe how staff and students can enact the vision and mission through specific behaviors. Articulate and model the importance of social-emotional and social responsibility skills and their connections to student success in school, college, and life. Build a school-level system of rewards and consequences that result from specific behaviors. Create an accountability system so that all infractions are addressed in a consistent manner, and hold staff responsible for consistently implementing rewards and consequences with all students, not only those they directly teach. Ensure that adults know how behavioral expectations translate to all parts of the school day, including opening of day, lunchtime, and class transitions.	There are multiple formal structures through which school values and expected behaviors are taught and reinforced; daily rewards and consequences are published and shared widely. Student social-emotional and social responsibility skills are included and explicitly named in the expectations of behavior. All members of the school community use common language to describe the school values, and they share a common understanding of expected behaviors. Rituals and public forums celebrate students who model expectations and demonstrate behaviors that reflect the values. All staff are taught and reinforce behavioral expectations while implementing the system of rewards and consequences.
Stage 2	Establish appropriate behavioral expectations for age and developmental stage. Create structures to implement frequent teaching and reteaching of behaviors. Expose staff continually to grade- and age-appropriate behaviors and supports. Use multiple forms of student data, including disaggregated discipline data, attendance, participation in activities, and who is publicly celebrated, to monitor and measure adoption of behaviors. Create structures and opportunities for students to teach other students and serve as role models. Develop the school's capacity to respond to students' behavioral and social-emotional needs in developmentally appropriate ways.	Induction systems are in place for new and returning staff, students, families, and communities. Adults use teachable moments and find time to reinforce and teach behaviors. Students who live the behaviors are given additional freedoms and demonstrate high levels of personal responsibility in social and academic settings. Staff consistently implement the discipline system and reinforce the established behavioral expectations. Social responsibility skills (service to others) are taught to all students. Systems are in place to review the number of referrals and analyze them to identify patterns or trends in referral data. Disaggregated referral data are regularly reviewed to ensure that consequences are not meted out differently based on race, class, or ethnicity.

Table 1.2 (*continued*)

	PRINCIPAL ACTIONS	SCHOOL ACTIONS
Stage 3	Build student capacity and experience in teaching the values and behaviors to others and for holding one another accountable for living them. Implement structures for peer mediation where students serve as role models for one another.	Students have a clear and consistent role in teaching behaviors to new and younger students. Students energize their peers and focus on achievement. Students hold one another accountable for living by the expectations for student behavior. Students mediate moments of conflict within the school.

however, the number of suspensions fell, reaching 16 percent of students by her fifth year.

Benjamin's and her staff's work around behavior has changed as the school evolves. First, with behavioral policies codified, known by all, and regularly enforced (stage 1 practices) during Benjamin's first year, the staff began to implement stage 2 actions of identifying and celebrating students who stood out as role models and exemplars. She went into the school wanting to make it "cool to be smart" so that students were motivated to do their best and persist through challenges. Also in her first year, the staff created competitions building from the Jeff Howard model of "work hard, get smart."[1] The school held competitions among advisory groups and grade levels, offering incentives such as a dress-code-free day or a grade-level celebration. These are stage 2 and 3 actions for behavioral expectations. The students "like[d] feeling smart" and they liked to "stand out," Benjamin said.

As important changes to the school culture took root in her first year, Benjamin doubled down on her focus on improving instruction. She had found that the general rigor of classes was low and most instruction consisted of teachers lecturing to students. Therefore, in her second year, she focused professional development for teachers on strategies for increasing student dialogue and engagement in the classroom. By Benjamin's fourth year at the school, the passing rate for tenth graders on the state English language arts (ELA) test had jumped to 89 percent and to 92 percent for math; two years after that, ELA and math proficiency continued to rise, to 94 percent and 96 percent, respectively, and 98 percent of students went on to college. "The new systems have fostered a sense of pride in students' ability to follow through, and there is a real commitment that no one will fall through the cracks," Benjamin said.

Having made so much progress around setting and implementing behavioral expectations, Benjamin and her staff in her third year were also able to put in place the stage 3 action of building students' capacity to teach values and behaviors to their peers and hold one another accountable for living them. Through an application process, juniors and seniors became peer leaders, responsible for running two orientations and attending a retreat for incoming freshmen before school started. At these events, the older students explained school policies and expectations. Not only did ninth graders come in to Richmond knowing what was expected of them, but the peer leaders were respected throughout the school, Benjamin said: "They shaped what other kids wanted to be like." To take student leadership development even further, in Benjamin's sixth year, one of her teachers created a class for peer leaders in which they learn leadership theory and training. At that point, peer leaders took responsibility for running weekly family meetings.

Two years later, Benjamin and her staff created a student ambassador role for older students as part of the school's home visit program intended to inform families about the school's college-bound culture. Each spring, the ambassadors accompany an adult school staff member on visits to the homes of eighth graders who will be attending Richmond the following fall. In those visits, the students talk about school expectations, trade stories about middle school, and discuss their own experiences at Richmond.

In Benjamin's eighth year as principal, only 4 percent of students were suspended, none of them freshmen. With that success, she and her team have created another structure for peer mediation, a stage 3 action: "I want us to move from telling students, 'If you do something wrong, you get in trouble with the dean,' to having students realize, 'I am a part of this greater community and I want to make the right choices because I feel committed to this community and my actions impact others.'" To do this, the school has created an honor council made up of students who apply for the position. The council will address low-level behavioral violations. Explained Benjamin, when students are sent to the dean, the matter is handled privately. Her hope is that by requiring students to explain their actions, or "poor choices," to a panel of their peers, they will feel more accountable to their community. "It's about the small choices you make," she said. "We have such a strong sense of identity and community, it felt like the perfect next step."

You can find more on how to move through the different stages of school culture in chapter 4.

Table 1.3 outlines the TLF practices Benjamin put in place, the data she used to identify her priorities, and the next steps she and her staff could take based on the sequence of actions in the framework.

Table 1.3 TLF Analysis of LPS Richmond

TLF ACTION	ARTIFACTS	EVIDENCE	TLF STAGE	PRINCIPAL ACTIONS TO MOVE TO NEXT STAGE	SCHOOL ACTIONS
Culture, behavioral expectations	Classroom observations; review of discipline reports; conversations with teachers	Disciplinary incidents high. Behavioral expectations not clear; incidents handled differently from classroom to classroom. Fractured relationships between students and staff.	Stage 0	Created an accountability system that set clear expectations for students and staff on attendance, tardiness, school cleanliness, and classroom performance so that all infractions were addressed in a consistent manner. Created a pyramid of interventions.	Student social-emotional and social responsibility skills are included and explicitly named in the expectations of behavior. Rituals and public forums celebrate students who model expectations and demonstrate behaviors that reflect school values.
		Over time, expectations are implemented consistently, with staff problem solving with students to correct inappropriate behavior and creating contracts and time lines for addressing challenges and regular check-ins to make sure things remain on track.	Stage 2	Implemented structures for peer mediation	Seniors took on the role of mentoring freshmen to help them acclimate to the school culture, meeting with them twice a week, and supporting them in developing their goals for the year.
	Course syllabus; Classroom observations	Teacher develops course for students to learn leadership theory and skills; students apply for and enroll in course	Stage 3	Work with teachers to continue to create leadership and peer mentor opportunities for students.	Hoping to make students feel more accountable to one another, the school created a student-run honor council to address low-level behavioral violations.

PUTTING THE FRAMEWORK TO WORK

As the work at LPS Richmond suggests, principals can use the framework to identify what school actions are evident in their school within each key lever of the TLF. After observing classrooms and talking with teachers and students, Benjamin quickly identified that her school lacked consistent expectations for student behavior. While LPS Richmond reached stage 3 for actions around behavior within the school culture category in its first year of making changes to principal and school actions, many actions in learning and teaching had not yet reached stage 1. Benjamin therefore chose to focus heavily on those lagging instructional practices in her second year.

Now that you have seen how the stages work and how you can use them to guide your own school improvement efforts, you are ready to move on to diagnosis and action planning. The next chapter is your gateway to making sense of and getting the most out of the TLF. It is there that we show you how the framework works as a tool for assessing and improving every aspect of your school.

Diagnosis and Action Planning

AS YOU KNOW FROM YOUR OWN WORK, NO TWO YEARS AT A SCHOOL ARE EVER the same. In the previous chapter, you saw how Shawn Benjamin, principal of LPS Richmond in California, developed a system of behavioral expectations in sequential steps over a number of years. How did Benjamin and the teachers decide to focus much of their work that first year on behavior and strengthening school culture? Why did they make that particular issue a priority? The answer is that they conducted careful, detailed diagnoses of their school's practices, a process they continue to undertake annually. This chapter explains how to do this work at your own school; it is the heart of this book.

"Every year we change and grow," Benjamin said. "We ask ourselves what is working and what's not working and how we can continue to meet the needs of our students." She and her teachers pore over student assessment results, observe each other's lessons, look at student suspension trends, and make note of how student behavior in and out of the classroom is affecting learning. They examine not only hard data but the actions Benjamin and the rest of her staff are taking around instruction, culture, and the operations of the school. What practices outlined in the TLF do they already have in place? And which actions are missing that they should prioritize for the coming year? They use that information to diagnose how well the school is doing in improving student learning.

You'll recall that when Benjamin arrived at the school, there was violence both surrounding and inside the school, and only a fraction of the students were performing at grade level in math or reading. During her first year, Benjamin examined student attendance, achievement, and discipline statistics. She reviewed suspension data to identify patterns within grade levels and classrooms and among individual students. She observed how teachers interacted with students during class and outside formal instructional time. She identified many fractured student-adult relationships, lack of clarity around even basic behavioral expectations, and inadequate social-emotional supports for struggling students.

Those findings, along with a belief that students will struggle to learn as long as the school lacks some basic structure and expectations, led Benjamin and her staff to focus primarily on improving the school culture in that first year. She made herself a regular presence, welcoming students at the gate every morning and wishing them a safe trip home every afternoon. She appointed deans to oversee discipline and counsel students who were regularly receiving infractions, deploying the intervention counselor on staff to provide crisis support. And she created a clear, coherent system of behavioral expectations for the entire school.

Benjamin's priorities at LPS Richmond have shifted from improving school culture, to improving classroom instruction, to expanding and strengthening opportunities for struggling students to get more support and ensure that all students are challenged with college-preparatory courses. With the TLF's stages of school development as their guide, each school year she and her staff undertake a new cycle of diagnosis and strategic planning. Based on their findings and conclusions, they select and implement a few priorities, careful not to take on too much change at once. They have made changes incrementally and in ways that produced quick wins—improvements in student achievement each step of the way. By taking a holistic view of her school through the diagnostic process, Benjamin said, she and her staff have been able to identify the changes they need to make to improve student learning and then can focus on how they all can work together to achieve those changes.

This chapter focuses on lever 1 of the planning and operations category: goal setting and action planning. While the other levers of this category are discussed in detail in chapter 6, this lever, the crux of diagnosing and planning, serves as an important frame for the rest of the book and is therefore given its own chapter.

A DIFFERENT APPROACH TO SCHOOL PLANNING

We have no doubt that planning is nothing new to you as your school's leader. Almost all school systems require principals to develop annual plans for school improvement. However, only effective plans with clear initiatives and responsibilities, that are consistently reviewed and updated throughout the year, lead to improved results for students.[1] Too often we have seen school leaders create plans filled with so many goals and initiatives that implementation becomes impossible. They contain so much detail that they lack focus,[2] or they neglect to assign responsibility for implementing portions of the plan to specific staff members. We have also seen principals create plans as compliance exercises in response to their district requirements, too often resulting in plans that are completed but never reviewed or updated by the school staff.[3]

Consider how you approach your school's planning. What steps do you follow to create a plan, and what do you do with the plan once it is down on paper? The Transformational Leadership Framework (TLF) can support you in getting the most out of your planning process and taking it several steps further. This chapter details each of the key steps around diagnosis and action planning that we have seen effective principals take to improve student achievement at their school, outlined in table 2.1.

Within the action of goal setting and action planning are four key steps.

Step 1: Diagnose. Review current school actions and data to identify the current stage of school actions for each category and lever.

Step 2: Prioritize. Select a few focus levers for improvement.

Step 3: Set goals, identify strategies, and create action plan. Set improvement goals using the school actions from the next stage in the TLF, and identify strategies that will help you reach those goals.

Step 4: Monitor and adjust the action plan. Review the efficacy of strategies and progress toward goals and adjust plan as needed.

We will bring each of these steps to life through a case study of one school that did this work well, but first we give a little more description of what each step entails:

Step 1: Diagnose. The first step of effective planning for school improvement involves regular diagnosis of the state of your school, looking for gaps in student learning and investigating the root causes of those gaps. To do this, you should examine multiple points of data and observe teacher and student activities both in and out of classrooms. You can then use the TLF to determine which effective principal and school practices are in place in different categories and which ones need work. You can also identify what stage the school is in for the actions within the framework. For this process to be effective, other staff must be involved in the diagnosis process.

Step 2: Prioritize. With detailed data in hand, you can determine your schoolwide priorities based on the stage your school is in for different practices (we recommend focusing first on areas that are in stages 0 or 1). A successful plan focuses on just a few areas in need of improvement, prioritizing those that are likely to have the greatest impact on student learning. This theory of simple and targeted planning has been found to work not only in schools but in companies of all sizes and complexities.[4] We have seen that principals whose school is in stage 0 have the most

Table 2.1 Lever 1: Goal Setting and Action Planning

	PRINCIPAL ACTIONS	SCHOOL ACTIONS
Stage 1	Assess the current state of the school and identify gaps that need to be addressed by analyzing student achievement data, teacher effectiveness data, and school practices. Determine the few and focused priorities for the current year using the results of the data analysis; limit any new initiatives to those that will receive adequate resources and time for implementation and monitoring. Develop an action plan that identifies clear end goals and strategies to make progress toward priority areas. At least two times per year, review student data and progress against strategically planned school practices and financial and operational information, adjusting strategies as needed.	Staff and families share their perspectives on school needs and performance to inform school goals. A strategic plan and priorities are in place and aligned to the urgent goal of making dramatic gains in student achievement. Grade-level and content-area teams use the goals and action plans to inform their planning.
Stage 2	Link each action plan strategy to metrics with which to measure progress against each strategic priority area. Set detailed milestones and benchmarks for implementation and student progress (e.g., interim assessments, attendance) in the school improvement plan. Identify leadership team members who are responsible and accountable for the implementation of aspects of the strategic plan. At least two times per year, review student data and progress against strategically planned school practices and financial and operational information; revise plans and priorities based on data in order to reach established goals.	Strategic plan priorities are public and easily accessed by multiple stakeholders. Each priority area has assigned staff responsible for implementation who share a common understanding of short- and long-term goals, strategies, and time lines. Progress is regularly tracked using leading indicators. If milestones and benchmarks are not met, contingency plans are created to reach the required result. The leadership team uses evidence and data to adjust strategies and action plans.

Table 2.2 (*continued*)

	PRINCIPAL ACTIONS	SCHOOL ACTIONS
Stage 3	Cocreate annual goals and a school improvement plan with a broad group of stakeholders before the school year starts. Use annual data, interim and formative data, and school improvement plan milestones to monitor, track, and review progress, systematically adjusting strategies where needed. Lead an ongoing planning process and multiple reviews of progress against plans each year, engaging all staff (e.g., at a summer retreat). Lead formal reviews of progress against the strategic plan and milestones at least two times a year, in addition to conducting regular reviews of school data.	The leadership team has institutionalized the practice of reviewing key data at every meeting. The leadership team meets regularly (at least once per week) to analyze a consistent set of key school indicators, including individual student-, classroom-, and grade-level data. The leadership team creates short- and medium-term action plans to address areas of concern and recognize areas of success. Targets for student subgroups and grade-level cohorts are included in the school improvement plan with milestones and benchmarks to track progress toward goals. Each teacher's targets are clearly aligned to the school's goal.

success when they start with a few high-priority actions. These include establishing a strong culture organized around clear norms and behavioral expectations, cultivating persistence and a love of learning among students, implementing consistent instructional strategies and routines, developing observation and feedback cycles, and helping teachers use data to set goals and improve instruction.

Step 3: Set goals, identify strategies, and create action plan. You can now set aggressive but achievable goals for your priorities and create an action plan to ensure those goals are met in the most efficient way possible. We recommend linking each goal to a few specific strategies that are designed to move you toward achieving the larger priority. We describe this work in greater detail later in this chapter, but to develop these strategies, principals can refer back to the TLF to identify school and principal actions that correspond to the school's priorities and the current stage of school development. A good action plan is realistic about the resources and time the staff has to implement and achieve the end goal.

Step 4: Monitor and adjust action plan. Plans are never perfect the first time. This step guides you through the work of regularly monitoring your action plan and your progress toward goals, making adjustments to your plan as needed.

CASE STUDY: THE FOUR STEPS OF PLANNING

In the case study that follows, we will demonstrate how the leader of an elementary school (fictionalized for case study purposes) used the framework to follow each of the four steps of planning. In telling this story, we also offer some tools on how to do this work with precision in your own school, based on your own context. Finally, we offer a sample action plan that we suggest using as a guide as you organize your planning work into a comprehensive and accessible document.

CHARTING A COURSE FOR SCHOOL IMPROVEMENT BY DIAGNOSING AND PLANNING: MOVING FROM STAGE 0 TO STAGE 2 FOR GOAL SETTING AND ACTION PLANNING

Jones Elementary School

When Gwendolyn Davies became principal of Jones Elementary, the school had been going through some growing pains.[5] A number of Spanish-speaking immigrant families had moved into the community, nearly doubling the number of English language learners (ELL) at the school. Meanwhile, the previous principal had been slow to adapt to the changes. Even with a growing achievement gap and pressure from the district to take action, he neglected to provide adequate professional development to his teachers.

Step 1: Using Multiple Data Points to Diagnose School Practices

As soon as Davies started in June, she began working with the existing leadership team and assistant principal to conduct an analysis of three years of trend data. For each piece of evidence, they looked for patterns by grade and subgroup (race and ethnicity, special education, ELL). They examined:

- Disaggregated state standardized test results, including subgroups and cohort progression
- Formative assessments, including the NWEA Measures of Academic Progress and district-created benchmark assessments
- Student mobility data
- Attendance rates by grade

- Student discipline data, including referrals and suspensions
- District targets and averages for academic performance and attendance

Davies and her leadership team also invited teachers and administrative staff in over the summer to talk to them about what they thought was working at the school and what needed improvement. Half of the staff voluntarily met with Davies.

The results of this analysis are outlined later in this chapter, but it is worth noting here that one of the key findings was that across grade levels, student performance on the state exams, particularly in English language arts, had been flat or slowly declining. Based on that trend alone, Davies hypothesized that improving literacy instruction would likely be a top priority.

At the same time, Davies knew that the available data alone were not enough to accurately identify the right priorities for improvement and the highest-leverage strategies and practices to address them. Using the TLF as a guide to examine a range of school practices and other data, she immediately engaged her instructional leadership team (ILT) in a deep diagnosis process. The members of the ILT, still intact from the previous year, were eager to participate in this work but needed guidance. Davies led a few training sessions for the team, helping them understand how to use the framework and honing in on some key data points on which they'd need to focus.

Over several meetings in July and August, they examined sections of the TLF categories that they thought could guide them in addressing their initial priority of improving ELA achievement across the school. "We tried to determine which practices were missing at Jones so that we could identify our current development stage for some key TLF categories. Once we did that, we would look to the next stage to determine what actions we would need to take to get to that level and support our larger goal of improving student reading and writing skills," Davies said. By revealing action areas in which the school was at or not yet approaching stage 1, Davies and her team could identify school practices likely holding back progress on student learning outcomes.

Davies presented the team's findings to the full staff during their August staff orientation. "I was very open in explaining that our initial assessment of the stage of each lever may shift as we learn more and continue to observe practices in the first few weeks of school," she said.

Davies also knew that she was going to have to assess her teachers in action and that she would have to keep modifying the diagnosis as she learned more about the school's instructional strengths and growth areas. During the first few months of the school year, she and the ILT continued with their TLF analysis.

For the operations category, they reviewed the school schedules and calendars and observed transitions between periods, looking for ways in which the master schedule did and did not align with the goal of increasing student learning, particularly in ELA.

For school culture, the team looked at discipline and attendance data, and observed student behavior inside and outside classrooms to determine if behavior and truancy were interfering with student learning. They read through school policies and spoke with each teacher individually about behaviorial challenges in their classes and how the teachers handled them. "We wanted to know if teachers were following established school procedures, and if not, why not," one committee member said. "Was it a matter of the procedures being unclear, hard to enforce, or just that some teachers disagreed with them and wanted to handle behavior issues their own way?"

Using the learning and teaching and talent management sections of the TLF as a guide, team members observed classrooms, reviewed lesson plans and student work, and observed teacher team meetings to assess where instructional practices did and did not align with state standards. This information, along with the previous year's teacher evaluations, also helped identify skill gaps across the staff to help them prepare early for staffing and hiring for the following school year.

The team members periodically brought their findings to the full staff for feedback, as well as to explain how upcoming changes would affect their work.

Finally, Davies issued a family survey to get parents' perspectives on the school's needs. When few parents responded to the survey, Davies solicited the help of three parents with whom she had developed a relationship, who helped her get more parents to complete the questionnaire.

Once the ILT identified actions within each category that best matched the actions at their school, they determined what stage of the TLF they were in and began to discuss their next steps. For example, if they identified stage 1 actions around scope and sequence at Jones, Davies looked at stage 2 principal actions within the scope and sequence section of the framework to see what actions she could take to help move the school forward around this aspect of curriculum alignment.

Table 2.2 shows key findings of their analysis of school actions and an initial brainstorm of possible next steps or strategies aligned to each finding, using ideas from the TLF.

Table 2.2 TLF Analysis of Jones Elementary School

TLF ACTION	ARTIFACTS	EVIDENCE	TLF STAGE AND LEVER	NEXT STEPS/ STRATEGIES
Operations, master schedule	Previous and current year schedules and calendars; conversations with teachers and leadership team	Collaborative teacher planning time is on the schedule, but staff play a limited role in creating the calendar.	Stage 1 Lever: Time use is aligned with schoolwide goals.	Give more support and responsibility to the leadership team to lead schedule assessment.
Culture, behavioral expectations	Discipline data; family survey; staff conversations; observations	Disciplinary incidents low. System of behavioral expectations in place, understood by most teachers, and posted in halls and most classrooms. Teacher-run student orientation held each August to introduce school rules and expectations.	Stage 2 Lever: Implement clear school mission, values and behaviors.	Create a peer mediation program to give students opportunities to teach good behavior to other students.
Learning and teaching	Classroom observations; meetings with individual teachers and teacher teams; lesson plans; student work	There is a process for creating and reviewing lesson plans, but many lesson plans still lack rigor.	Stage 1 Lever: Aligned curriculum.	Implement common expectations of rigor and ensure all staff understand how they apply to their subject areas. Develop the capacity of the leadership team to review lesson plans for alignment and rigor.
		Instructional routines and strategies are inconsistent across classrooms.	Stage 0 Lever: Classroom practices and instruction.	Identify, teach, and monitor three to five consistent classroom procedures that support student learning and support staff in gaining the skills they need to implement those practices.

(*continued*)

Table 2.2 (*continued*)

TLF ACTION	ARTIFACTS	EVIDENCE	TLF STAGE AND LEVER	NEXT STEPS/ STRATEGIES
		Some data are used to develop interventions, but regular classroom instruction is not deeply informed by data analysis and feedback.	Stage 1 Lever: Data.	Develop and support staff ability to analyze data and to use those data to identify and prioritize student needs.
		Some good intervention systems in place, but varied student needs are not identified and addressed by regular classroom instruction.	Stage 2 Lever: Student-centered differentiation.	Identify effective and aligned community resources like college tutors or parents to increase time and talent dedicated to system interventions. Build consistency with teachers and teacher teams on how and when to adjust pacing of instruction.
Talent management	Classroom observations; one-on-one meetings with teachers; review of professional learning plan	The ILT is in place, but not all members are able to regularly provide effective coaching and model schoolwide core values.	Stage 1 Lever: Development of high-performing ILT.	Build the capacity of ILT members to conduct observations and provide effective feedback; develop reporting systems for sharing feedback.
		Infrequent teacher observations and feedback to teachers.	Stage 0 Lever: Monitoring and management of staff performance.	Create an observation protocol for walk-throughs, which are done often with a schoolwide focus, and find creative ways to give teachers feedback.
		A comprehensive professional learning plan is in place, but it does not align with whole school areas in need of improvement.	Stage 1 Lever: Professional learning structures to drive instructional improvement.	Develop a clear plan for adult learning that aligns with school's areas in need of improvement, teacher team areas of focus, and individual development priorities. Create structures for job-embedded collaborative learning.

The following guide lays out the steps you can take as you conduct your own diagnosis.

Diagnosis Process Guide

1. Examine at least three years of data, looking for trends by grade and subgroup (assessments, student mobility, attendance, discipline data, district targets and averages).

2. Collect evidence on the state of the school by examining school documents and handbooks; school improvement plans; district evaluation of the school; conversations with staff, family, and community members; discipline data and discipline code; newsletters; mission statement; celebrations and rituals; hiring processes; curriculum materials; and professional development schedule.

3. Observe classrooms, teacher team meetings, and all professional learning sessions.

4. Consider which staffers will be your strongest allies in completing an effective diagnosis and creating your action plan (e.g., ILT members, assistant principal).

5. Train ILT and other key staff in how to use the TLF to diagnose school practices.

6. Work with the ILT and other staff to use the TLF to determine practices that are in place and those that are missing, identifying what stage your school is in for actions within the TLF.

 Potential Pitfalls

In conducting a diagnosis, we have found that school leaders sometimes jump to judgments in three ways that can distract them from a deeper understanding of school actions.

1. *Using limited evidence to assess the school.* Leaders might rely solely on student achievement data when diagnosing the current stage of school development. However, to make substantial and sustained improvements in outcomes, leaders must think more comprehensively about the school actions that underlie these outcomes. Having high student achievement may not mean that a school has all stage 3 practices in place. For example, a school that has stagnant student achievement scores may need to implement stage 1 practices even though 70 percent of their students are proficient.

2. *Looking at the forest and ignoring the trees.* School leaders should be wary of assuming that all school actions fall into a single stage across all key levers. A principal might refer informally to her school as a "stage 2 school." However, while these practices often do flow together and are at similar stages of development, the most effective diagnoses of

school actions identify the few key levers where practices are at a lower stage, allowing for effective plans to improve in those targeted areas.

3. *Assessing principal effectiveness using the TLF.* Although the TLF might resemble principal evaluation tools used by systems, we do not recommend the TLF for that purpose (see chapter 8 on principal supervision for our recommendations on principal evaluation).

Principal's Tool 2.1: Possible Data Sources for Your School Diagnosis

Step 2: Bringing the Outputs of the Diagnosis Together to Identify Priorities

As Davies and her team analyzed student outcomes and TLF data to identify a few focused priorities for her first year, an important stage 1 action for goal setting, they looked specifically for areas where there had been underperformance across a number of grades or departments and where stage 1 or stage 2 actions from the TLF were lacking. In particular, they chose actions that they thought would boost student learning in the immediate term. To determine next steps, they looked to the next stage for each priority action.

Davies brought together her assistant principal and a few lead teachers to group the data they had collected, including the results of the TLF analysis, into three categories:

- *On track:* Areas where the school has met or will meet its target and where performance is aligned to school vision

- *Almost on track:* Areas where the school almost met the target or is making progress to the target, or where alignment to school vision is improving

- *Off track:* Areas where targets for the previous year were missed (stagnant or declining); where the school is performing well below the district or peer schools; where performance is misaligned with the school vision; or key levers where the school is at or below stage 1

Areas identified as off track could become priorities for improvement. In schools where many stage 1 actions are lacking, leaders and their teams need to be careful not to prioritize every area that needs improvement to prevent making the work of making changes overwhelming and unmanageable.

To effectively categorize their findings, Davies and her staff also needed to be mindful of district policies and priorities. After meeting with the deputy superintendent,

Davies learned that as part of a renewed effort to improve schools across the district, the district had set its own target of increasing the district-wide percentage of students scoring proficient or higher on the ELA test to 70 percent from its current level of 50 percent. That meant every school was expected to have 70 percent proficiency on ELA for every grade the following year. For math, the district's goal for each school was 60 percent proficient or higher. Table 2.3 outlines the key findings from the staff's TLF diagnosis.

Table 2.3 Key Findings for Jones Elementary School

NOT ON TRACK*	
Math achievement	Schoolwide: 5 points below district average
	Fourth grade: 36 percent of students scored proficient or advanced
Reading achievement	Third grade: 48 percent of students scored proficient or advanced
	Fourth grade: 49 percent of students scored proficient or advanced
	Fifth grade: 49 percent of students scored proficient or advanced
Planning and operations	Schedule lacks certain details like key dates for data review, interventions, professional development, and talent reviews
	Staff role in schedule review and creation, including that of the leadership team, has also been limited, making it hard for the principal to manage effectively on her own.
Learning and teaching	Instructional routines and strategies are inconsistent across classrooms and often lack rigor.
	Teachers do not regularly use data to inform instruction, particularly to differentiate instruction and create and revise interventions.
Talent management	ILT members do not regularly provide effective coaching.
	Teacher observations and feedback to teachers are infrequent.
	The comprehensive professional learning plan does not align to whole school needs for improvement.
ALMOST ON TRACK	
Math achievement	Fifth grade: 49 percent of students scored proficient or advanced
ON TRACK	
Math achievement	Third grade: 60 percent of students scored proficient or advanced
Attendance	Average attendance 5 percent above district average
School culture	System of behavioral expectations in place, understood and followed by most teachers and students
	Disciplinary incidents are low

*Including those school actions diagnosed as being at stage 0 or stage 1 from the TLF.

Davies focused on the not-on-track areas to identify a few priorities for the next year. She considered the following questions to determine priorities, choosing those that would have the greatest impact on the entire school:

- Which school actions, if improved, would be most effective in improving the off-track student outcome data?

- Are there some off-track areas that need to be tackled together to increase the impact on student performance?

Following their analysis, Davies and the ILT set the following priorities for the next eighteen months:

- Improve ELA mastery for each grade over the next year.

- Improve overall literacy levels for all students.

- Increase rigor and expectations around literacy.

⬇ Potential Pitfalls

All of the priorities for Jones Elementary had a schoolwide focus. While a leader might see one or two grade levels emerge as "weak grades" where students are not achieving growth, we advise against making those grades alone the areas of schoolwide focus. Rather, make them priority areas for the leadership team and potentially for informing staffing choices. Identifying one grade area as a schoolwide priority sends a message to the rest of the staff that their content area is less important or essential (the same holds true for tested grades and subjects). Priority areas should be able to touch most (if not all) grade levels and subjects.

Step 3: Set Goals, Identify Strategies, and Create an Action Plan

Davies then set about determining what set of strategies would best enable her staff to address each priority. "Once we knew what our focus was, we needed to know what work was required to make those improvements," she said.

To identify the right strategies, you have to (1) carefully assess why there is a gap to be sure you design strategies that address the root of the problem, and (2) determine what resources will be needed to effectively implement the strategy and where the school can get those needed resources. Any new initiatives based on these priorities should be limited to those that will receive adequate resources and time for implementation and monitoring.

You can begin this process with your staff by asking, "Why?" Why, after students' reading scores spiked with the implementation of a new reading curriculum a few years ago, has reading growth leveled off or fallen? Or, why has the achievement gap among different groups of students persisted despite our efforts to give those students more targeted instruction? The answers to many of these questions around student outcome challenges are often found in the lower-stage school actions from the diagnosis. By wrestling with these questions, you can begin to identify the underlying cause of some of your school's challenges. Too often schools move directly from identifying academic needs into selecting targeted instructional programs or interventions to address these identified needs without first taking a deeper look at school actions that are often the root cause behind student performance challenges.

Your next question is, "Now what?" What actions should you take to make the greatest impact on student learning with the resources available to you—what we call in this book "high-leverage" actions?

As was clear from Jones's TLF analysis, there were some likely reasons that students were not performing well in literacy: the ELA instruction across grade levels lacked consistency and rigor; staff were not regularly using data to inform instruction; the school lacked systems for ensuring rapid interventions were in place to support the lowest-performing students; and several ILT members lacked the ability to coach and give effective feedback to teachers on a regular basis.

As they considered a number of strategies, Davies and her team considered the following questions:

- What would the staffing implications be? What professional development or job-embedded support would teachers need to change their practices?

- What resources in addition to staffing would be needed?

- What kind of time and how much time would the principal need to spend, and where in her schedule could she find that time?

- Looking across stakeholders' groups, what, if any, skill or belief gaps contributed to areas going, or remaining, off-track?

- What actions would the principal leadership team need to take to support changes in skills and beliefs to reverse that trend? What, if any, changes were needed in the curriculum?

- What, if any, changes were needed to make to assessments?
- Looking at operations, had systems or structural deficiencies contributed to a priority area's becoming or remaining off track? What changes to the schedule, calendar, or other systems would allow staff to address that priority more effectively?
- What principal actions would Davies (and members of the leadership team) need to take to redress operational deficiencies? Were there district supports they could access to remedy logistics and other operational deficiencies?

These strategies then become part of the action plan. Too often schools don't create a true plan of action or don't maintain consistent focus on the plan.

You can use the action planning process to determine how you will implement your strategies and then, as we will discuss in more detail in the next section on step 4, monitor the effect of the strategies and your progress toward your goals.

Action plans are detailed documents that are intended to meet short- and long-term priorities and goals. They include:

- A set of specific strategies that will be put in place
- Specific people responsible for implementing each strategy
- Skills the principal and other staff have to implement the strategy
- Resources required for each strategy
- Time line for completing each strategy
- Benchmarks for measuring success or lack of success for each action

In terms of the content of the plan, strategies should include:

- Professional development targeted to school priorities and data collection and analysis, customized to support teachers' specific needs
- Plan for periodic collecting and analysis of data

The action plan shown in exhibit 2.1 outlines each of the strategies Davies and her colleagues selected and why they were chosen, along with proposed steps to implement and periodically assess how things were going.

EXHIBIT 2.1: SAMPLE ACTION PLAN FOR JONES ELEMENTARY

Urgent Concern: The high and increasing percentage of students who have not reached proficient or advanced in the annual ELA assessment.

Target Goal: Increase the percentage of students who are proficient or advanced by 15% by improving ELA instruction and implementing interventions that support students struggling with reading and writing.

Measurable Progress:

- Students who are at risk of failing are identified for services by the 2nd–3rd week of every quarter.
- 90% of students who were in the bottom quintile at the end of last school year move into the next quintile.
- Interim assessment results show 80% of students meeting or exceeding their expected growth target.
- Interim assessment results show 40% of students exceeding their expected growth target.
- Parent engagement to support the development of reading skills increases by 45%.
- 80% of teachers will have a literacy block routine of consistent instructional practices.

Activities/ Deliverables	Person(s) Accountable	Time Line for Activity	Benchmarks	Use of Data
Strategies, interventions, and practices that will help us to attain the goal	*Person responsible for planning, organizing and ensuring implementation*	*When this will take place*	*Indicators of progress*	*What data will we use to measure progress?*
Students identified for early intervention by 2nd or 3rd week of every quarter	Classroom teachers, intervention team, and ILT	Ongoing Sept–June	Improvement on interim assessments and improved performance on classroom assessments and assignments for identified students Students improve to the point where they are no longer assigned interventions	Interim assessment data, classwork and assessments
Quarterly student goal setting and on track reflections	Classroom teachers	Five times throughout the school year	Progress on student goals	Teacher logs and student reflections

(*continued*)

EXHIBIT 2.1: (*continued*)

Activities/ Deliverables	Person(s) Accountable	Time Line for Activity	Benchmarks	Use of Data
Strategies, interventions, and practices that will help us to attain the goal	*Person responsible for planning, organizing and ensuring implementation*	*When this will take place*	*Indicators of progress*	*What data will we use to measure progress?*
Family reading night to share resources and student progress with families	Classroom teachers	Beginning of every quarter	Family attendance at events and increase parent engagement via phone and e-mail	Family report card and conference log, attendance at family events
Reduce interim assessment data turnaround time from one week to 48 hours	Test coordinator and ILT	Sept–June	Reduction in data turnaround	Data analysis time lines
Observation and feedback schedule	ILT	Weekly Sept–June	Improved differentiation in classrooms	Lesson plans, class group listed
Identify schoolwide instructional focus	ILT and classroom teachers	Aug–Sept	Consistent practices across classrooms • Whole group instruction (30 minutes) • Small group instruction (60 minutes) • Guided reading time • Writer's workshop • Daily independent reading (15–30 minutes)	Lesson plans Weekly walk throughs

EXHIBIT 2.1: (*continued*)

Professional Learning Activities	Person(s) Accountable	Time Line for Activity	Stipends and Fees	Other Budget Allocations
Professional learning sessions that will help each teacher to improve their practice in support of goal attainment	Person responsible for planning, organizing, and ensuring implementation	When this will take place		What activities require specific budget allocations
Creating a common definition of rigor with the ILT	Principal	Two days in August	$5,000 for ILT stipends	$5,000 for books $1,500 for printing
Planning for Rigor	Principal, AP, Literacy Coach	Monthly for Sept–Nov	$7,500 for consultant coaching	
Levels of Questioning	Principal, Literacy Coach	Nov–Jan		
Data Analysis Support	ILT	Weekly at teacher team meetings	$1,000 for consultant support	
Providing effective feedback on instruction	Principal	Weekly at ILT meetings	$1,500 for consultant support	
Creating consistent routines and instructional strategies for literacy	Principal, AP, Literacy Coach, ILT	Weekly at ILT meetings	$1,000 for consultant support	

There is no one-size-fits-all approach to planning. Whatever process you and your staff use, it is critical that within that work, once you settle on a few key priorities and strategies, you set appropriate goals and targets that will help you periodically evaluate whether your plan is advancing your core priorities. We recommend you align school-level, classroom-level, and individual student goals.

You can set targets by examining student-level data with your teachers. In high-functioning schools, teachers tend to recommend a class- and grade-level target based on the past performance of their incoming students and the assessments used by the district or state. Targets should be ambitious but attainable. If they are set too high, they might be dismissed as unrealistic, and goals that are modest do not help students make sufficient progress. To close achievement gaps and help students who are not at grade level begin to catch up with their peers, you should help teachers set targets that represent more than one year's worth of growth. The exact target will vary depending on the assessment, but these need to be achievable to avoid burnout and frustration across staff and students alike.

Each target must be quantifiable and achievable, based on what you know about your students and what they have already learned. You and your school will be most successful if you can justify a goal and target with hard data, and that goal has to be connected to a plan of action that is implementable and concrete.

To identify the target that is just right for a student, a grade, and your school, consider your context by looking at trends over time to understand how the school has been progressing. Examine the student cohorts to see how groups of students are performing (this is especially important for high schools, where credit accumulation determines graduation) while also looking at individual student performance using analyses from their teacher teams. We have found there is real benefit to considering both proficiency and value-added measures when setting targets.

Savvy leaders also use goal setting to map the work of their schools to the goals of the district. This does not necessarily mean that your school's goals must directly match the district-level goals, but you will find there is a benefit to being aware of district and state priorities.

The staff at Jones Elementary chose to establish more targeted professional development, particularly around ELL support, as one of their strategies for improving ELA instruction and, in turn, student learning. They tracked the consistency of routines and instructional practices across classrooms with a focus on literacy instruction. They set a goal that specified the time period, the people the goal targets, how the goal will be measured, and what school practices will change.

▼ Potential Pitfalls

Often we have seen leaders pull their targets seemingly from thin air, not taking into account past performance, the performance of similar schools within the district, or resource alignment. In other cases, some schools make the mistake of aligning their targets to the average achievement across the district, when in fact schools across the district are performing at low levels and each individual school should strive to exceed district norms and set sights on state or national averages. In the last ten years there has been a focus on using SMART goals (goals that are specific, measurable, achievable, results-oriented and time-bound). New Leaders teaches this paradigm in our programming, but we urge school leaders to keep in mind that setting goals is just a starting point. We have seen staff in schools that are struggling to implement changes devote most of their time to the work of setting SMART goals while failing to invest in identifying the strategies needed to achieve those goals. In these cases, staff members are often uncomfortable with planning and the school has not yet reached stage 1 in many categories, setting the stage for failure and frustration when goal setting should really provide the opportunity to map out a path to success.

Questions to Guide Goal and Target Setting

- What is typical growth on this metric in a year?

- What targets need to be hit in each of the goal areas in each of the next five years to achieve the school's vision? If the targets reached from aggregating class and grade data do not project sufficient growth to close achievement gaps, how will you adjust your strategies or targets? Given current priority areas, strategies, and resources, how might you adjust annual targets to reach the achievement level outlined in the long-term vision?

- Given the identified priority areas, strategies, and resource allocation, are there some areas where the target should be higher?

- Have there been any changes to student composition that would make your goals less or more feasible?

- Are there additional assessments or metrics that should be included to measure student learning outcomes?

Step 4: Monitor and Adjust Action Plan

So far you have followed Jones Elementary through the following actions:

- Diagnosing school practices and determining the school's current developmental state

- Identifying priority areas for improvement based on the diagnostic work

- Determining strategies to address these priorities and milestones to track progress on an ongoing basis

It is critical to understand that action plans are living documents that must be regularly monitored and revised as needed. School leaders don't always choose the right strategy the first time, or perhaps they miss a critical step that would enable them to implement that strategy more effectively. Consider, for example, a school that identified improving writing across the curriculum as a critical priority. If, after several classroom walk-throughs, the principal sees that teachers are not consistently using lesson plans on writing, she will realize that she and her team missed a step of providing guidance to teachers on how to infuse writing into unit and lesson plans. She therefore introduces a new strategy around lesson planning that precedes the strategy around increasing writing instruction in all lessons. She also creates a plan to give her science and math instructors, who had limited experience teaching writing, more robust and well-defined supports so that she can better track their progress and hold them accountable for advancing the schoolwide initiative. (See chapter 5 for more on professional development.)

Effective leaders reference strategic plans on a regular basis and build in regular periods of review that encourage staff members to reflect on how strategies are working in their classrooms. As staff members become more adept at reviewing progress toward goals, more of the implementation responsibility can live with members of the instructional leadership team, teacher teams, and, ultimately, students, a hallmark of stage 3 in school development.

At Jones Elementary, the principal adopted the stage 1 action of reviewing student data and progress against strategically planned school practices and financial and operational information at least twice a year, and grade and content teams used the action plan to inform their own planning cycles.

NEXT STEPS

We hope, after reading this chapter, that you and your team feel equipped to begin the work of diagnosing the most pressing school improvement priorities for your school and planning a productive strategy to address them. The four key steps we have detailed here—diagnose, prioritize, identify strategies and set goals, and determine leadership actions—will ultimately become second nature as you use them regularly. But we encourage you to return to this chapter as often as needed, whether for your initial diagnosis, smaller diagnoses you conduct throughout the year, or each annual planning cycle for years to come. The stories of LPS Richmond and Jones Elementary are meant to serve as exemplars by showing that other schools have done this work and, despite the occasional roadblocks, achieved real success. The diagnosis process guide and the sample action plan and template should serve as a reminder of the steps you can take to achieve similar results.

You are now ready to dig in to the categories of the TLF, to begin to determine what promising practices your school already has in place and which actions you and your staff should begin to take to improve student learning.

 Principal's Tools for Diagnosis and Action Planning

Principal's Tool 2.1: Possible Data Sources for Your School Diagnosis

PART TWO
THE TRANSFORMATIONAL LEADERSHIP FRAMEWORK

Chapter Three
Learning and Teaching

Chapter Four
School Culture

Chapter Five
Talent Management

Chapter Six
Planning and Operations

Chapter Seven
Personal Leadership

Learning and Teaching

WHEN DAVID O'HARA BECAME PRINCIPAL OF EXPEDITIONARY LEARNING SCHOOL for Community Leaders in Brooklyn, New York, only two of the sixty ninth graders were on track to graduate from high school, and the district had put the school on its list of schools in danger of being closed. O'Hara developed a new vision with staff: high expectations, rigorous instruction, and the mission to get all students to and through college. Given that 90 percent of his students would be the first in their families to go to college, he knew he needed to shift both instruction and school culture.

During O'Hara's first year, he and his staff rolled out two instructional strategies that O'Hara had seen help students improve their reading skills and better prepare them for college-level work: textual annotation and Socratic seminar. In every class, teachers helped students read text closely and then discuss the text using evidence to support their arguments. "There is a strong focus on complex reading, sophisticated writing, and oral presentation," O'Hara said.

Meanwhile, the staff worked to make sure the curriculum aligned to state standards. In addition to work over the summer, department teams completed regular cycles of inquiry, designing and implementing lessons, debriefing what worked for students with different needs and what didn't, and changing the lessons to strengthen them. O'Hara also credits his school's work developing teachers as leaders for enabling teachers in every classroom to implement these strategies effectively. (For more on developing teacher leaders, see chapter 5.)

With more rigorous instruction in place, the staff created assessments that hold students to high expectations. These new performance-based assessments required each student to write several research papers for every class during all four years at the high school. Students spend a few months researching a single topic through fieldwork and service and produce a project that they present to a panel of teachers, students, and parents. For one chemistry/physics culminating assessment, for example, a group of students wrote a forty-three-page research paper on hydrofracking, which they presented to staff in Senator Kirsten Gillibrand's office.

With all of these changes, O'Hara said, "Students start to understand that this [college] is very possible for them and that this is an expectation." A few years into O'Hara's tenure, every senior at Community Leaders was accepted to college, and when alumni came back to visit the school, they unanimously reported that annotation and Socratic seminar best prepared them for college.

THE IMPORTANCE OF INSTRUCTIONAL LEADERSHIP

The story of Community Leaders and David O'Hara demonstrates the importance of creating clarity across a school community not only about what students need to learn but also how they will learn most successfully. O'Hara set a vision for high expectations for students, worked with his staff to create a shared definition of rigorous instruction to meet those expectations, and aligned assessments to ensure students could demonstrate learning at those high levels. These are three of the key actions that we found in our research to be hallmarks of successful instructional leaders.

Learning and teaching is at the core of every school's work. As we emphasized in the introduction to this book, the most important work you can do at your school is to serve as a strong instructional leader. Teachers need a leader they can go to for guidance on a range of instructional issues—someone who will set a vision for effective instruction with high expectations and ensure all school practices are in line with that vision. Much research has found that when a principal does this critical work as an instructional leader, student achievement improves.[1] Principals who do this work well shift their school's work from basic coverage of material to teaching true mastery of skills.

What does excellent instructional leadership look like? In recent years, this term has taken on a broad definition that often includes not only leadership around quality curriculum and instructional strategies, but also the creation of a strong culture for learning and professional learning structures and practices that help teachers develop their skills. At New Leaders, all of these elements are crucial to the role of school leadership, and we have therefore incorporated all of them into multiple categories of the Transformational Leadership Framework (TLF).

The learning and teaching category detailed in this chapter focuses on the quality and rigor of curriculum and instructional planning, the consistency and quality of instructional strategies and classroom routines, the use of data and assessments to improve instruction, and the process of differentiating instruction to meet the needs of all students. We expect that most or all of these key practices sound familiar to you. There are great resources available in the field around effective curriculum planning, research-based instructional strategies, data-driven instruction, and differentiation and intervention. We use these resources in our own trainings for aspiring principals, and we will refer to a number of them in this chapter.

When we visited schools in our research, whether they were schools making consistent improvements in student outcomes or those struggling to make progress, school leaders told us that they were working hard on curriculum alignment, using data, and differentiating learning for students. But as we spent more time observing classrooms in their schools, sitting in on teacher team meetings, and talking with students, we recognized a number of key distinctions in how the rapidly improving schools were implementing these key practices versus the schools demonstrating slower growth. The detail in the framework and in the vignettes that follow will help you distinguish the practices of schools that believed they were effectively working on curriculum and instruction from those that were truly improving results for students.

We identified four key levers that principals use to improve achievement at their schools:

Lever 1. Aligned curriculum: *Aligning curriculum to both state and college-readiness standards.* Schools are most successful when staff have a deep understanding of the standards and how those standards connect to daily instruction; principals work with all their teachers to define and implement rigorous instruction; and together the principal and staff hold all students to high expectations of learning.

Lever 2. Classroom practices and instruction: *Ensuring consistent and high-quality classroom practices, routines, and instructional strategies across classrooms, which drive student achievement.* Implementing such routines, procedures, and strategies requires regular support for teachers, as well as monitoring and adjusting to ensure efficacy.

Lever 3. Data: *Using diverse student-level data to drive instructional improvement.* Moving beyond analysis to action, school leaders help teachers use data and insights to create corrective instruction plans that resolve student misconceptions, build deeper understanding, and provide students with clear goals and targeted feedback.

Lever 4. Student-centered differentiation. *Focusing on student-centered instruction.* Differentiation is not easy, but scaffolding instruction and tailoring it to individual students' learning needs is critical to student achievement. Principals can play an important role in supporting teachers in effective differentiation.

 **LEARNING AND TEACHING CATEGORY MAP**

**Lever 1:
Aligned Curriculum**

*Aligning curriculum to
both state and college-
readiness standards*

Actions

- **Action 1: Scope and Sequence:**
  Articulate clear sequence of
  key learning outcomes
  across grade levels aligned
  to standards.
- **Action 2: Units of Study:**
  Plan effectively to translate
  curriculum into lessons and
  units with clear objectives,
  activities, strategies, and
  assessments aligned to the
  standards.

**Lever 2: Classroom
Practices and Instruction**

*Ensuring consistent and high-
quality classroom practices,
routines, and instructional
strategies across classrooms
which in turn drive student
achievement*

Actions

- **Action 1: Classroom routines
  and instructional strategies:**
  Implement effective
  procedures, routines, and
  practices that support and
  facilitate student learning;
  match instructional methods
  to student need and use
  them consistently to improve
  student engagement,
  performance and development
  of critical thinking skills.

Lever 3:
Data

Using diverse student-level data to drive instructional improvement

Actions

- **Action 1: Identifying Data Sources and Assessments:**
  Collect data and develop learning targets using multiple assessments aligned to standards to inform student grouping and adjust curriculum pacing.

- **Action 2: Data Analysis and Action Planning:**
  Analyze multiple sources of data to track and assess student progress.

- **Action 3: Feedback on Progress:**
  Provide multiple opportunities to discuss progress toward goals with students.

Lever 4: Student-Centered Interventions

Focusing on student-centered instruction

Actions

- **Action 1: Interventions and Accelerations:**
  Put in place a pyramid of support for students below grade level, and preventions for students at risk; create expanded learning opportunities for those who have attained proficiency.

LEVER 1: ALIGNED CURRICULUM

As educational standards have gone through major changes in most states over the past few years, we have seen many school leaders and teachers struggling to align their curricula, assessments (both formative and summative), and instructional materials to those standards. In this era of increased expectations for college and career readiness, many successful leaders and schools have demonstrated similar practices to those we found in the TLF research schools. These school leaders and staff worked together to build a shared understanding of the standards and the level of instructional rigor needed to support student learning and success. They then aligned their year-long scope and sequence, unit plans, and daily lesson plans to those shared expectations and developed systems to consistently review these instructional plans to ensure they were meeting the needs of their students.

When we've shared these actions with principals in our own community of New Leaders–trained principals and with others in the field, we often hear from principals that they don't set curriculum for their schools because their district or school system has a mandated scope and sequence. In cases where the district (or state) determines many aspects of the curriculum and scope and sequence, we have seen school leaders closely review the curriculum and scope and sequence with their teams. They create systems that ensure that the full staff has a shared understanding of the standards and the curriculum, and that teachers can tailor the content for their students. As we saw in the schools we studied, effective curriculum planning and review processes allow teachers to adjust strategies as needed and help teachers provide a depth and pace of instruction rigorous enough to hold all students to high expectations.

In this lever of aligned curriculum, we describe two sets of actions: one that involves setting and consistently following a scope and sequence and the other that creates units of study. As you know from your own work, scope and sequence are critical for ensuring that your students are learning what they need to be ready for the next unit of study, the next grade, the next school, and, ultimately, college. The scope of material students are expected to learn and the pace at which they are expected to learn it must be well thought out, challenging, and achievable.

In the second action in this lever, units of study, we outline a number of practices that effective leaders have taken to regularly review and refine unit and lesson plans to make sure they remain aligned and are taught in ways that meet the learning needs of all students.

Lever 1: Action 1: Scope and Sequence

New Leaders found that the stages of principal and school actions around scope and sequence, outlined in table 3.1, led to improvement in student achievement.

Table 3.1 Lever 1: Aligned Curriculum: Action 1: Scope and Sequence

	PRINCIPAL ACTIONS	SCHOOL ACTIONS
Stage 1	Articulate a common definition of rigor in order to develop a shared understanding of what rigorous student work looks like in every course and grade. Ensure that curriculum maps clearly recommend pacing and address standards for each grade level and content area. Identify and address gaps between written, taught, and tested curriculum. Lead an analysis of the standards with the instructional leadership team to identify learning targets, curricular activities, and performance tasks that will inform units of study.	Teachers, staff, and students work toward a common definition of rigor aligned to the vision. Scope and sequence are broken into units, and assessments are aligned to grade-level standards as defined by the state assessment or state standards. A curriculum map delineates key ideas, essential questions, and several recommended texts for each unit.
Stage 2	Analyze the curriculum and standards to ensure vertical alignment of content across all grades and subject areas. Build the capacity of teacher teams to analyze and align standards, curricula, instructional strategies, and assessment tools. Ensure that curriculum teaches students how to use the process of inquiry to solve complex problems. Ensure that interim and formative assessments are aligned to the standards. High school: Intentionally increase the number of opportunities for students to participate in Advanced Placement (AP) and honors-level courses.	Vertical alignment allows users to see how skills connect and scaffold across grade levels. Grade-level and content teams review the standards together to analyze what students need to know to demonstrate mastery of each standard and what students would need to be able to do to demonstrate mastery of a standard. Teams analyze similarities and differences between these expectations and what is currently taught in the curriculum. High school: Admittance policies and entrance criteria for AP and honors classes are reviewed to ensure that all students have access to rigorous content.
Stage 3	Lead annual review process in which staff collaborate to assess alignment to college readiness standards across grades. Ensure that the curriculum requires students to routinely address and engage with complex integrated problems.	Staff demonstrate a shared understanding of how standards translate to rigorous expectations of student work and ensure that they are defining mastery consistently. Teachers find opportunities to surpass the state standards to require higher levels of learning that will lead to college and career success.

Stage 1 of the scope and sequence actions focuses on creating a shared definition of rigor that all teachers, students, parents, and support staff know and live by and that is conveyed in the scope and sequence and instructional plans. Consider what level of content and skills students must know for a particular grade or subject area. What kind of performance tasks and assessment items must they be able to complete successfully to demonstrate this level of knowledge? What does your daily approach to instruction need to look like if it is going to build this level of student knowledge and capability? If you surveyed your teachers on what rigor looks like in their classrooms, you might very well get a variety of answers. Working with your staff to create a clear definition and descriptions of rigor will help you and your teachers hold every student to the same level of high expectations and make sure every student is challenged in every class.

The staff at Powell Bilingual Elementary School in Washington, DC, made unpacking standards and creating a curriculum and assessments aligned to rigorous 21st Century Learning Standards the most important first step toward improving student learning. Later in this section, you will see exactly how they did that and moved successfully through the stages of development for curriculum alignment.

A leader's practices are in stage 2 when she has set up systems to ensure that curriculum is aligned across grade levels and content areas, all assessments are aligned to the curriculum, and teachers have the capacity to analyze alignment and refine curriculum as needed. We have all seen schools in which teachers spend time at the beginning of the school year teaching skills that their students should have learned the previous year, making it hard to get to all the material designated for their course. Frequent discussions about vertical alignment among teachers ensure that expectations are clear from grade to grade and allow teachers to identify persistent gaps in student learning from grade to grade.

As alignment to standards becomes more developed, so does the rigor of instruction. In stage 3, a school's instructional practices enable students to reach and surpass mastery of the state standards. In this section, we outline how principals in our study gauged the level of rigor in their lessons and made adjustments as needed, and we give you tools to do this work with your own staff.

DESIGNING YOUR OWN CURRICULUM

Designing curriculum is a time-consuming and resource-intensive undertaking that requires both adequate resources and a particular type of expertise. Some principals choose to lead their staff through the process of creating curriculum as a way to inspire staff buy-in to the curriculum and all teachers' deep understanding of instructional concepts, strategies, goals, and the connections among those concepts that could foster a more cohesive year for students. In this case, effective school leaders often bring in outside consultants to work with the administrative and teaching staff. Staff members bring their knowledge of student achievement and learning needs, and the outside expert understands the details of curriculum design and its integration with standards and assessments. Still, for most schools, there are now so many resources available that creating curriculum from scratch, especially for schools that are not yet in stage 1, would not be a good use of time and resources, as the process can stretch staff and take away from instructional planning.

If you decide to use existing curricular materials or if your curriculum or scope and sequence are provided by the district, you still benefit from sitting together as a staff and reviewing materials. This will ensure that you have a shared understanding of the scope and sequence, that it is well matched to the needs of your students, and that you have a shared definition of rigor across teams and grade levels.

Creating a Common Definition of Rigor

States, districts, and schools frequently use the word *rigor* to describe instruction and expectations, but they often do not have a common definition. What educators mean by *rigor*, however, is critical for shaping a school's expectations of students and teachers. The effective leaders we observed in our TLF research worked with their staffs to develop a common definition so that teachers are clear as to what constitutes rigorous lessons and units. To do this work, some principals start by reviewing the rigor of the tasks the students will be asked to complete to demonstrate what they have learned.

Examining the rigor of standardized tests can be a good place to start, particularly for schools whose students are not demonstrating full proficiency on those exams. Of course, as you do this, it's important to look for evidence that your state's summative exam is truly aligned to college-readiness standards. For example, if NAEP gives very different results or if students scoring proficient or advanced on the summative test still struggle on the ACT or SAT or end up taking remedial postsecondary classes, you have evidence that the state summative test may not be aligned to college-readiness expectations. In that case, it is worth using questions and tasks from those other assessments, in addition to your state exams, to help you define rigor for your school.

Once effective principals determine what their students need to know and be able to do, as evidenced in performance assessments, they use those assessments as guides for aligning the rigor of curriculum and instruction. They ask themselves, How rigorous is the content and the way we deliver that content? Are we scaffolding appropriately and preparing students for the rigor of the assessments? They examine lesson plans and units of study, instructional strategies and materials. One way to do this is to study lesson plans aligned with college-ready standards and analyze the rigorous strategies and activities found in those plans.

As these principals identify or develop learning tasks aligned to the standards, a stage 1 action, they consistently turn to a few widely respected and well-used tools designed to gauge the rigor of the tasks:[2]

- Bloom's taxonomy uses a multitiered scale to determine the level of expertise and type of thinking a student needs to use to complete a performance task. Organized from least to most complex, the taxonomy looks at the complexity of the work students need to do to complete the task to demonstrate knowledge, comprehension, application, analysis, synthesis, and evaluation.

- Webb's depth of knowledge (DOK) can be used to measure the level of complexity of a task by examining how deeply a student has to understand content to interact with it successfully. Organized from least to most complex, the DOK describes five levels: recall and reproduction, skills and concepts, strategic thinking and reasoning, and extended thinking.

- Hess's cognitive rigor matrix brings together Bloom and Webb, creating a tool that helps determine both the type of thinking required and the complexity of the task.

When applying these tools, principals look at the consistency of rigor between assessments (both their state or college-readiness summative assessments and any school-developed tasks or formative assessments), the planned curriculum, and the actual day-to-day instruction. They review school-based assessments to see if they build up to the same level of expected rigor as the state assessments. They review unit and lessons plans to see if the planned content and activities require the same levels of rigor and student work. And when observing instruction, they listen closely for the depth of the questions students are asked and the complexity of the required tasks. Do the students just need to respond to simple questions, or are they asked to create a product that demonstrates what they have learned in the unit? Principals use these questions and observations to continuously review the level of rigor and alignment of rigor between all assessments, curriculum plans, and daily instruction.

> Principal's Tool 3.1: Reflection Questions for Observing and Assessing the Rigor of Instruction

After the next section on developing effective units and lesson plans, we will give you the story of Powell Elementary and how the staff there used the standards as a guide to develop an agreed-on definition of rigor and then created a curriculum that challenged each of its students and increased their ability to meet standards.

 Potential Pitfalls

When schools are moving into stage 1 in any of the learning and teaching actions, there is little, if any, rigorous instruction. Principals in underperforming schools should be careful not to unconsciously lower expectations for rigor to match the current state of teaching in the school. It is important to stay in tune with effective teaching by continually referring to the district or state's rubrics and exemplars for effective teaching. We have seen principals support teacher development around increasing rigor in instruction by leading learning groups and professional development and by taking teachers to visit schools with similar student populations but stronger results to observe more rigorous instruction in practice.

Lever 1: Action 2: Units of Study

The principals and schools that we studied to inform the TLF were all relentless about planning for quality instruction. They built systems for teachers to develop and review strong unit plans aligned to the scope and sequence and expectations they had set in lever 1. They and their leadership team members reviewed unit and lesson plans on a regular basis for alignment and rigor, and they provided regular support and feedback to teachers on their planning. By breaking the scope and sequence into a series of detailed unit plans, teachers were better able to understand how the concepts to be taught that year built off one another.

The goal of unit planning is to create a cohesive series of lessons so that teachers are not planning day to day but rather are deliberately planning with an end goal in mind. Many of the successful schools we observed used protocols and practices from Jay McTighe and Grant Wiggins's understanding by design (UbD) framework to support their unit planning.[3] This framework helps school teams unpack standards and define specifically what students must know, understand, and be able to do by the end of a unit, and then plan units of study backward from their goals of meeting specific standards. These frameworks and approaches also serve as effective tools to help a staff define rigor.

We have found the backward planning process of UbD to be an effective approach to unit planning, a stage 1 action in the TLF (see table 3.2, which sets out the stages of development we found for developing and effectively using units of study). It has served as a training tool for principals trying to build the capacity of the ILT to assess units for rigor and alignment to standards (stage 2) and ensure that all instructional

Table 3.2 Lever 1: Aligned Curriculum: Action 2: Units of Study

	PRINCIPAL ACTIONS	SCHOOL ACTIONS
Stage 1	Articulate clear expectations for common planning time, and create standard unit planning and lesson planning templates. Model effective approaches to unit planning, and regularly review unit plans to provide teacher teams with feedback on their plans. Review the curriculum materials to ensure that they are aligned to the curriculum and lesson plans. Create and institute criteria for making judgments about the instructional design of curriculum materials. High school: Offer courses that support the development of 21st Century Skills and dismantle tracking practices that prevent some groups of students from participating in college preparatory classes.	Unit and lesson plans are developed by teacher teams and reviewed on a regular basis. All lesson plans include clear objectives, opening activities, multiple paths of instruction to a clearly defined curricular goal, and formative assessments. All materials are examined for clarity of purpose and relevance to students.
Stage 2	Lead staff in creating high-quality lesson plans that consistently include differentiation, corrective instruction, and formative assessment. Develop the capacity of the instructional leadership team to review unit and lesson plans for alignment and rigor. Lead teachers in planning for curriculum units that align to the state and college-readiness standards, and build their capacity to review and assess lesson quality. Implement common expectations of rigor, and ensure that all staff understand how they apply to specific subject areas. Make certain the curriculum materials match all areas of the curriculum, and ensure access to materials that are culturally relevant for all students.	Systems are in place to ensure that lesson and unit plans are written and reviewed on a set schedule. All unit plans include regular formative assessments of student learning. Teacher teams have deep and frequent conversations about formative student data and strategies to adjust instruction for every student. Students develop the skills to engage in complex problems through a process of inquiry, discovery, and self-questioning to solve complex problems. Grade-level and content-area teams review curriculum materials to ensure that they align with the standards and support the development of critical thinking skills. Unit and lesson plans consistently implement cognitively challenging tasks, and classroom instruction demonstrates connection to students' lives. Systems are in place to ensure that lesson and unit plans are aligned to the scope and sequence.

Table 3.2 (*continued*)

	PRINCIPAL ACTIONS	SCHOOL ACTIONS
Stage 3	Ensure that all curriculum materials include rigorous content and require students to apply knowledge. Ensure that staff are actively looking for connections among content areas.	Staff work to ensure that students know the necessary content to successfully transition from elementary school to middle school and from middle school to high school. Curriculum materials and unit plans are revised quarterly based on student achievement results.

materials include rigorous content and require students to apply their knowledge (stage 3).

Unit Design

Unit plans, which often span about six weeks, provide teachers with a broader view of what students will be learning by capturing all of the content in the scope of a unit. A complete unit plan will likely include the standards each lesson covers, the pacing of the lessons, instructional materials to use, and questions for inquiry and assessments. These plans, when they are clearly mapped out, also enable teachers to adjust instruction to accommodate students who have not yet learned the material without losing track of the end goal of the unit.

As a school leader, you can support unit planning by regularly reviewing the strength of the plans and how well teachers are implementing them. Are they aligned to college-ready standards? Do the classroom materials and unit assessments identified in the unit plan represent a consistent and high level of rigor? Are standardized strategies being introduced and scaffolded at each grade level? Throughout the year, this means leading teachers in examining levels of student mastery within curricular units to determine if the students are on pace with the scope and sequence. Some principals at low-performing schools have found it helpful to analyze units of study and sample student work from high-performing schools for guidance and inspiration.

Teachers and school leaders can apply rigor to unit design and redesign by asking:

- What are the overall learning goals, expectations, and cognitive demand of the unit?
- Do the learning activities in the unit have the coherence and increasing cognitive rigor to enable students to meet the goals of the lesson?

We have found it incredibly helpful to visually plan out units of study. You can do this be creating a table that outlines pacing, standards, instructional materials, and assessments to be used. When the unit of is planned out in this way for all teachers to use consistently, then you and your teachers can regularly monitor how well students are learning the material and adjust instruction as needed.

Principal's Tool 3.2: Sample Unit Plan for Fourth-Grade ELA

In schools in stage 1 of unit planning, school leaders regularly review instructional materials to make sure they are aligned to curriculum and lesson plans, but the school lacks alignment across grade levels. In those cases, you might find two second-grade classes on different parts of the scope, making it unlikely that the teachers are collaborating and sharing best practices. When common templates and processes for both unit and lesson plans are in place across grade levels and subject areas, another key stage 1 practice, the principal and teachers can clearly explain how each part of the lesson propels student learning toward meeting specific standards. At stage 2, the instructional leadership team takes on some responsibility for giving teachers regular feedback on their unit and lesson plans.

In a school at stage 3, teachers can identify connection points among content areas and, where possible, create common connections. For example, a teacher whose students are reading a piece of literature might also have students read a history text from that same time period, making the connections clear in class discussion and written assignments. At this stage, students should be able to explain what they are learning that day and how it fits into other lessons and into their own lives. This work requires the leadership of grade-level and content-area teams are aware of standards and expectations for the subsequent year and work to ensure that students will be prepared not just for their current challenges but also for future ones.

To show you what both actions in the aligned curriculum lever can look like in practice, we give you the story of an elementary school that raised math and reading achievement thanks in part to the staff's initial work aligning curriculum.

DESIGNING AND REGULARLY REVISING UNIT PLANS TO ENSURE RIGOR: MOVING FROM STAGE 1 TO STAGE 3 FOR ALIGNED CURRICULUM

Powell Bilingual Elementary School, Washington, DC

You might remember from the introduction to this book that when Janeece Docal became the principal at Powell, the school had been on the district's list of failing schools for a few years. After speaking with staff and families and reviewing student performance data, she made one of her top priorities developing a shared definition of *rigor*, a stage 1 action for scope and sequence. At the same time, teachers told her through a staff-wide survey that they wanted more support with developing assessments, curriculum, and lesson plans based on examinations of student work. To do this, she and her leadership team created the Curriculum Development Institute, a system for teachers to regularly work together to ensure that their curriculum and assessments are aligned with standards, and to revise lesson plans as needed to better meet all students' learning needs. Using high school Advanced Placement course work as the bar they wanted all of their students to be prepared to eventually meet, Docal and her teachers designed a curriculum that flowed seamlessly from college back to preschool, putting McTighe and Wiggins's backward design to work. "We really want to make sure that that pipeline exists," Docal said. They reviewed Washington, DC's standards to identify all of the distinct skills that are part of each standard so they could determine what students needed to know and be able to do when they leave each grade level.

With this scope and sequence in place, the teachers began to design unit plans. To ensure rigor in their instruction, they decided early on to use portfolio projects as their primary assessment tool. "Because we had, and still do have, a large number of students who are English language learners, the portfolio was the best method for all students to show what they know in nontraditional ways," Docal said. In fact, when the PARCC assessments were introduced, she found that Powell students were well prepared thanks to the rigor of the project-based learning they had been doing. For their projects, students had to think critically, problem-solve and analyze, and ask good questions. They required a lot of extended evidence-based writing and, in math, explanations of reasoning.

To complete the projects, students have weekly research expeditions and conduct interviews, taking field notes. For example, when studying a unit on plants and their connection to the environment, third graders grew rice in their classrooms and then went to Kenilworth Aquatic Gardens and the Anacostia River to plant it. They created a report and display that was mounted in the exhibit room of the Friends of Kenilworth Gardens. ("Another reason why partners are so important," Docal said.) To further ensure a level of rigor, Docal trained her teachers to lead inquiry-based discussions with their students, pushing students to think critically and engage in complex problems, a stage 2 action for units of study.

"All students at each grade level complete the same portfolio projects at Powell so that there were not just classrooms with pockets of excellence, but all teachers collaborated to design and score the student work and all students had the same expectations and opportunities to succeed," Docal said.

The Curriculum Development Institute (CDI) creates time for teachers in all grade levels to meet before and after every unit of study to discuss the standards and the projects, and it builds the capacity of the entire teaching staff to analyze and align standards, curricula, and instructional strategies, a stage 2 action for scope and sequence and units of study. Some teachers did push back at first, saying they felt micromanaged and distrusted in their ability to teach well without help from others. To counter these arguments, Docal spoke often about the benefits to collaborating on designing curriculum, lessons, and assessments. Because teachers were working in teams, those who believed in the work could talk to their colleagues about the positive changes they were seeing in their students' learning. Early on, Docal also gave teachers credit for trying the collaborative approach, rating them "effective" in their contributions to school community in collaboration simply for showing up to meetings.

The institute meets for the first time each year over the summer, for which Docal reserves funding to compensate teachers for putting in the extra time (see chapter 6 for more on budgeting). Teachers then meet for CDI six times throughout the year to develop projects for both literacy and math (teacher teams also meet twice a week to look at lessons and examine interim assessment data). For half-day retreats, Docal and her team arrange classroom coverage so teachers can attend, and extra funds are also budgeted for teachers who opt to meet for further planning after school. They discuss the standards and the level of rigor they have been seeing in the classrooms, analyze student work looking for student growth, and develop the next unit. "They talk about, is that good enough, is that rubric really going to get students to where we want them to be?" said Docal. Outside observers have praised the projects for being just what high-quality student work should look like, Docal said, because "it comes from being vetted by the staff, and then the teachers really own it, they love the projects. It comes from their passion as well as the standards."

The institute is "a full circle, the cycle of continuous improvement: developing, evaluating, implementing, reflecting," Docal said. "We're looking at what students are creating, whether it's before they create or afterwards, and then the teachers are tuning it and develop from there." To make sure all students are challenged, sometimes teachers swap classes. For example, if one teacher's students did well on one part of an assessment and another teacher's students did not, the teacher who had greater success might teach her colleague's students a mini-lesson, and her colleague would do the same for the other class on what was successful for her. "Teachers are then working as teams and are the experts," Docal said.

The entire staff also meets at the end of the year to examine student work again, a stage 3 action for scope and sequence. "We take a step back and say, 'How did this go? What tweaks do we want to make? Do we want to make any changes to our cornerstone or anchors assignments?'" Docal said.

At first, Docal led the work of the institute. However, once teachers developed the capacity to do the work, she asked her instructional coaches and teacher leaders to facilitate the sessions, allowing for a gradual release of leadership responsibility to her staff. (For more on distributing leadership, see chapter 5.)

Over time, students grew in both reading and math achievement: ELA proficiency nearly doubled during Docal's first five years at the school, and math proficiency rose by 15 percent. In addition, Powell became a Teacher Leader Initiative School as a result of their work to develop teacher capacity.

Principal's Tool 3.3: Reflection Questions for Aligned Curriculum

Principal's Tool 3.4: Diagnostic Tool for Lever 1, Aligned Curriculum

LEVER 2: CLASSROOM PRACTICES AND INSTRUCTION

As leaders we need to know the instructional improvements teachers must make, provide coaching and support to help them make those improvements, and monitor implemented strategies. In many cases, that means we have to retrain ourselves on what constitutes good instruction and help teachers make sure the instructional strategies they identify will help all students reach the instructional standards.[4]

At New Leaders, we think about routines and instructional strategies as closely related yet distinct components of instruction. The routines outline how students are expected to interact with the physical classroom space, the teacher, and their peers; instructional strategies are the teaching techniques used to move all students toward mastery. Table 3.3 outlines routines and instructional strategies that support student learning, the only action in this lever.

Procedures and routines outline how students should conduct themselves within classrooms. Creating consistency across rooms helps each adult enact common structures and expectations. More broadly, common routines are one way to bring the school's culture into the classroom (for more, see chapter 4). Think for a minute about how the routines in your school reflect your school's culture. How are students greeted and how does the school day open in each classroom? How and when can students request to leave the classroom? How is recess organized?

Whatever classroom routines you and your staff design, when they are clear, teachers and students can devote more of their time and attention to the content of the lesson. Routines include things like a regular lesson flow from whole class discussions or presentations to small group or station work and how efficiently and quickly students transition from activity to activity. In some classrooms, this means that every class starts with a "do now" that connects to the previous day's lessons. In other classes, students know there will be a mini-lesson and then some applied practice.

Although we don't prescribe a specific set of routines for New Leaders–trained principals, we do recommend that school leaders help their teachers arrive at common expectations and routines across classrooms so students know what is expected of them in multiple classrooms rather than having to learn different routines for each class they attend or teacher they interact with. These consistent routines are particularly important for English language learners.

> Principal's Tool 3.5: Questions to Consider When Establishing Common Routines

As schools move into stage 1, we often see a lot of variation across classrooms based on the teacher's style and experience level. Newer teachers in particular may struggle

Table 3.3 Lever 2: Classroom Practices and Instruction: Action 1: Classroom Routines and Instructional Strategies

	PRINCIPAL ACTIONS	SCHOOL ACTIONS
Stage 1	Identify and teach three to five consistent instructional strategies, classroom procedures, and routines that support student learning. Ensure that every staff member has the skills to implement the identified strategies, procedures, and routines. Monitor the implementation of the three to five nonnegotiable procedures and routines. Assess instructional strategies currently being implemented across grades and classrooms for alignment to student needs and standards. Lead schoolwide professional development that focuses on creating meaningful learning experiences that lead to mastery.	Classrooms share some common procedures, routines, and practices. Staff maximize learning by using transition time effectively. All staff participate in schoolwide professional development to learn and practice high-leverage instructional strategies.
Stage 2	Review and revise procedures and routines based on student learning data. Ensure that staff are identifying strategies that will meet all students' needs and ensure that all students master content. Monitor and make adjustments to the instructional strategies on the basis of student progress. Model effective instructional strategies and provide feedback to teachers about the implementation of instructional strategies.	Instructional time is maximized through consistent and efficient structures for class opening, homework collection, within-class transitions, and formative assessments. New staff and students are introduced to shared procedures and routines. Students lead and facilitate schoolwide practices. Teachers consistently use a variety of instructional strategies to differentiate content based on student learning needs. Students have frequent opportunities to lead through peer teaching. Students understand the ideas specified in the standards and draw on them in a variety of contexts. Students are regularly asked to defend their positions and to debate with others. Classroom instruction builds conceptual understanding, procedural skills, and fluency and gives time for practice and application.

(continued)

Table 3.3 (*continued*)

	PRINCIPAL ACTIONS	SCHOOL ACTIONS
Stage 3	Monitor and reinforce the routines and practices regularly. Systematically and regularly review the effectiveness of instructional strategies.	All teachers and students implement the schoolwide classroom practices and routines consistently and with quality. Classroom instruction incorporates high-quality experiences of rigorous dialogue and critical thinking skills. Students use problem-solving strategies in a variety of settings.

to identify, establish, and maintain consistent routines in their classrooms. If you find that you have a lot of variation, tool 3.6 in the Principal's Tool Kit can help you and your team arrive at some common routines.

Principal's Tool 3.6: Activity: Identifying Common Routines

By implementing common routines and procedures, you and your team can add precious instructional minutes to each day. Over time, those minutes will add up for your students and allow them to accomplish more in each school day.

Instructional Strategies

Perhaps one of your teachers asks students to talk to the text, while another tries reciprocal learning and two-column note taking. What works? Instructional strategies are techniques teachers use to facilitate student mastery of concepts and help students become independent, strategic learners. Because different strategies are suited to different types of content and lessons, teachers must be purposeful when choosing strategies.

We recommend identifying three to five instructional strategies that are used consistently across classrooms, a stage 1 action in the TLF. You might want to begin by introducing strategies that can be used in multiple content areas so that all teachers can be engaged in this process. You or your leadership team can facilitate professional development that adds to the teachers' tool kit and outlines how teachers can create meaningful learning experiences that lead to mastery. To determine the instructional strategies that your students need, you might look closely at trends that you are seeing in your data. For example, if students are struggling to make logical inferences from fictional and nonfictional texts, you might try to identify strategies to address that growth area.

Keeping to that example, you may determine that you want all teachers to focus on logical inferences; your next step, then, is to differentiate the strategy for each grade band. For example, kindergarten teachers can work on prediction as well as inference to build a solid foundation of literacy skills. These teachers may determine that they are going to begin read-alouds with a picture walk where students predict what will happen. Next teachers can pause in the story to ask students to reflect on what they know and to infer why they think a character has taken a specific action, how the character is feeling, or other ideas that the author alluded to without explicitly stating.

For older grades, teachers build the same skill using more complex texts and additional strategies. For example, they might practice the strategy of Questioning the Author, which gives them license to explore an author's intent and clarity.[5] Or they might hone using inference to interpret figurative language, advertisements, or political cartoons.

Across grades, you may also choose to implement some similar structures, such as response journals, graphic organizers, or culminating projects, that include the same or similar components to unify the focus area across the school.

 Potential Pitfalls

Teachers may choose strategies based on their comfort with the strategy. Throughout this section, we discuss ways you can build your teachers' tool kit of strategies, but we also recommend that you and your team practice asking, "How is this strategy going to help students meet this outcome as you plan lessons?"

 TEACHING AND IMPLEMENTING A CONSISTENT INSTRUCTIONAL STRATEGY MOVING FROM STAGE 0 TO STAGE 2 FOR CLASSROOM ROUTINES AND INSTRUCTIONAL STRATEGIES

ASPIRE Centennial, Huntington Park, California

When Jennifer Garcia made an initial assessment of the state of ASPIRE Centennial (now ASPIRE Ollin University Preparatory Academy) during her first couple of months on the job as principal, her own observations, along with anonymous surveys she took of staff and students, showed that classroom instruction was not engaging or challenging students. "I am in classrooms asking kids about their learning, and kids are not giving me answers," she said. On top of that, nearly half of students said in a survey that they did not like going to school. "I am getting red flags all over the place," Garcia said of the indicators of low rigor.

With English language learners, the majority of the student body, Garcia looked for instructional strategies that would push them to talk to each other about what they were learning. "They are never going to get to academic discourse if they don't learn to talk to each other," Garcia said. She introduced the staff to reciprocal teaching, which offers four clearly defined roles for engaging with and discussing text: summarizing, generating questions, clarifying meaning, and making predictions. To support teachers in implementing the strategy, Garcia led schoolwide professional development that focused on creating meaningful learning experiences for students, a stage 1 action. In those sessions, Garcia took feedback from teachers on how reciprocal teaching was going in their classrooms and addressed issues of management necessary to implement the strategy successfully. In each session, they also delved deeply into one aspect of the teaching strategy, doing the kind of work they would ask of their own students.

The teachers spent the entire year implementing and revising the reciprocal teaching strategy. "I don't expect you to go to one professional development session and start it the next day," Garcia told them. "That's an unreasonable expectation. It's not sound for you as a teacher, and it's not sound for kids. You need to read about it; you need to see it in action; you need to make it work for you and your classroom." In addition to providing professional development, Garcia also regularly observed teachers in their classrooms, gave immediate feedback, and offered one-on-one coaching.

Teachers scaffolded their instruction when they introduced the new strategy, a stage 2 action. One teacher first had each group of students focus on one strategy each day. Working in groups, the teacher said, enabled students to teach one another the concepts, a stage 2 school action: "A student can explain things in a way that a teacher can't."

Another teacher chose to start her lessons on reciprocal teaching with summarizing because that was a foundational skill she knew most of her students were already familiar with: "It's something they can be successful at from the beginning. Once they can do that, they can clarify meaning; then they will be able to make predictions and then question the things they are reading.

If they don't have a sound idea of what's in front of them, they won't be able to do those other things."

In both the initial professional development and the subsequent follow-up, Garcia incorporated practice, feedback and refinement that teachers could use broadly.

Implementing the stage 1 actions of improving instruction that we just outlined can be easier said than done. This work requires adults to change their practices, which is not always easy. Understandably, change can be met with resistance. In chapter 7, we go into detail about how you can manage change by honing certain leadership skills. Some of this work requires building agreement with the staff that there is benefit to making change—for example, moving away from every classroom being its own island and choosing consistent approaches that are good for students and allow teachers to learn from and support each other around implementation. As leaders, we can help teams see the benefit in making changes to practices by inviting them into the process of determining the focus areas and outlining the rationale. A new principal at an elementary school in Memphis was able to do just that in her early efforts to improve instruction.

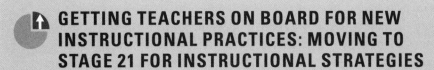

GETTING TEACHERS ON BOARD FOR NEW INSTRUCTIONAL PRACTICES: MOVING TO STAGE 21 FOR INSTRUCTIONAL STRATEGIES

LaRose Elementary School, Memphis, Tennessee

When Tonya Cooper became principal of LaRose, she immediately saw the need to improve literacy instruction. She set out to do so by creating some common routines across classrooms. Teachers in her previous school had had success with work stations in their classrooms, and she thought it could work well at LaRose too. However, the concept of work stations was foreign to most LaRose teachers. Cooper knew she had to be sensitive to concerns about change and not do too much at once. "Telling them, 'Well, this worked in my other school and we will do it here,' was not the right approach," she explained. She needed to demonstrate to teachers that her ideas could work, particularly since her staff was a little wary of her knowledge of elementary education, as Cooper's experience was entirely in high schools. Some teachers suspected that students would see work stations as play time, while others worried about the amount of work creating effective work stations would require.

To help her teachers learn more about work stations, Cooper invited the academic support team from her previous school to talk to the LaRose teachers about their experiences and then sent a group of teachers, including the lead teacher from each grade, to that school to observe work stations in action. Teachers at LaRose started to open up to the strategy when they saw instructors at other schools having success with work stations.

Cooper then led her staff through a thoughtful and systematic approach to understanding and rolling out work stations. "We were sensitive to make sure we didn't throw teachers out and expect them automatically to perform or to do work stations at optimal levels," she said.

She created time in the schedule for teacher teams to meet three times a week to examine data and classroom trends and to discuss when to use small group instruction, whole group, or work stations based on students' levels of mastery. Cooper expected each teacher to have differentiated work stations, a stage 2 action for instructional strategies, so they used those meetings to discuss those strategies too. Initially Cooper sat in on one of those meetings each week; once she had created an academic support team of coaches and teacher leaders, she asked them to support team meetings.

Cooper also changed full faculty meetings from gatherings that dealt with housekeeping matters to professional development sessions. She expected teachers to bring materials they were using for their work stations and take turns simulating their work stations for their colleagues. She pushed them to think about the work they were doing in their classrooms. "Why did you select those activities?" she asked one teacher after her demonstration.

"[Cooper] takes a tremendous amount of time and allows us to practice, practice, practice routines and procedures," one second-grade teacher said. The teachers introduced work stations to their classes at the beginning of the year, one new station per week, making sure they understood how one station worked before introducing a new one. Teachers did a lot of modeling for students. "We saw the one [station] work, and then we incorporated a few more and a few more," one teacher said.

Cooper and members of the leadership team regularly observed classrooms and gave teachers feedback. "I wanted teachers to feel that when the literacy coach walks into the classroom, that this is not an indictment against your teaching abilities. We are not trying to catch you in anything; we want to act as a support base and listen to you and know what we can do to make your school day work," Cooper said.

Said the second-grade teacher, "With Ms. Cooper's guidance and her leadership, I am able to see tremendous results with my children, great achievement.... That is the biggest thing that has given me buy-in to her vision, because her vision makes sense."

Cooper's personal leadership practices also helped her develop collaborative and trusting relationships with teachers. She had an open door policy, teachers said. One teacher described Cooper as "genuine, honest, open, there for us, letting us know we can come to her anytime. If there is something she is doing and we don't like it, we can go and talk to her about it." At the same time, she has held teachers to high expectations. While at times that can be daunting, one teacher said, Cooper was also very encouraging. "I always feel like my principal is in my corner," she said. And her work paid off: during Cooper's last four years at the school, ELA proficiency rose by 15 percent and math proficiency by 9 percent.

Monitoring and Adjusting Strategies

In stage 2, once you and your teachers are deeply familiar with the standards, all of you can monitor and adjust instructional strategies based on student progress. Looking closely at instructional strategies will allow your team to complete a review of the effectiveness of the strategy selected to teach a lesson. In stage 2, you want teachers to be asking themselves: Are students still struggling with key concepts or assessment tasks? If so, does that point to a need to identify additional or different instructional strategies for that content area and grade level? Or do students simply need more practice?

As you prepare to move into stage 2, we recommend you start by reviewing each teacher's knowledge of instructional strategies so that you can focus your coaching, development, and feedback.

> Principal's Tool 3.7: Stage 2 Instructional Strategies Practice Activity

Once you do that, you will likely find that teachers are better able to build conceptual understanding and fluency in their classrooms, and students will understand what is expected of them for each lesson.

> Principal's Tool 3.8: Diagnostic Tool for Lever 2, Classroom Routines and Instructional Strategies

LEVER 3: DATA

After more than a decade of mandated school data collection, most schools are well versed in the importance of using student data to inform instruction. A number of authors have identified detailed strategies and concrete recommendations for effectively analyzing and using data at the school level.[6] However, as we noted in the introduction to this chapter, even with so much focus on the use of data and so many high-quality resources for doing so, we saw large variation across schools in their approaches to using data to inform instruction. The results were startlingly uneven. Even more concerning, all of the schools we visited, regardless of their approach to data use and their results for students, thought they were using data well. For this lever, we will focus in particular on the differences between stage 1 and stage 2 practices around data so that the sequence of implementation is clear and also so you have some questions to use with staff to reflect on your own current practices around using data to improve instruction.

In our research on how schools use data, we found three essential sets of actions that lead to improved student achievement: Identifying data sources and assessments (addressed in table 3.4), data analysis and action planning, and providing feedback on progress to students and families.

Lever 3: Action 1: Identifying Data Sources and Assessments

Action 1 focuses on having diverse and accurate data sources about student learning, student outcomes, and culture and climate indicators to inform key decisions throughout the school, especially choices about instruction at the classroom level. This set of data begins with a focus on student academic assessment results, but also includes a wide range of information about students and schools. In our research, we observed teacher teams comparing student grades to state test results to test the alignment of their grading policies to the state expectations. We sat in on grade-level teams poring over student attendance and behavior referral data to identify students needing additional social-emotional supports beyond their academic interventions. And most important, we listened as teachers reviewed interim assessment data and examples of student work to identify specific areas of student misunderstanding. While these are just some of the data sources available to inform instruction, they all provide examples of intentional gathering and use of student data.

As we began our research into how different schools were using data, we saw schools that were using only summative state test data to inform instruction. Today, almost all schools we visit have some form of interim assessments—tests given three to four times a year to provide more frequent information about student performance, aligned to the year-end state test. However, to fully meet our definition of stage 1 for identifying data

Table 3.4 Lever 3: Data: Action 1: Identifying Data Sources and Assessments

	PRINCIPAL ACTIONS	SCHOOL ACTIONS
Stage 1	Determine the most important student learning data points, including attendance and discipline, that will drive decisions, and use those data to make decisions. Ensure that staff are looking at multiple measures to assess student progress, including informal checks for understanding and performance tasks. Implement an ongoing common interim assessment cycle and ensure a quick (forty-eight-hour) turnaround of data so that leading data trends and gaps in learning are used to guide decisions. Analyze interim assessments for alignment to state standards and written curriculum; if interim assessments are not available, pick or develop an assessment that is aligned with state standards and written curriculum. High school: Build initial systems to track attendance, grades, and credit earning for secondary students to identify early off-track warning signs.	Interim assessments are given three to four times per year to determine if students learned what was taught, and time for corrective instruction is built into the scope and sequence. High school: Performance of secondary students is tracked closely throughout the school year to ensure that they remain on track to graduate in four years. Every teacher differentiates instruction or reteaches key concepts on the basis of formative student achievement data.
Stage 2	Train staff in the effective development of rigorous performance tasks that should be created to truly assess mastery, particularly against the state and college-readiness standards. Set the expectation, and provide time for teachers to develop larger projects and rubrics for assessing mastery.	Interim assessments are aligned to college-readiness standards. In addition to regular interim assessments, teachers use multiple assessments to inform instruction and guide corrective instruction.
Stage 3	Make every instructional and student support decision using evidence of student progress. Hold teachers accountable for knowing how their students are progressing. Carefully select assessment items to align to the level of cognitive rigor associated with a given learning target or standard.	Teachers track the learning of every student using multiple measures to determine individualized student goals and plans. High school: School staff review college acceptance, matriculation, persistence, and graduation data to improve schoolwide learning and teaching, culture, and college supports.

sources and assessments, the data from these interim assessment need to be available to teachers immediately after the tests are given. All too often this doesn't happen when larger districts administer the tests.

Beyond having interim assessments in place, the other key factor for stage 1 in this action is mostly relevant for middle and high schools. The effective secondary schools we studied were all gathering and regularly reviewing key on-track data on every student, as defined by the Chicago Consortium on School Research.[7] By tracking individual course grades, attendance, and credit earning for each student, focusing especially on the ninth grade, these schools were more quickly identifying critical student needs and supports.

In stages 2 and 3, teachers develop additional projects that require students to apply knowledge in new ways and demonstrate full mastery of a particular set of content and skills. The semester-long projects described in the Expeditionary Learning School for Community Leaders vignette that opens this chapter are a good example of teacher-developed projects and assessments. Though they don't provide data as frequently as interim assessments, they offer the best sense of whether students are fully able to apply their knowledge. At this stage, school leaders also expect teachers to have a detailed awareness of each student's current data and to use that information for instructional planning.

Principal's Tool 3.9: Reflection Questions for Identifying Data Sources and Assessments

However, as important as it is to ensure availability, alignment, and timeliness of student data, it has little impact on instruction without the next major action: data analysis and instructional action planning, described in table 3.5.

Lever 3: Action 2: Data Analysis and Action Planning

Imagine this scene. Twenty teachers are sitting in the small chairs of a third-grade classroom for their weekly professional development session. Small groups of teachers have pulled student desks together and are marking up printouts of the recent benchmark testing scores, looking for trends in the data. Are there items that most students answered incorrectly? Are there other items that assessed that skill? Was the misconception the result of a poorly worded question, or did the students struggle on all questions related to that skill? Where did the students show evidence of growth and improvement? Where do teachers still need to redouble their efforts to clarify concepts for students?

Table 3.5 Lever 3: Data: Action 2: Data Analysis and Action Planning

	PRINCIPAL ACTIONS	SCHOOL ACTIONS
Stage 1	Hold regular meetings with teacher teams to review student work and other forms of student-level data. Explicitly link conversations about assessment to conversations about how to change instructional practice.	Teachers review assessments at the beginning of each interim assessment cycle and use evidence to predict student performance. Student data are consistently used as the basis for decisions around instruction and adult professional learning. Staff have data on the achievement gap in their school and use those data to intentionally prioritize closing the gap.
Stage 2	Develop and support staff ability to analyze data and use those data to identify and prioritize student needs, guide student grouping, and design corrective instruction strategies. Provide evidence of progress and student work toward an established goal when giving feedback to staff. Create action plans for whole school professional development with and for teachers in order to address any learning gaps that exist across classrooms. Observe and provide feedback on corrective instruction to support effective use of data.	A continuous data review process is in place (including aligning assessments, analyzing interim and formative assessments, and taking action based on results through corrective instruction and other strategies) to ensure that student misconceptions are addressed through instruction and students learn taught material. The instructional leadership team reviews disaggregated data to track and monitor the progress of all students and provide evidence-based feedback to teachers. Teacher teams frequently analyze data for root causes; on the basis of this analysis, students are regrouped and targeted, and the curricular scope and sequence is revisited throughout the school year. Instructional decisions throughout the year, including student grouping/differentiation and interventions, are based on interim, daily, and weekly formative assessments.

(continued)

Table 3.5 (*continued*)

	PRINCIPAL ACTIONS	SCHOOL ACTIONS
Stage 3	Implement a comprehensive student assessment process that creates common expectations for corrective instruction action planning. Hold teachers accountable for using multiple sources of student learning data during common planning, classroom observations, and observation debriefings.	Teachers use a corrective instruction action planning process to identify trends in student misconceptions, identify why students may not have learned the concept, and plan to create a revised approach to instruction and assessment using the data. Teacher teams have deep and frequent conversations about formative student data and about strategies to adjust instruction for every student.

In stage 1 of data analysis and action planning, the key action is making the connection between interim assessment data and instructional improvement. By making data available to all teachers and developing protocols for teachers to look at these data, teachers are also given the tools to successfully analyze the data. Frequent assessments are one of the best tools teachers have to improve their own practice and meet the needs of their students. In New Leaders' training, we provide a range of articles and vignettes that leaders can use with staff members to build a positive culture around data use.[8]

Once teachers understand how data analysis can support instruction and data become a public part of teacher conversations and culture in the school, leaders can move rapidly to stages 2 and 3 in data analysis and action planning, though these actions require significant capacity building and professional development for many teachers and staff members. Leaders develop the skills of teachers to analyze the data in their teacher team meetings and, most important, create detailed action plans with their teacher teams or individual classrooms based on the data analysis. In many of the schools we visited in which staff honestly felt they were using data effectively but they were not seeing improved results for students, this was the crucial missing step. Teachers were not creating detailed plans based on the data, and school leaders were not following up to see if these plans were enacted and if they succeeded in addressing student misconceptions and challenges.

An important term to clarify in our framework is *corrective instruction*, which we use in our training and support of principals in place of *reteaching*. We have found that even in schools where teachers are successfully identifying student gaps, the response is too often to teach the same material in the same way in the hope that students will better understand through repetition. In corrective instruction, as originally defined by Robert Sternberg and referenced by Thomas Guskey, the teachers plan a different approach to teaching and assessing the content, based in large part on identifying and resolving the underlying misconceptions of students that are leading to assessment errors.[9] Rather than "reteaching" content the same way, they identify alternative instructional strategies and approaches that are more likely to lead to clearer student understanding and skill mastery.

In the following vignette, we look at how the leaders of one school in Washington, DC, supported their teachers to analyze data and use those analyses to improve their instruction, with a particular structure for corrective instructional planning.

CREATING A SYSTEM FOR CORRECTIVE INSTRUCTION: MOVING TO STAGE 2 FOR DATA ANALYSIS AND ACTION PLANNING

E. L. Haynes Public Charter School, Washington, DC

When students' scores on district exams were mediocre, the directors and instructional leadership team at E. L. Haynes Public Charter School realized they and their staff were not putting the assessment data they were gathering to good use. "While we had laid a solid foundation of looking at interim assessments, teachers were not putting down a concrete plan once they completed their instruction," Eric Westendorf, the chief academic officer, said. "Without that, it's hard for teachers to hold themselves accountable for following through, and it's hard for school leaders to hold teachers accountable and provide them needed support."

To help teachers take the crucial next steps once they determined what material students were struggling to learn, the school's leadership team created what it called the Reteach Action Plan (work that New Leaders calls corrective instruction in the TLF) to codify in concrete terms next steps for data analysis, a stage 2 action for data collection and analysis. In conjunction with expanding the set of interim assessments the school was using, teachers were given a template to plan next steps after each assessment. The plan outlined for the whole class, small groups of middle- or low-performing students, and individual students of major concern:

- What standards and areas were strongest
- What standards within each area warranted more time for more instruction
- Why students did not learn the standard or show improvement
- Instructional plan for the next six weeks

During the staff's weekly professional development sessions, Westendorf led teachers through sessions on scoring, analysis, and using the form to draft next steps. He also met with each teacher for about twenty minutes after school or during a free period to discuss the plans, the thinking behind them, and how they connected to improvement goals, making explicit links between assessments and how to change instructional practice, a stage 1 action in data analysis and action planning and stage 2 for identifying data sources and assessments. Within a few days after each assessment, teachers also met for a full day in grade-level teams to examine the data and create their corrective teaching plans. (A quick turnaround of assessment results is important; it allows teachers to use gaps in learning to guide instructional decisions, a stage 1 action for identifying data sources and assessments.)

Leaning on the work of Paul Bambrick-Santoyo's *Driven by Data*, teachers used data to hypothesize why students did well on some questions and not others, Westendorf said.[10] They looked at which standards the incorrectly answered questions were linked to, stage 2 for assessments. They examined not only which questions the students got wrong, but also the answers they gave, looking for clues into what students were thinking when they answered the question. This level of analysis helped teachers plan ways to correct their instruction. For example, Westdendorf said, if you see that students are incorrectly answering questions about main idea and students are selecting responses focused on an interesting fact in the story rather than the main idea, then you know you need to plan your corrective instruction not just on what a main idea is but how to differentiate between remarkable details and main ideas.

When creating a corrective instruction plan, teachers looked at these patterns for whole classes, groups of students within classes, and individual students. In their action plans, they summarized their analysis for each concept they planned to revisit, listed which students were struggling with each concept, wrote out how they planned to correct their instruction, and gave a time line for correcting the concept. They also devised a plan for monitoring the effect of their corrective instruction. Teachers did their analysis and action planning in grade teams, with lead teachers and other school leaders circulating among the teams to offer advice and ask questions.

Said Westendorf, "The use of the common planning template was probably the most influential aspect of our interim assessment cycle in terms of moving our teachers' practice because it forced them to do something with data." In the spring after the templates were first implemented, students saw a 19 percent gain in math proficiency. Improvement in reading was not nearly as strong—only a 3 percent gain. Westendorf attributed this small gain to the content of the interim assessments, which, after a close analysis, he realized were not aligned closely enough to the DC standards. After they changed the assessments, students saw an 18 percent gain in reading the next year and another 19 percent increase in math.

Based on our observations of schools effectively using data for corrective instruction such as E. L. Haynes, we have developed our own template for planning corrective instruction that we teach across our leadership development programs. The template, in the Principal's Tool Kit in the appendix, shows the blank template we recommend, and tool 3.10 shows a complete example of the corrective instruction template.

Principal's Tool 3.10: Corrective Instruction Action Planning Template

Creating plans from data doesn't stop with the teacher or teacher team–level corrective instruction plans. At stage 3, data on every student are also used to inform whole school professional development focus areas and the professional development plan. These data are also used frequently to update and revise student intervention schedules and plans. Rather than setting one schedule for student interventions that is static through a whole year, the schools we saw at stage 3 made adjustments to their intervention plan for each student after each interim assessment, ensuring that all students in need of intervention were receiving support but also recognizing and celebrating when students had successfully mastered a particular skill or content area and were no longer in need of deeper support.

Lever 3: Action 3: Feedback on Progress

While the first two actions within the data lever focus deeply on teachers and school leaders and their use of data to improve instruction, action 3 focuses on the importance of engaging students and their families in similar cycles of reflection and action (see table 3.6 that describes assessing progress and providing feedback). Students and their families need to fully understand the goals and expectations for each grade level and content area, they need frequent and accurate information about where they are relative to that standard, and they need feedback about how they can improve and meet the objective. Previous writers have pointed out that students make the best use of feedback when it is detailed and directly connected to a goal, such as a standard.[11] When students see that the feedback from their teachers is directly and explicitly tied to their learning and is not just an exercise in compliance,[12] they feel more connected

Table 3.6 Lever 3: Data: Action 3: Feedback on Progress

	PRINCIPAL ACTIONS	SCHOOL ACTIONS
Stage 1	Create expectations for assessing progress toward proficiency and specified actions. Build a practice whereby students are given frequent feedback on their work, including clearly outlined areas for improvement. Establish grading practices and summative judgments that align to learning targets.	Staff understand criteria for mastery of specific tasks. Summative assessments and grades are given after multiple rounds of feedback.
Stage 2	Define and implement a feedback policy that focuses on specific criteria for success. Require teachers to separate the consequences for missing time or work from the assessment of mastery or progress toward goals. Implement a standards-based grading policy characterized by the attainment of learning targets.	Expectations are consistent and known by all. Feedback is specific and helps students understand and correct their mistakes and misconceptions. Summative assessments and grades use multiple measures to assess student progress. Students track their own goals and progress data, know their current level of proficiency, and receive frequent feedback on their performance and on areas of improvement.
Stage 3	Build interrater reliability so that assessment of student work and student progress is consistent across classrooms. Create systems to make daily or weekly grades visible to families.	There is interrater reliability across classrooms. Students are assessed for what they know and are able to demonstrate. Students and families can continually monitor progress using an online grading system.

to and responsible for their learning. When done well, feedback reinforces the expectations teachers are placing on students and offers a clear and encouraging pathway for the work students need to do and the materials they need to learn and to reach their goals.

Many of the high-gaining schools that we visited also made a powerful link between work on student feedback and student efficacy, which we discuss in greater detail in chapter 4. In these schools, students believe, and their teachers believe, that with hard work, they can succeed and reach expected standards, regardless of their current level of proficiency. This belief is best expressed by psychologist Carol Dweck in her work on mind-set.[13] She describes a "growth mind-set" for individuals who believe that they have the ability to improve and therefore take data and feedback as key information to help them in the process. They remain focused on the goal, see failure as a learning opportunity about what not to do, and welcome feedback and suggestions for new strategies.

These schools taught students about the concept of growth mind-set and that success comes through effort, and then they connected that concept to the frequent information and feedback coming from formative and interim assessments. This work goes hand in hand with giving students a clear understanding of what is expected of them, how they are doing in a particular lesson, and what they need to learn to master a particular task.

As an example, one elementary school in Denver saw great improvements in students' writing skills after the principal and her teaching team taught them to be responsible for their own learning to analyze their achievements, identify areas in need of improvement, and devise plans for how they would make those improvements. These practices enabled the school to put in place the stage 2 action of students tracking their own data and progress and owning their own strategies for success.

 USING DATA TO SET BETTER STUDENT GOALS: MOVING FROM STAGE 1 TO STAGE 2 FOR FEEDBACK ON PROGRESS

Steck Elementary School, Denver, Colorado

When the Denver school district encouraged schools to set SMART goals as a way to increase student achievement, La Dawn Baity, principal of Steck Elementary School, took the opportunity to create a schoolwide system for every teacher to use data to set student goals. Many of the teachers at Steck were already using assessment results to identify students' learning needs and set goals, but, Baity said, the goals were too generic and goal setting was not happening in every classroom. "To really monitor progress and get a handle on moving all of our students, we needed to set better goals," Baity said.

She started by having vertical teacher teams meet every six weeks to set and revise SMART goals. In these meetings, teachers analyzed different forms of student work and made projections based on each student's progress. The teams also identified proficiency rates for particular skills or concepts in order to choose an area of instruction to focus on. For example, one literacy team identified a need to focus on identifying main ideas and supporting details. Teachers then wrote a SMART goal to reflect their projection.

After attending a workshop run by Robert Marzano, author of many works on instructional practice, about goal setting, Baity and some of her teachers were inspired to shift some of the responsibility for setting goals and monitoring progress to the students. "We had the adults taking all the responsibility and holding all the power," said Baity. By giving students frequent feedback on their work, a stage 1 action, and having them engage with that feedback, Baity hoped students would better understand what skills they needed to learn.

The teachers started by teaching groups of students to analyze their own work and identify areas they needed to focus on improving and then to set challenging but attainable goals for those areas. Baity and the teachers created self-assessment and goal-setting rubrics and worksheets for students to use. On those sheets, in addition to writing in the most recent assessment score and a goal, students also chose what strategies they would use to meet those goals.

After each assessment, teachers facilitated class conversations about how students did, asking who reached their goals and what strategies they used to get there. Students created graphs to chart their progress and then set goals for the next unit assessment based on that progress. Having students complete this work themselves, said one teacher, "gives students buy-in and makes them more accountable for their learning." For example, the literacy team of third-, fourth-, and fifth-grade teachers created self-assessment tools for students to regularly monitor how well they were doing on identifying the main idea and supporting details in a passage, and identify strategies to address their areas of need.

Some teachers also held individual conferences with students a few times a year after each major assessment to look at the test results and talk about whether they reached their goals. Together they then devise strategies the student can use to reach her next goal. "The goal-setting conference really falls under the umbrella of efficacy training," a fifth-grade teacher said. "If they can realize that their effort has a direct, tangible impact on their work, they will continue to do it. And when we codify it in a goal-setting meeting, they know 'I did X, I did Y, and I wound up at Z,' and they will continue to do that process because it breeds success."

The goal sheets that students fill out show student performance in a particular subject throughout the year so that they can see their progress and the strategies that helped them get there. In a goal-setting meeting with another fifth grader who did not meet his goal, the teacher talked with him about what strategies he had used over the previous few weeks. He showed that he had been working hard at them, and the teacher commended him for that. They then looked at some sample questions he got wrong and came up with a new strategy he can use to continue to improve: asking the teacher and his classmates questions when he does not understand material.

The teacher told the student, "Goals are all about work completion and taking ownership, and that is where you really are starting to grow. With your confidence and the actions you are starting to do, I think you are going to get there at the end of the year too."

This fifth grader noted it was good to have the strategy written down so that he could look back at it in his notebook when he needed a reminder. Added another fifth grader, "If you have a goal, you are going to work really hard on that specific thing," the student said. "A good goal is a goal that you know with a little bit of work you can achieve. It also tells how you are going to reach that goal."

After two years of student goal-setting work, students' writing scores rose by ten points. Teachers also said students were working harder and were more focused, and several students improved their classroom behavior and work habits. This process is not without its challenges, though. Baity noted that one of the big challenges moving forward is being able to support teachers to meet with every student individually. The math facilitator was able to meet with every fifth-grade student, and the literacy support teacher was starting to do the same with fourth- and fifth-grade students. Several teachers also said they struggled to get students to be specific about their goals and were trying to get them to better describe how they will address each area of need they have explicitly identified.

Principal's Tool 3.11: Reflection Questions for Providing Student Feedback

Principal's Tool 3.12: Diagnostic Tool for Lever 3, Data

LEVER 4: STUDENT-CENTERED DIFFERENTIATION

Students come into our schools with a variety of academic skills, strengths, and areas of growth. Our challenge is to support and respond to the needs of all students regardless of where they enter at the start of a school year. As leaders, we have to establish supports and systems that equip teachers to respond quickly and effectively to the needs of all students. In this lever, we discuss supports for students who are performing below grade level as well as for students who have already attained mastery of a skill. Table 3.7 shows the stages of practices principals put in place to differentiate instruction.

Lever 4: Action 1: Interventions and Accelerations

System of Interventions

We define a system of interventions as a set of intentional strategies that helps assess the needs of each student so the teachers can accurately determine what supports and resources that student needs to master skills and content. Creating a schoolwide system of interventions requires a school team to develop multiple supports that will help students learn. At the core of effective interventions is the ability to ask and answer the question: What do I do when a student has not mastered the content of a lesson? Thinking about interventions in this way requires teachers to be creative problem solvers and to look closely at individual students and patterns across their classrooms and at their own practice.

When we work with teachers, we break our core question into three component parts: Which students are struggling to master content? Why are they struggling? and How can we support their learning? Once students are identified, they have to be monitored closely to track their progress and adapt their supports as needed. Determining why students are struggling can be challenging and requires a close look at data, as we discussed in lever 3; examining patterns in data can help us to identify skills that the student needs to develop and to pinpoint the specific intervention that will be needed. The goal with interventions is to help students catch up to their peers who are performing on grade level.

In stage 1, when systematic interventions are likely not in place, we recommend leaders work with their teachers to identify students who are furthest from grade level. Creating such a system that identifies students who need additional support is a critical stage 1 principal action.

Once you have identified target students and determined their current skill level, work with your teams to develop plans for these students. In stage 1, some interventions should occur within the classroom, so ask teachers to brainstorm: How can the lessons support the students who are below grade level?

While there are times when pulling students out of class to give them additional support is needed, our research and that of others has found that preventions and

Table 3.7 Lever 4: Student-Centered Differentiation: Action 1: Interventions and Accelerations

	PRINCIPAL ACTIONS	SCHOOL ACTIONS
Stage 1	Articulate a system of interventions that include classroom-based practices and strategies that all teachers implement. Identify the lowest-performing students, and create plans to support them. Allot extra time in the school day for core subjects for all students not yet achieving at grade level (e.g., creating two literacy periods—one to teach at grade level and one to teach developing skills for those not on grade level). Dismantle any adult or student beliefs that students who excel will fit a specific gender, race, or socioeconomic profile. Ensure that teachers and teacher teams plan for the learning needs of students who are performing at the proficient and advanced levels.	Rapid interventions target groups of students who have significant learning gaps or who lack key foundational skills. Individualized education plans are clearly written and identifies multiple strategies that are closely followed. Students who are in danger of failing a course receive interventions immediately upon the first warning sign; services are provided prior to any failure. Teachers include acceleration opportunities for all students in most lessons.
Stage 2	Continue to develop an explicit range of interventions. Create a process for the development of an individual plan for every student in your school, addressing interventions. Provide students who need additional supports with required interventions. Ensure teachers and teacher teams create lessons and units that facilitate the original thinking of all learners. Lead sessions to develop and implement strength-based accelerations for students who mastered content. Provide enrichment activities to students above grade level.	A student tracking system is in place that uses assessment information, course grades, teacher referrals, and attendance to track each student and his or her intensity and schedule of interventions. Students not making progress at the anticipated pace are given extra support in class; differentiation is implemented in every classroom. Teachers consistently differentiate lessons to include parallel experiences for students who have previously learned or mastered content. Students who master content and complete work quickly are not asked to complete additional work repeating the skill and are not penalized with heavier workloads than their peers.

(continued)

Table 3.7 (*continued*)

	PRINCIPAL ACTIONS	SCHOOL ACTIONS
Stage 3	Identify effective and aligned community resources to increase time and talent dedicated to system interventions (e.g., college student tutors, parent support, resources and space provided by local businesses). Build consistency with teachers and teacher teams on how and when to adjust pacing.	School staff and leaders engage students in the creation and implementation of their intervention. Regular classroom instruction identifies and addresses varied student needs and includes prevention and scaffolding to reduce the need for additional interventions. Students receive rapid, data-driven interventions matched to current needs, and intervention assignments and schedules are frequently updated to reflect student needs and progress. Teachers work with students to modify pacing to ensure that students who master content more quickly are able to accelerate their exploration of a concept. When they have completed required tasks, all students are given opportunities to pursue independent projects based on their individual interests.

interventions are most effective when they are woven into classroom instruction; this requires teachers to create lesson plans that account for how to engage the variety of learners in their classrooms. You may need to help teachers successfully differentiate lessons to meet multiple learning styles, as well as the needs of students currently performing at varied levels of proficiency. In addition, since some students may also need out-of-classroom supports, you may need to review the schedule to identify additional intervention time for students. (See chapter 6 for more on scheduling.)

When you are beginning to implement stage 1 practices, you might have to help teachers shift their mind-sets as well as their instruction. It is not uncommon for struggling students to be over-identified in special education and for all intervention to occur out of the classroom. In these settings, a leader faces the challenges of building a teacher's technical skills while reorienting the teacher to her or his role in the intervention process. When building a culture of interventions, our leaders ask:

- How does your school identify struggling students?
- What happens when a student is below grade level? How are students who are performing below grade level supported?
- What diagnostic assessments and procedures are used to determine why students are struggling?
- How are lessons planned to support learners at different skill levels?

These questions can serve as a baseline to help you target support of teachers. We also recommend leaders review individualized education plan data to see if overidentification is a challenge for your school.

As your school moves into stage 2, teachers will be able to better delineate the needs of their students. At this stage, your team has the opportunity to focus on early identification of students who are at risk of getting off track if they are not given extra support. Teachers in stage 2 demonstrate an ease with data analysis and consistently differentiate instruction in their classrooms. With those systems in place, you can then be better prepared to create a process for developing individual plans for each student in your school, a stage 2 principal action. We encourage you to create a student tracking system that uses assessment data and other information (e.g., attendance) to help develop those plans. Among other things, those plans will enable teachers and other educators in your building to give targeted support to students who need it. With those pieces in place, you can then identify resources within the school community—parents, college students—that can further support students' learning needs and increase teachers' abilities to adjust pacing of instruction as needed, both stage 3 actions. One commonly used intervention framework, response to intervention (RTI), helps schools create a continuum of support using a three-level system:[14]

- Primary prevention: High-quality core instruction that meets the needs of most students
- Secondary prevention: Evidence-based intervention of moderate intensity that addresses the learning or behavioral challenges of most at-risk students
- Tertiary prevention: Individualized intervention of increased intensity for students who show minimal response to secondary prevention

Because RTI is used in a variety of contexts, the language of its three-level system may help your team as it develops your school-level system of interventions.

When planning time for intervention work, some schools slot it in place of lunch, arts courses, or other electives. Students cannot afford to lose those classes, however, as they have been found to increase student engagement and support higher attendance. We have also seen a number of schools plan for interventions during class time—for example, having a student leave the literacy block to work with a reading coach. The most effective intervention systems do not pull students out of core instructional time. This may create a scheduling conundrum, but we recommend creating intervention blocks as a part of your schedule if possible. As we mention in the scheduling section of chapter 6, a creative approach to rostering and scheduling can help support attaining your goals.

One high school in Denver approached the work of differentiation head-on and created a comprehensive system that has seen improved learning for all students and supports those who need additional time to master material while holding every student, regardless of skill level, to high expectations.

CREATING A COMPREHENSIVE SYSTEM FOR IMPROVING LEARNING FOR EVERY STUDENT: MOVING FROM STAGE 1 TO STAGE 3 FOR INTERVENTIONS AND ACCELERATIONS

East High School, Denver, Colorado

When a quarter of ninth graders at East High School in Denver failed to meet the school's course credit and GPA requirements to be on track for graduation, the school staff set out to raise the percentage of students on track to graduation from 75 percent to 90 percent by the end of the following year. They wanted to do this while maintaining high expectations for all students, in particular, by helping more students do well in honors classes.

They began by prescreening incoming freshmen. The spring before the new students arrived, a small committee of educators—the principal, assistant principal, intervention coordinator, and a counselor—examined incoming students' performance on state standardized tests. (To be able to do this, the school worked with their feeder schools and the district's central office to get those scores in March.) Students who scored "unsatisfactory" on the reading, writing, or math exams were immediately placed in an RTI class. Students who scored partially proficient on any of the tests were registered for a supplemental support class for the appropriate subject area. And for students whose cases were not as clear—who, for example, scored high on some state tests but not as well on others—the committee also looked at their grades, attendance, and suspension records for the previous three years. This entire process was a stage 1 action.

The support classes, called academic success classes (ASC), are small, typically twelve to fifteen students, and meet daily. In the program's first year, East offered eighteen ASC sections of algebra, geometry, literature, earth science, and biology. Students in these classes are also taking the honors class in that subject. The ASC not only offers supplemental academic support in that subject area; it also helps students develop as learners, building resiliency and the ability to develop trusting relationships with teachers and their peers.

"Many students come in with this idea that education is not for me," said an ASC teacher. "It is important to develop self-confidence, to instill a sense of self-worth. . . . In ASC, someone is cheering for them."

Added principal John Youngquist, "It's about being a successful student at East High School ... on being a self-advocate, going and talking to teachers when your grade is not what it needs to be, setting goals and reflecting on whether they have achieved those goals."

As a way to offer challenging course work for all students regardless of incoming skill levels, a stage 1 action in the TLF, the school had begun a couple of years earlier to offer honors classes comprising 60 percent proficient or advanced students and 40 percent mid-to-high partially proficient students. Over years of teaching, several teachers found that students learned best in classes of peers with a range of skill levels, as the higher-level students can challenge their less proficient classmates and vice versa.

While many of the lower-level students were succeeding in the honors classes, some struggled. The ASC was an antidote to that, an intervention strategy that pulled students of similar skill levels together every day for additional work with the honors course material. One of the important features of these classes is that they are all taught by the honors class instructors. This allows the teachers to assess what students do and don't understand during the honors class time and then structure the ASC sessions around material that students need added support with. The ASC is not just about catching up, though. The teacher also previews discussions on material to be covered in the next session of the honors class so that students are prepared to participate in that class' discussion. In a lead-up to an honors class lesson on Shakespeare's *Julius Caesar*, for example, the teacher helped the ASC students parse lines of text and understand challenging vocabulary. The teachers also make time to talk with students one-on-one during class or after school to further assess what they still don't understand.

And they do all this while holding them to high expectations. "I don't just want them to get basic plot," English teacher Jeremy Hoffer said. "I want to provoke them into deeper thinking about the characters, about their motivations. . . . That is where I aim to take them with my questions." Through regular classroom instruction, teachers are able to identify and address varied student needs, reducing the need for additional interventions, a stage 3 school action.

Noting that his ASC students have made a lot of academic growth over the course of the year, Hoffer said, "The thing I look for is, can I really make a kid realize, 'Whoa! I didn't realize that I had that in me.'"

To further support students, ASC teachers meet with students individually every week to review and revise goals and create an action plan for the next week, a stage 2 action, asking them if they are happy with their grades and if there is anything they need to improve on.

Students have been responding to these expectations. "Mr. Hoffer always tells us we can go above and beyond; he always pushes us to do better," said one student. "ACS has made me as a person feel a lot more confident and prepared and organized."

Recalling how she used to be embarrassed to ask teachers questions because she did not feel as smart as her classmates, another student said, "My teacher told me it's okay to ask the teacher to explain it one more time. It doesn't mean you're not smart; it just means you don't get it as fast as other kids. I am more confident now than I have ever been."

Of course, for this program to be successful, it cannot be isolated to a few classrooms. Youngquist and his staff created an explicit schoolwide system, a stage 2 action. They screen each of their twenty-one hundred students for a range of academic and social-emotional risk factors. Each week, the school's intervention team of counselors, teachers, and interventionists meets to discuss the most at-risk students, brainstorming solutions for that individual child.

"We are able to adjust their school experiences so quickly," said Youngquist. "This system has helped us shift the culture of our school in a way that is much more student focused than we were in the past."

The school saw an increase in students taking honors classes in their sophomore year and AP classes in their junior and senior years. The number of African American and Latino students taking AP classes increased by 32 percent and 43 percent, respectively, in the first two years of the program.

TLF Analysis of East High School

Now we take a look at the principal and school actions implemented at East High School to make these improvements.

Principal Actions

- Articulate a system of preventions and interventions that include classroom-based practices and strategies that all teachers can implement (stage 1).

- Provide students who need additional supports with required interventions (stage 2).

- Through regular classroom observations and feedback sessions, the principal ensured that teachers create lessons and units that allow creativity and original thinking to support all learners (stage 2).

School Actions

- Through the schoolwide intervention committee of educators, staff identified the lowest-performing students and created plans to support them (stage 1).

- By screening incoming ninth graders based on their past academic and behavioral performance, staff have rapid interventions to target groups of students who have significant learning gaps (stage 1).

- Students not making progress at anticipated pace are given extra support in class (stage 2).

- Regular classroom instruction identifies and addresses varied student needs and includes prevention and scaffolding to reduce the need for additional interventions (stage 3).

Accelerations

In striving to support all students, we can often focus all of our attention on students who are behind grade level, but we also want to call out the importance of focusing on students who are on or beyond grade level. To assess the current state of your school for differentiation, you might want to look at the rates of growth for students who start the year performing at the proficient level. Is their growth consistent, or is it stagnating? The data will help you to determine the right entry point for your work with your teachers.

For schools building stage 1 practices, part of the work is making these students visible to teachers by bringing a focus to the spectrum of student needs. Consider how your teachers plan for students who have mastered a skill or are currently performing at a proficient level.

Teachers can struggle to work with students who have mastered a skill or a concept, and they can resort to two strategies that do not serve the students. The first pitfall is to assign additional work or practice of the same skills to keep students busy. This strategy can be viewed as a punishment for mastering a skill and can discourage students from demonstrating mastery in the future. The second pitfall is to ask students to support other students who have not yet mastered content. While it can be helpful for students to have an opportunity to work with and/or teach a concept to others, when this becomes an expectation it places an undue burden on students who have mastered content.

As you move into stage 2, work with teachers to create open-ended lessons that give students the opportunity to deepen their work and help teachers create tiered assignments. At stage 3, teachers are able to adjust the pacing to allow students to accelerate and extend their learning as needed.

Principal's Tool 3.13: Diagnostic Tool for Lever 4, Student-Centered Differentiation

NEXT STEPS

You are now equipped to begin the work of improving instruction at your school. Look back at the tools for this chapter as often as needed to determine the level of rigor in your teachers' instruction, develop or improve your unit plans, and assess whether your school has effective classroom routines and what you can do to improve them. Do your teachers have the means to correct instruction when students do not grasp the material? Is instruction differentiated to meet the learning needs of all students, whether they need support catching up or are ready for accelerated learning? When pondering each of these questions, keep in mind how the principals in each of the vignettes in this chapter tackled these challenges. While the situation at your school might vary from theirs in some ways, those principals still offer valuable lessons on how to do some of this work in ways that improve student learning.

 WATCH LEARNING AND TEACHING VIDEO: In this chapter's companion video, you'll learn about great work being done at schools across the country in the category of learning and teaching. To access the video, go to www.wiley.com/go/newleaders.

Principal's Tools for Learning and Teaching

Principal's Tool 3.1: Reflection Questions for Observing and Assessing the Rigor of Instruction

Principal's Tool 3.2: Sample Unit Plan for Fourth-Grade ELA

Principal's Tool 3.3: Reflection Questions for Aligned Curriculum

Principal's Tool 3.4: Diagnostic Tool for Lever 1, Aligned Curriculum

Principal's Tool 3.5: Questions to Consider When Establishing Common Routines

Principal's Tool 3.6: Activity: Identifying Common Routines

Principal's Tool 3.7: Stage 2 Instructional Strategies Practice Activity

Principal's Tool 3.8: Diagnostic Tool for Lever 2, Classroom Routines and Instructional Strategies

Principal's Tool 3.9: Reflection Questions for Identifying Data Sources and Assessments

Principal's Tool 3.10: Corrective Instruction Action Planning Template

Principal's Tool 3.11: Reflection Questions for Providing Student Feedback

Principal's Tool 3.12: Diagnostic Tool for Lever 3, Data

Principal's Tool 3.13: Diagnostic Tool for Lever 4, Student-Centered Differentiation

School Culture

SCHOOL CULTURE IS THE ESSENTIAL FOUNDATION ON WHICH EFFECTIVE SCHOOLS are built. We often hear the same thing from principals of struggling schools: "I can't improve teaching and learning until I get a handle on the school's culture, until my school has a clearly articulated and understood vision of academic excellence, until we have a set of consistent behavioral expectations and strong relationships with students to improve their attendance and openness to learning." But how can we assess whether those conditions are in place and take steps to bring that kind of culture to life when it is lacking?

You can get a sense of a school's culture from the ways adults speak to each other and to students, the ways students are disciplined, and the ways students talk about their ability to complete challenging assignments. This chapter examines the actions school leaders and their staffs take to create and maintain school cultures that support academic success. While both the methods and the outcomes of this work look different from school to school, there are some deep consistencies as well. Our research indicated that schools with sustained improvement in student learning use three key levers to build positive and productive school cultures:

Lever 1. Shared mission and values: *Establishing shared school mission, values, and behaviors focused on college success for every student.* Having a collectively agreed upon vision and a shared belief that all members of the school community play an integral role in carrying out that vision are strong predictors of student success.[1] The vision and mission then inform a set of core values that the school staff, students, and families live by. These values have the maximum impact when they are woven into every classroom, school activity, and practice; are regularly reinforced in conversations among students, teachers, family members, and school staff; and can be seen in the behavioral expectations set for students every day.

CULTURE CATEGORY MAP

Lever 1:
Shared Mission and Values

Establishing shared school mission, values, and behaviors focused on college success for every student

Actions

- **Action 1: Vision, Mission, and Values:** Collaborate to create a clear and compelling vision, mission, and set of values.
- **Action 2: Behavioral Expectations:** Translate vision, mission, and values into specific behavioral expectations for adults and students that are described, taught, and consistently implemented.
- **Action 3: Adult and Student Efficacy:** Ensure that adults and students believe in their ability to reach ambitious academic goals through hard work, effective instruction, and feedback.
- **Action 4: Social-Emotional Learning Skills and Supports:** Teach behavioral and social-emotional skills and ensure that supports are in place to guide students' navigation of their academic and personal lives.

Lever 2: Relationships

Building and maintaining meaningful relationships among teachers and staff, focusing on creating a culture where all students are valued

Actions

- **Action 1: Supportive Adult-Student Relationships:** Build strong relationships with students.
- **Action 2: Cultural Competency and Diversity:** Leverage the strengths of a diverse community to create an equity-focused school community.
- **Action 3: Student Voice:** Create structural opportunities for students to provide input and leadership within the school.

Lever 3: Family and Community Engagement

Purposefully engaging families and communities in the academic and social success of students

Actions

- **Action 1: Involving Family and Community:** Support student aspirations and success by engaging families and the community.

Lever 2. Relationships: *Building and maintaining meaningful relationships among teachers and staff, focusing on creating a culture where all students are valued.* Schools with strong cultures support students' social and emotional development and help students negotiate academic and nonacademic challenges. Just as it is important that teachers build relationships with one another and work collaboratively (see chapter 5), so the school needs structures that enable the adults in the school to establish supportive relationships with students. Adults must help students believe that with hard work, they can succeed. They are responsible for creating and maintaining the school culture and, ultimately, creating structures through which students also contribute to developing the culture.

Lever 3. Family and community engagement: *Purposefully engaging families and communities in the academic and social success of students.* A healthy school culture engages families and communities in supporting student aspirations and success. Because parents' perceptions and actions have an enormous influence on their children, families are a critical partner in any school's vision to prepare students for success in college and careers.

The school culture category map lays out these levers and their associated actions.

LEVER 1: SHARED MISSION AND VALUES

While your school's primary purpose is to educate students, leaders have the greatest success when their vision of excellence goes beyond academic achievement. Consider what your ultimate goal is for your students: What do you want your students to believe about themselves and their potential? What's your vision for their success beyond your school, from college to careers to citizenship? What values should your community members model in order to help students reach that goal?

It can be easy to get lost in the day-to-day work of running a school, for your teachers to become consumed with the work of managing their classrooms, and for students to just focus on completing that day's assignments. However, our observations and experience indicate, and research confirms, that students are more successful when school leaders look beyond daily work and develop a clear picture for the long-term success of the school and its students. This includes mapping out how the school will get there and making sure the plan is known and integrated into the work of every member of the school community.

Lever 1: Action 1: Vision, Mission, and Values

Table 4.1 outlines the actions that effective principals and their staff take to create a mission and vision that is a part of their school's daily life.

Table 4.1 Lever 1: Shared Mission and Values: Action 1: Vision, Mission, and Values

	PRINCIPAL ACTIONS	SCHOOL ACTIONS
Stage 1	Collaborate with aligned staff members to create (or revise) a compelling and aligned vision, mission, and set of values focused on college success factors. Scaffold the communication of the vision, mission, and values in phases that staff can digest. Create ongoing structures and opportunities for adults and students to reinforce the values and behaviors.	The leadership team and/or a small group of leaders demonstrate alignment to and support for the school mission, vision, and values. The vision, mission, and values are informed by students and staff. The values include some variant of these: • Every student can and will be ready to succeed in college. • Consistent effort, not innate ability, leads to success. • Adults and students share ownership for student success. School staff members share a common understanding of vision, mission, and values in practice; can describe the vision and the mission; and can explain how they are present in the daily life of the school.
Stage 2	Establish systems to consistently review and revise the vision, mission, and values with a broad group of stakeholders. Ensure that the values promote successful social-emotional skills, such as resilience, self-awareness, and optimism, that will help students succeed in college. Explicitly link academic success in school to consistent effort.	The leadership team translates the vision and mission of the school into a step-by-step school improvement plan. The leadership team owns the communication and modeling of the vision, mission, and values of the school. Stakeholders are deeply involved in the process of refinement and revision of the vision, mission, and values.
Stage 3	Benchmark success against other high-performing schools (conduct visits) to evaluate and refine the vision, mission, and values. Put systems in place that will maintain a focus on attaining the vision.	Staff rely on vision, mission, and values for all major decisions and planning. Staff compare data to goals set in the vision and mission. Staff on a regular basis reflect as to whether their actions and decisions are congruent with the school's values. Students drive school direction in alignment with the school vision and mission.

Crafting a Vision and Mission

Your school probably has a vision or mission statement that appears on your website and perhaps hangs on the wall of the school's main office. But simply having a vision is not enough. Consider how you and your entire school community use your school's vision. Does it shape how you develop and implement practices and programs? Does it infuse the language you use with one another and with your students? The extent to which your vision permeates actions and mindsets at your school is what makes it more than words on a wall.

You will find your school vision most effective if it grows out of your school's needs. A compelling school vision includes a description of what success looks like for students (college, careers, citizenship, and other focus areas for student learning). We have consistently found some version of the following three elements of mission and vision statements in successful schools:

- Every student can and will be ready to succeed in college and careers.
- Effective effort that leads to success is expected and taught.
- Adults and students share ownership for student success.

> The terms *vision* and *mission* are often used differently by different schools and organizations. New Leaders generally relies on the following definitions: A *vision* is an aspirational statement that captures the ideal future state for the students and teachers in the school. A *mission* is a concise, concrete pathway to achieve the vision. The mission should guide the choice of particular strategies and describe the unique approach of this school to reach the long-term vision. A leader or leadership team's core beliefs inform the vision and mission, along with input from the goals and needs of the school community. Out of the vision and mission then come a set of *values*, the ways in which students and the adults in a school are expected to work together and engage with one another. What matters here is not what you call each of these statements, but that you have a clear sense of purpose for the vision or mission that everyone in the school community knows and accepts and is the basis for all of the school's practices.

The vision and mission are the foundation of the school's goals and underlie the rationale for specific strategies. Staff need to see where they will be going, particularly when a school is experiencing major transitions. When a vision truly lives in a school, it is clear and well understood and can be used to inform major school decisions. In this way, decisions are depersonalized and instead are framed around guiding questions such as, Will this new program or change move us toward our vision? The mission describes the "how": How will the school approach the work in a way that will move us toward our vision? A good measure for this is regularly assessing the alignment of programs and initiatives to the mission.

The work of creating and maintaining a shared vision and mission at your school starts with the drafting process, as noted in stage 1. You can do this with a small group of "thought partners," such as fellow school founders or a school leadership team, or you can solicit ideas from a broader range of stakeholders within the school community. It is most important that the vision and mission reflect the perspectives of staff, students, and parents and that they be responsive to the needs and values of the community. Your school will be more likely to fulfill its vision and achieve its mission if the entire school community is invested in those ideas and believes they are relevant to their work at the school.

Principal's Tool 4.1: Activity: Creating and Sharing a School Vision

Once the school leaders and teams we studied settled on a school vision and mission, they created structures that enabled everyone in the school, including students and families, to regularly assess and refine them, and aligned their school practices with the vision, stage 2 actions. When your staff refers to the vision, mission, and values for all planning and major decisions and your students are regularly engaging in ways that reflect the vision, you have reached stage 3.

To see what this work looks like in practice, we turn to the story of a high school leader who, as he designed and prepared to open his school, collaborated with his school cofounders to define the vision, mission, and values. He, his staff, and his students then successfully infused these into all aspects of school life.

 ## USING CORE VALUES TO GUIDE STUDENTS TOWARD SUCCESS: MOVING FROM STAGE 0 TO STAGE 3 FOR VISION, MISSION, AND VALUES

Sci Academy, New Orleans, Louisiana

Students and teachers at Sci Academy are reminded every day of the core values they are expected to embody: achievement, respect, responsibility, perseverance, teamwork, and enthusiasm. Teachers start each day with a meeting in which they praise a colleague for some achievement based on a particular value. In the words of the school founder and principal, Ben Marcovitz, "The nature of the positive picker-upper is actually value based, so what we're thinking about during those moments is why we're here and the values that guide us, so that teachers know that they're centered in them before they start to talk to kids that day."

From the meeting, Marcovitz heads to the school entrance, where students know to use some variation of the core value terms when he asks them, "Why are you here?" "What will it take?" Students gather around Marcovitz in the hallway for a final word about one of the core values before heading to class. One morning he told the students about some of their schoolmates who, while serving detention in the cafeteria the day before, decided to clean up a mess left by students from another school in the building. Explaining that the Sci Academy students did not want the custodians to think they had left the mess, Marcovitz told them, "At the end of a long day, being in detention and still doing things like that, showing both responsibility and perseverance, that's what makes us who we are." Such everyday routines, starting with the morning rituals, have helped make the core values a regular part of daily life at the school. Of course, this came about only through much thought and hard work and started with the principal.

When he founded the school, Marcovitz's goal was to be able to take any entering ninth grader at any achievement level and get that student ready for college in four years. He wanted to close the gaps and see "if we could do a whole lot more with high school. The first step for me was to be really honest about what my values were in starting this school and actually making those the values of the school." At this point he turned to thought partners, a cohort of school founders. With their help, he said, "I reflected on the purpose of my own work in education, the purpose I think a school should serve, what I've seen work in schools, what I believe works in schools. What were the primary statements and philosophies that govern all my thinking on education? I wanted to be really, really clear about them."

For Marcovitz, that meant "focusing on results and doing whatever it takes to reach our goals. Responsibility means we look to ourselves first to get done what needs to be done. Getting really specific about what these values mean to me makes it very easy to communicate to other adults."

Sci Academy Core Values

- Achievement: We focus on results and do whatever it takes to accomplish our goal.
- Respect: We treat every person and every thing as we want to be treated.
- Responsibility: We look to ourselves to do what needs to be done.
- Perseverance: We never give up.

- Teamwork: Helping a member of our team is helping ourselves. When one succeeds, we all succeed.
- Enthusiasm: We remain positive. We show our positivity. This positivity gives us strength.

These values all supported a clear vision of success for the students at Sci Academy: to prepare all scholars for college success, equipped with the passion and tools to pursue their long-term ambitions.

Once the vision and values were established, Marcovitz said, they became the basis for the rest of the work at the school. When hiring staff, he noted, "I framed all my interview questions around those values." The values also formed the basis for the four-week staff orientation before school started. The entire staff planned a student orientation to familiarize students with the school values and designed activities and lessons to reinforce them. Marcovitz and his staff were effectively taking stage 1 actions for setting mission and vision by creating ongoing structures for adults to reinforce core values.

As the school grew and added students and teachers, Marcovitz had to continually teach and reinforce the vision to make sure that new members of the community became familiar with the values that were integral to the school culture. He used this as a time to ask his leadership team: Are these the right values? Do we need to adjust our vision? Are there things we want to shift in how we hold students and adults accountable? These conversations, a stage 2 action, gave the leadership team space to reflect and refine the foundational document that supports the school's culture and affirm that the values continued to serve the needs of the students.

The values started to rub off on student behavior. Said one tenth grader, "Every time we had an altercation, something had to be reflected back to the core values. They taught us to treat each other with respect … and to help each other no matter what."

Still, as the student body doubled in size, Marcovitz said teachers became less likely to enforce school values when they saw students acting out in the hallways. To put systems in place that would maintain a focus on attaining the vision, a stage 3 action, he and his team developed a mantra: "Accountability. Close every loop. Every kid is my kid" (ACE). They structured professional development sessions around giving teachers strategies for handling difficult situations and conversations with students. They also created a culture rubric for teachers to use across classrooms to assess how well they and their students were living the vision. Measures included how well students acted with urgency to be prepared for class to start and whether they followed the dress code. Finally, Marcovitz created a student survey that asked, among other things, how important academic achievement was to them, whether they considered their classes to be interesting and fun, and whether they thought classmates and other students spoke well of them. School staff used all of these data points to shape professional development and guide teachers on how to better reinforce the school values inside and outside the classroom.

"What we do is essentially make academics the new sports for high school," Marcovitz said. "We have pep rallies around academics; kids are praised for academic success in ways that are very socially acceptable for kids." Students receive awards and give each other "shout-outs." That mutual respect, he said, reduces anxiety and allows students to function better in class.

Through such methods, students have internalized the school's mission and values, a key indicator that the school has reached stage 3. "The kids know that the moment you step into this building, the absolute coolest thing you can be is a high-achieving student," Marcovitz says. "These are all things that are specifically designed to serve the vision of preparing our kids for college."

Sci Academy's positive and clearly defined vision and values have supported striking gains in student achievement. The school's ninth graders typically entered on a fourth-grade level for reading and math, and many had been expelled from other schools. During their time at Sci Academy, students on average improved their reading skills by three grade levels each year.

Reflecting on Your Current Vision

Does your vision include these components?

- Brief and easy to remember. Is it concise?
- Motivational and moving. Is it inspirational and passionate?
- Vivid and descriptive. Does it paint a picture of your school and students?
- Inclusive. Does the vision include all of the stakeholders in the school community?

 Potential Pitfalls

Don't fall into the trap of trying too hard to perfect the wording of your vision. We have all heard guidance that vision statements need to be short and pithy, but the goal is not to reach perfection in the fewest possible words. It is most important that the school community know and understand what the statements mean and that they are able to connect them to their daily work.

The sample statement in exhibit 4.1 integrates elements of a vision statement—the future picture of success for students—and mission statement—the image of the school community and how it will reach that vision. You will notice that this statement highlights the particular skills the school leaders would like students to attain. Some of those skills are subject specific, such as proficiency in reading, writing, and algebra. Other skills apply across all subject areas.

EXHIBIT 4.1: A SHARED VISION AND MISSION STATEMENT: KINGSBURY MIDDLE SCHOOL, MEMPHIS, TENNESSEE

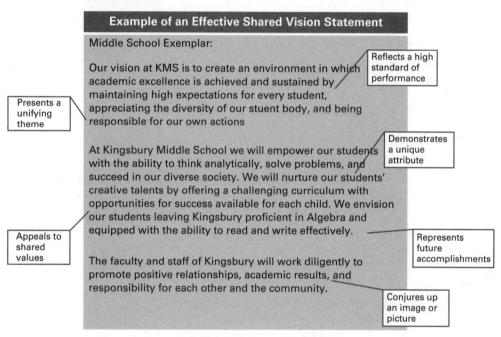

Principal's Tool 4.2: How Visible Is the School Vision at Your School?

Lever 1: Action 2: Behavioral Expectations

As the previous section made clear, effective leaders integrate the school vision and values into all aspects of the day-to-day work of the school. They are not mere platitudes displayed around the school building. They inform, among other things, a set of behavioral expectations for all members of the school community.

In schools with strong and productive cultures, behavioral expectations are explicitly tied to the school's core values and are consistently taught to both adults and students. These expectations are communicated clearly in adult and student orientations, and

Table 4.2 Lever 1: Shared Mission and Values: Action 2: Behavioral Expectations

	PRINCIPAL ACTIONS	SCHOOL ACTIONS
Stage 1	Describe how staff and students can enact the vision and mission through specific behaviors. Articulate and model the importance of social-emotional and social responsibility skills and their connections to student success in school, college, and life. Build a school-level system of rewards and consequences that result from specific behaviors. Create an accountability system so that all infractions are addressed in a consistent manner, and hold staff responsible for consistently implementing rewards and consequences with all students, not only those they directly teach. Ensure that adults know how behavioral expectations translate to all parts of the school day, including opening of day, lunchtime, and class transitions.	There are multiple formal structures through which school values and expected behaviors are taught and reinforced; daily rewards and consequences are published and shared widely. Student social-emotional and social responsibility skills are included and explicitly named in the expectations of behavior. All members of the school community use common language to describe the school values and share a common understanding of expected behaviors. Rituals and public forums celebrate students who model expectations and demonstrate behaviors that reflect the values. All staff are taught and reinforce behavioral expectations while implementing the system of rewards and consequences.
Stage 2	Establish age- and developmentally-appropriate behavioral expectations. Create structures to implement frequent teaching and reinforcing of behaviors. Expose staff continually to grade- and age-appropriate behaviors and supports. Use multiple forms of student data, including disaggregated discipline data, attendance, participation in activities, and who is publicly celebrated, to monitor and measure adoption of behaviors. Create structures and opportunities for students to teach other students and serve as role models. Develop the school's capacity to respond to students' behavioral and social-emotional needs in developmentally appropriate ways.	Induction systems are in place for new and returning staff, students, families, and communities. Adults use teachable moments and find time to reinforce and teach behaviors. Students who live the behaviors are given additional freedoms and demonstrate high levels of personal responsibility in social and academic settings. Staff consistently implement the discipline system and reinforce the established behavioral expectations. Social responsibility skills (service to others) are taught to all students. Systems are in place to review the number of referrals and analyze them to identify patterns or trends in referral data. Disaggregated referral data are regularly reviewed to ensure that consequences are not meted out differently based on race, class, or ethnicity

Table 4.2 (*continued*)

	PRINCIPAL ACTIONS	SCHOOL ACTIONS
Stage 3	Build student capacity and experience in teaching the values and behaviors to others and for holding one another accountable for living them. Implement structures for peer mediation where students serve as the role models for one another.	Students have a clear and consistent role in teaching behaviors to new and younger students. Students energize their peers and focus on achievement. Students hold one another accountable for living by the expectations for student behavior. Students mediate moments of conflict within the school.

teachers are expected to find moments throughout the school year when they can draw connections between the school's expectations and its values. As principals and their teams move through the stages of the Transformational Leadership Framework (TLF), these expectations evolve from abstract schoolwide policies to consistent classroom practice, from being uniform across the school to being customized for different age groups, and, finally, from being imposed by adults to being taught by students to their peers. Effective leaders take many of the actions shown in the table 4.2 to make such evolution possible.

Creating a System for Consistent Behavioral Expectations

Do you and your staff believe your students should wear a uniform? How should students conduct themselves in the cafeteria? At sports games? During a classroom debate? What rules should everyone follow on the playground? Behavioral expectations like these grow out of a school's values. A strong school leader describes the specific behaviors that bring the school's vision and mission to life, creating systems for teaching those expectations and ensuring they are implemented consistently.

An important aspect of the stage 1 actions for behavioral expectations is consistency. In chapter 1, we saw Shawn Benjamin, principal of LPS Richmond Public Charter School in California's Bay Area, create a tiered set of discipline responses that ensured all students knew what to expect if they broke the rules and that teachers addressed discipline in the same way for all students. The result was a dramatic decrease in suspensions over time.

A key piece of this work, associated with stage 2, is supporting students and staff in understanding and internalizing expected behaviors. Many schools begin the year with some form of shared expectations, but they struggle to maintain them throughout the year and across classrooms. The principal of the Bruce Randolph School in Denver,

Colorado, avoided this pitfall by establishing structures for reinforcing behavioral expectations and responding consistently to discipline challenges.

CREATING A SYSTEM FOR TEACHING AND REINFORCING EXPECTED BEHAVIORS: MOVING TO STAGE 2 FOR BEHAVIORAL EXPECTATIONS

Bruce Randolph School, Denver, Colorado

When Kristin Waters became principal, Bruce Randolph was in danger of being closed. The school was the lowest-performing middle school in the city, with only 11 percent of students proficient in reading and just 6 percent in math. The school struggled with gang activity and violence. In class, students threw things across the room, chewed gum, passed notes, and used their cell phones, because, as one student explained, "The teachers wouldn't say anything." The state was considering closing or taking over the school when the superintendent hired Waters to try to turn it around.

As a first step, Waters created a school improvement plan that, among other things, outlined clear and consistent expectations and routines; created a process for teaching all students, staff, and parents those expectations; and established a plan to ensure consistent, effective implementation. Called Challenge 2010, the plan revolved around the school's mission to ensure that all sixth graders would graduate from high school on schedule in 2010. The routines outlined in the plan included specific practices to use at the start of every class, along with a referral ladder and consequences for discipline problems. The plan focused on five simple values and defined behavioral expectations across all classrooms: Be prompt, prepared, polite, productive and positive ("the five Ps"). The motto at the top of the plan, "Cultivating individual expertise in a collaborative school," served as a reminder of Waters's vision.

Waters knew her next critical step was getting teachers to commit to faithfully implementing the plan, a stage 1 action. She used the hiring process to initiate this shift. While interviewing returning teachers, she discovered that many had concerns about the plan and doubts about students' ability to achieve at a high level even when given the right supports. Most of those teachers left, and as Waters filled vacancies, she asked each new teacher to read the plan, ask questions, and commit to following it. She recognized that what she was asking was not easy for some teachers, as it meant giving up certain personal preferences and routines that they had been using in their classrooms. But, she told them, "Consistency is huge for the good of the whole."

"When the same procedures are used in every classroom by every teacher, we find that students don't have to ask themselves when they go from classroom to classroom, 'How do I behave in this teacher's classroom?'" said Waters. Instead, "the student is focused on learning and the content that the teacher is delivering."

With clear expectations defining how specific behaviors advanced the school's mission and vision, the school invested heavily in training aligned to those priorities, a stage 2 action. New teachers received three days of training, a portion of which was spent discussing school expectations and rules.

The school launched an annual orientation program for students before the start of each school year, where the staff introduced and reinforced the school values and expectations in a variety of ways. In small groups, students talked about their hopes for the school year, creating connections to student success in school and life, a stage 1 action. Students read sections of the school handbook focused on rules, homework, celebration traditions, attendance, tardiness, detention, and dress code policies, exploring connections between those expectations and their short- and long-term goals. At the end of the orientation, they had to pass a series of quizzes to ensure that they acquired a clear understanding of the school policies and procedures. These rules were posted in every classroom, with ample opportunities to revisit and discuss them as needed during the year. The school also introduced an orientation for parents and students to attend together so that they had a place to sit down and discuss school expectations and policies as each school year begins.

Waters began staging events to celebrate students who met academic growth goals and had strong attendance, a stage 1 action. At these events, students who met attendance goals for the first time received special recognition. To keep all students optimistic and engaged, those who did not meet attendance goals worked with counselors to set new goals and come up with strategies to achieve them.

Some teachers were immediately enthusiastic about the system when it was implemented, noting that it reduced classroom discipline problems. "Students know how to behave and what to expect," one teacher said. However, others found it challenging to faithfully and consistently implement some rules while teaching lessons. Realizing teachers needed more support, Waters built on her initial program by adding regular guidance for teachers around applying these approaches in their classrooms, a stage 2 action. She also created a one-on-one coaching program that paired new teachers with more experienced educators, usually one of the school's five instructional coaches. Periodic coaching sessions focused on classroom-management strategies and implementation of the Challenge 2010 plan. When observations revealed that a teacher was struggling to follow school routines and expectations, Waters scheduled a conference to discuss what was and was not working in her classroom. She also took steps to ensure that struggling teachers got more frequent observations, detailed feedback, and additional support to address their individual growth areas.

These efforts contributed to major improvements in student learning, particularly in reading. Four years into Waters's tenure, the percentage of ninth graders meeting or exceeding proficiency standards in reading nearly tripled, to 40 percent. In Waters's second year, only 18 percent of sixth graders were proficient or advanced in reading. By the time those same students reached eighth grade, their proficiency rate had doubled.

↓ Potential Pitfalls

Value statements like "be respectful" can mean different things to different people. In a school, that could mean that value is implemented differently across classrooms. In some classrooms, it could mean, "don't leave your seat," and in another, "get up and get a pencil rather than interrupt the teacher." Cultures are stronger when expectations, rules, and consequences are consistently understood and implemented. New school leaders should not assume a school will automatically have a strong culture in place, and even longstanding leaders need to make ongoing culture building a priority. As schools grow and new students and staff join the community, the culture needs to be nurtured by introducing those individuals to school expectations and providing consistent reminders of those expectations and values to reinforce them.

Principal's Tool 4.3: Reflection Questions on Behavioral Expectations

Principal's Tool 4.4: Behavioral Expectations Self-Study

Lever 1: Action 3: Adult and Student Efficacy

"The view you adopt for yourself profoundly affects the way you lead your life," writes psychologist Carol Dweck.[2] There is no such thing as being bad at math, she would argue. If you work hard and seek out new strategies when you struggle, you can improve and excel. For students to increase their achievement, all students and adults in a school, including parents, must believe in each student's ability to reach ambitious academic goals through hard work, effective instruction, and feedback.

Effective school leaders make a growth mindset—the idea developed by Dweck that hard work and actionable feedback results in improvement and excellence[3]— central to their values and vision, and they work to ensure that this belief shapes the attitudes and actions of every member of the school community. They focus most importantly on helping students develop this growth mindset and what we call "student efficacy"—the belief that they can accomplish significant academic and personal goals through consistent individual effort and improvement. These leaders consistently reinforce the importance of learning from mistakes, persisting at difficult tasks, and seeking frequent feedback and help in the learning journey. We've seen many of them use stories and examples of famous leaders, musicians, and athletes to show how effort and persistence are crucial to any long-term success. They help students to set short- and long-term goals, build awareness and aspirations around college and potential careers, and explain the connection between success in school and achieving their larger aspirations.

Principals focused on student efficacy also work hard to ensure that all adults in the building demonstrate this belief in the potential of students, and they reinforce these growth mind-set messages for students. As you will see in detail in chapter 5, such principals use the new staff interview process as a first step in ensuring that everyone in the building supports and lives by the school's values and vision. They ask targeted questions like, "Give an example of a time when you were able to build a relationship with a student whom others had difficulty reaching," and, "Why do you want to teach at this school?" By asking these questions, they can quickly weed out candidates who believe that innate abilities or external factors like poverty make it impossible for students to succeed.

Of course, efficacy is not just for students. Before teachers can believe in the growth potential of all their students, they have to believe that they themselves can continuously grow and improve their own teaching and the support they provide to students. Do your teachers believe that through their own diligence, learning from challenges, and through intentional, ongoing development, they will be able to grow as educators and be better able to help students reach success? This sense of adult efficacy is also a crucial part of building school culture, and it is reinforced by the structures and supports for adult learning and growth that we describe in chapter 5.

Table 4.3 shows the stages of development for adult and student efficacy.

Table 4.3 Lever 1: Shared Mission and Values: Action 3: Adult and Student Efficacy

	PRINCIPAL ACTIONS	SCHOOL ACTIONS
Stage 1	Create opportunities for students and staff to observe schools with similar populations of students succeeding. Teach adults how to support and teach effective-effort strategies. Shape the environment to make explicit links between student aspirations, effort, and achievement (e.g., publicly displayed school symbols and rituals). Model and create a system through which staff and students develop and track short- and long-term goals. Provide opportunities for adults to receive feedback, and track their improvement.	Clear messages about effort leading to near- and long-term success are visible and vocalized by all. College and career aspirations are a visible part of students' everyday experience in the school. All students engage in a college-going and career development process that includes setting short- and long-term learning goals and college and career goals. Students have opportunities to experience mastery in multiple settings to reinforce their sense that they can achieve.
Stage 2	Create conditions where students are able to take intellectual risks, make mistakes, and analyze the impact of their actions. Create college and career access experiences for all students. Set expectations that all teachers will develop mastery experiences for their students to build student efficacy.	Students have multiple opportunities to make decisions about their learning experiences. Students and staff develop short- and long-term goals and strategies for how they will attain their goals. Students and staff value feedback and view it as an integral part of their learning. Students engage in rich college-going and career access experiences High school: Dedicated staff are in place to help students understand the college admissions process (research colleges, apply to college, and apply for financial aid and scholarships).
Stage 3	Celebrate staff and students who persist in the face of challenges and adversity.	Students and staff energize their peers by making public their progress toward goals. Students and staff do not give up when faced with adversity. Students and staff see challenges as part of the learning process and seek help when they need it.

The vision at LPS Hayward is for every student to attend and graduate from college. With that in mind, the school has created systems that ensure students are challenged to work hard and excel in ways that will prepare them for success in college.

In setting this priority, the school wanted to play a role in reversing the nation's dismally low four-year college completion rates—around 10 percent—among first-generation, low-income students, said principal Michael De Sousa, who took over the school from another New Leaders–trained principal, Lauren Klaffky. Because the two leaders shared similar core beliefs, the school's vision and mission remained constant during the leadership transition. The school staff was already focused on creating a culture in which everyone, adults and students, believed that with hard work, all students could complete college. When De Sousa took the helm as principal, he intensified that focus.

The school's vision influenced how De Sousa interviewed teachers for open positions. "I wanted to make sure teachers believed in the transformative nature of higher education," he said. He looked for teachers who saw every student as an Advanced Placement student and believed "it's a matter of time and effort that teachers and students need to put in, but they can reach that goal." These efforts ensured that new teachers were aligned with the values and vision of the school and sent a message to staff that they were expected to challenge students with rigorous course work and help them master it, a stage 2 action.

Hayward also established a strong structure to develop and support teachers in raising rigor in their classrooms and consistently improving their teaching. Said math teacher Rose Zapata, "We wanted to make sure kids are growing as individuals. We try to keep that at the center of all our conversations. . . . If my students are underperforming, then I am going to ask for help so that I can better support my students." Teachers now meet regularly to examine assessment data, plan lessons, watch videos of their practice, and give each other feedback on their instruction. They also collaborate to ensure that students understand the connections between hard work and high achievement, not only in theory but through their day-to-day experiences in the classroom. (For more on teacher team meetings, see chapter 5.)

Parents as Partners in Teaching Efficacy

The staff at Hayward also invested time and energy in engaging families in the work of getting students ready for college, particularly in helping students develop a belief in their own capacity to excel and the resilience to persist in the face of obstacles that they will inevitably confront. "No one alone can do this work of making sure students feel supported, successful, ready, and eager to learn and to develop and to go to college," said school counselor Claudia Aguilar. "If we really want to reach the goal of sending 100 percent of students to college, we have to work with parents from the beginning."

To the staff at LPS Hayward, working with parents does not mean treating them as "blank slates," talking at them for an hour and sending them home, as some other schools do. "We want to make sure students inherit and take on this belief that they are college bound," said Aguilar, and part of that, she added, is having a conversation with parents, understanding who the parents are and who they can be as team members on this path of getting their kids to college.

"Students spend most of their life with their families," Aguilar said. Because many families at the school are recent immigrants who did not attend college, Aguilar acknowledges that they "may not have necessarily received the message that we are sending here at school."

To address this reality, the school began hosting frequent workshops on different aspects of the school and college application process for parents, which are now offered on the first Wednesday of every month, with three additional meetings annually to which both students and parents are invited. During one conversation about the college admissions process, the facilitator told parents, "We have a lot of information to share with you, but you are experts too. You are an expert on your children, so we want to give you resources to help your children meet their goals." The conversations, held in both English and Spanish, cover how to calculate grade point averages and understand their significance and how to make a student more competitive for college admissions. Parents work together in small groups to explore issues related to the topic. In one recent workshop, parents shared ideas for helping their children, including making sure they did their homework every night and turned it in on time, providing resources like a dedicated, quiet study area and access to a computer, teaching their children time management and organizational skills, and finally asking their children how they can help them.

Said one father, "There is no reason why a kid coming to this school shouldn't be getting A's. They give them opportunities, they give them the right education. It's up to us to help them. If they are just playing video games and watching TV, that's on us too."

Student Efficacy

The Hayward staff makes it clear that their primary goal is for every student to finish college. College banners hang in the hallways, and each classroom is named for a university. Teachers talk with students about college and how higher education will advance their salaries, open doors to exciting careers, and enable them to fulfill their ambitions and better support their future families. Through these efforts, teachers make college and career aspirations a part of students' everyday school experience, a stage 1 action.

Students also regularly set long- and short-term learning goals at the beginning of each year, a stage 2 action for student efficacy. For instance, after receiving mediocre grades as a younger student, one eleventh grader set her sights on a 4.0 GPA. "I wanted to push myself as hard as I could," she said. While she knew that goal was ambitious, she believed that it was achievable because of all the incremental goals she and her classmates had been asked to set throughout the year and the support they received from teachers to help them stay on track to meeting those key milestones along the way.

Hayward students set goals before every test and keep them next to them as they do their work. After reviewing his students' goals before a quiz, math teacher Michael Fauteux said, "Some people are going back and trying to become proficient or advanced in something they already finished. I love that: Don't settle. The key message is, wherever they are, that's okay. Wherever they are, the goal is to get better. They have the whole year to get where they want." During the math test, Fauteux tells them to be brave about making mistakes, that they will learn from them, an important lesson in perseverance, a stage 3 action.

Students set goals based on how they have done in the past. For quizzes, students often use a computer program that allows teachers to immediately see on their own computer how students are doing. Teachers can then give immediate feedback and correct misunderstandings.

Students also hold each other accountable for their work, another stage 3 action. They track their progress on their own data sheets, which are publicly displayed. "They begin a process of owning wherever they are," said math teacher Fauteux. "The message is, 'Let's accept where you are, set some goals, and just get better.' It's not about getting to a specific finish line; it's about improving." This message seems to have sunk in. Said one twelfth grader, "I make sure my effort is more important than my grade."

De Sousa is certain that the school's work to raise students' sense of personal accountability for reaching their goals has contributed to the school's success. A few years after Lauren Klaffky, the initial New Leaders–trained principal, started at Hayward, student proficiency in ELA rose over two years from 57 to 77 percent and in math from 51 to 85 percent. That progress has continued under De Sousa. The most recent data (from 2014) showed 98 percent of students proficient in ELA and math and a 98 percent graduation rate.

We can map the TLF to the work at Leadership Public Schools Hayward as shown in table 4.4.

Principal's Tool 4.5: Reflection Questions on Student Efficacy

Lever 1: Action 4: Social-Emotional Learning Skills and Supports

Schools must establish systems for handling challenges students face beyond the classroom and for teaching behavioral and social-emotional skills. They also must ensure that supports are in place to guide students as they navigate their academic and personal lives. At schools with strong cultures of social-emotional support and development, teachers regularly encourage students to name their emotions and help them find appropriate ways to manage stress, pressure, and conflicts with other students. For many students, regular reminders from teachers and targeted instruction focused on the school's core values and behavioral expectations are all the support they need. For students who need more than this baseline level of support, effective principals establish a pyramid of social-emotional interventions.

Effective principals have put some of the practices in table 4.5 in place and seen student improvement over time.

Pyramid of Behavioral Interventions

Different students need different levels of support to manage social-emotional challenges. Once your school has set and implemented consistent behavioral expectations, or while you are putting them in place, you can begin to create a pyramid of interventions to help students who struggle to demonstrate the schoolwide behavioral expectations. Figure 4.1 shows a pyramid that ranks specific behavioral interventions, from most intense at the apex to least involved at the base. At each level, the interventions are matched to specific infractions or patterns of misbehavior.

Many schools get overwhelmed trying to serve large numbers of students who need intense intervention and support. For such schools, creating a pyramid like this one is an important stage 1 action. Interventions at the top of the pyramid may require the involvement of outside mental health providers. These interventions need to be closely linked with the academic interventions addressed in chapter 3. Be mindful that many behavioral issues that seem intractable might actually be resolved through good,

Table 4.4 TLF Analysis of LPS Hayward

TLF ACTION	ARTIFACTS	EVIDENCE	TLF STAGE AND PRINCIPAL ACTION	SCHOOL ACTIONS
Culture, Adult and student efficacy	Teacher schedules; teacher meeting observations and agendas	Teachers have regular meeting times, often daily, to examine data and student goals, discuss and plan instruction, and give each other feedback.	1, teach adults how to support and teach effective-effort strategies 1, provide opportunities for adults to receive feedback	1, Clear messages about effort leading to near- and long-term success are visible and vocalized by all.
	College banners; classroom observations	College banners hang in the hallways; teachers talk with students about what college means for salaries and for families.	1, shape the environment to make explicit links between student aspirations, effort, and achievement	1, College and career aspirations are a visible part of students' everyday experience in the school.
	Classroom observations; student goals	In class discussions, teachers tell students it is okay to make mistakes. Students are expected to set short- and long-term goals at the beginning of the school year and before each test.	2, create conditions where students are able to take intellectual risks, make mistakes and analyze the impact of their actions	2, Students value feedback and view it as an integral part of their learning. 2, Students develop short- and long-term goals.
	Data sheets and club memberships displayed in hallways	Students track their progress on their own data sheets, which are then publically displayed. Students are put in clubs based on proficiency in different subjects, which are displayed.	3, celebrate staff and students who persist in the fact of challenges	3, Students energize their peers by making public their progress toward goals. 3, Student see challenges as part of the learning process.

Table 4.5 Lever 1: Shared Mission and Values: Action 4: Social-Emotional Learning Skills and Supports

	PRINCIPAL ACTIONS	SCHOOL ACTIONS
Stage 1	Ensure that all teachers have some training and support in teaching social-emotional skills. Create a pyramid of behavioral interventions that mirrors the academic intervention pyramid with social-emotional development support. Design and implement systems to gather positive and negative data on school culture and behavior. Establish a basic system of identifying students who need more interventions or additional supports. Create a student intervention team to support students in crisis.	Teachers encourage all students to name their emotions and find appropriate ways to manage stress and pressure. Students begin to practice describing their emotions and to manage their behavior even when they are upset. Data systems exist to track all discipline referrals and interventions. Data are used to identify structural issues that need to be addressed (e.g., transitions that consistently cause problems, times of day that are problems for students). Teacher team structures exist to identify students with significant behavioral and learning challenges.
Stage 2	Create a highly effective and efficient pyramid of social-emotional interventions and additional supports (including wraparound services for the students with the most significant needs) and ensure that mental health support is provided to students in need of additional supports. Lead conversations with staff about social-emotional development and defusing challenging situations. Ensure that all adults are trained to identify and support students in need of nonclassroom-based supports. Monitor data to ensure that no child is invisible and that every student has access to supports within and beyond the school.	Students demonstrate empathy toward others, resist negative social pressure, make ethical decisions, and exhibit respect. Crisis intervention teams train and support all adults to learn how to support students in crisis. Students in crisis are referred and receive their first intervention within forty-eight hours. All staff receive professional development on how to implement the social-emotional and career skills curriculum.

Table 4.5 (*continued*)

	PRINCIPAL ACTIONS	SCHOOL ACTIONS
Stage 3	Weave social-emotional learning and personal development into the academic program so that students, staff, and families recognize how these skills support academic achievement. Ensure that interventions support academic, social, and emotional needs for all students. Use proactive strategies to support students' and staff members' emotional well-being.	Students can analyze how their thoughts and emotions affect their decision making and behavior and can use that knowledge to make informed choices. Students who are at risk are identified prior to incident and receive additional supports. Multiple members of the staff have the skills to serve on the crisis intervention team. Students implement strategies to work in teams, manage time and projects, and make responsible decisions.

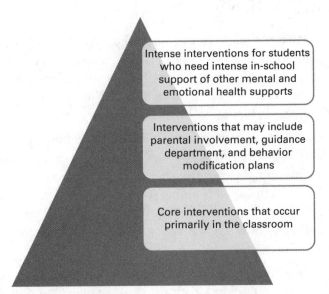

Intense interventions for students who need intense in-school support of other mental and emotional health supports

Interventions that may include parental involvement, guidance department, and behavior modification plans

Core interventions that occur primarily in the classroom

Figure 4.1 Pyramid of Behavioral Interventions

consistent responses in the classroom. Once a strong behavioral management system is in place, it will become clearer which students really do need the supports at the higher levels of the pyramid.

When entering a school with culture practices that are either approaching or in stage 1, many leaders find that they are providing intensive behavioral interventions and supports to large numbers of students. This quickly results in substantial amounts of administrators' time to manage these supports and often pulls too many students out of classroom instruction too frequently. As an alternative, leaders we studied were more successful when they began the school year by implementing the kinds of consistent behavioral expectations and responses described earlier in this chapter. Once they and their staff members began teaching and reinforcing these common expectations, they found that many fewer students were demonstrating the kinds of significant and consistent behavioral challenges that required intensive intervention. By starting with a stronger and more consistent base of core interventions and teaching expectations to all students, they were better able to identify the students in most need of intensive support.

LEVER 2: RELATIONSHIPS

Do you remember that one adult, possibly a teacher, who believed in you and whom you trusted enough to talk to about some of the personal details of your life? The adult who knew how you were doing beyond school and supported and counseled you when times got particularly hard for you? Many of us have had one particular adult in our lives who made it possible for us to realize our own potential.

School leaders can build a school culture in which it is far more likely that adults and students will have these kinds of connections. Effective principals create systems and structures to foster meaningful, positive relationships between staff and students. These relationships are critical for building students' belief in themselves and their ability to meet behavioral expectations. Students become more motivated to take positive risks when they know teachers and other adults in their schools will support them in moments of success and failure.

In schools that are building stage 1 culture practices, the principal explicitly creates structures that will connect every student with at least one adult in the building. These structures ensure that the school moves beyond positive intentions toward concrete supports and systems that ensure no student is forgotten or overlooked.

Advisories and Referrals

In middle and high schools, where students are moving from room to room and teacher to teacher, advisories can be an important and effective structure for developing supportive relationships between students and the adults in the school. Through advisories, adults can focus on the entire experience of a small set of students and get to know more about them than the results of their latest math test. You can also accomplish this with homeroom teachers who gather information on students and regularly follow up on their goals and results.

At the elementary level, where most classroom teachers work with the same group of students all day, this work involves creating time and structures within and beyond the classroom for small group and one-on-one conversations that help educators tailor support to individual student needs.

Relationships can also be fostered through the school's tiers and interventions for responding to negative student behaviors like the system we described at LPS Richmond in chapter 1. There, students must meet with at least one adult for each tier of the discipline process, giving students a chance to reflect on and discuss their actions with an adult who has kept track of their behavior. At Bruce Randolph, all disciplinary actions, including tardiness and missed homework, are recorded in a database that is accessible by the entire staff. If a student has missed a few homework assignments in one class, her teacher can look in the database to see if she has also failed to complete homework for another teacher. In that case, both teachers might meet with the student to discuss the situation.

To develop supportive adult-student relationships, effective leaders have implemented some of the actions in table 4.6.

Lever 2: Action 1: Supportive Adult-Student Relationships

 CULTIVATING RELATIONSHIPS THROUGH ADVISORIES: MOVING TO STAGE 2 FOR SUPPORTIVE ADULT-STUDENT RELATIONSHIPS

Benjamin Banneker Academic High School, Washington, DC

Principal Anita Berger sat in a circle of students with their latest report cards in her lap. "How do you think you did?" she asked the group.

"It's not as good as I think it should be," one student said.

"It's not as good as you *know* it should be, right?" Berger replied.

Berger meets with her advisory group of students once a week not only to discuss how they are doing academically, but also to talk both one-on-one and

Table 4.6 Lever 2: Relationships: Action 1: Supportive Adult-Student Relationships

	PRINCIPAL ACTIONS	SCHOOL ACTIONS
Stage 1	Create time, structures, and processes for adults to build strong relationships with students. Design a plan for every student to have at least one one-to-one caring adult relationship in the building. Create structures to facilitate adults' developing the skills to provide authentic care for students.	Every student has at least one adult who checks in with her regularly to provide support and who knows all aspects of her academic and behavioral progress to date. Staff members have a profile for every one of their students that includes the student's strength and growth areas. Middle and high school: Staff and students meet on a regular daily or weekly basis to explore academic and nonacademic topics.
Stage 2	Create teacher team structures that look at the whole student, not just his or her results in a particular content area. Organize the student community into cohorts with supporting rituals and routines that build positive cohort identity and foster strong relationships among and between students and adults.	Adults take responsibility to support each student's overall academic and social success. All staff feel comfortable reinforcing behavioral expectations and supporting students and school spaces beyond their own classrooms.
Stage 3	Create times and structures for adults across content areas to discuss students' performance and behavior in multiple settings. Provide space for adults to talk about the social-emotional needs of students. Facilitate cohort and grade relationships among students to support student learning.	All students are known well by multiple adults. Adults meet frequently to identify individual student needs and work together to support and monitor individual student progress, behavior, and social-emotional development. Staff lead culture-building activities with students and with parents and families.

as a group about the outside factors affecting their academic performance. Organizing the student community into groups that foster strong relationships among and between students and adults is a stage 2 action. "The teacher advisory program is so critical because it provides an opportunity for students to look beyond the academic constraints of a classroom to develop those other skills they are going to need to be successful," Berger said.

During the session on report cards, when a younger student started laughing as Berger discussed GPAs, she asked the rest of the group to remind that student of how important their academic performance now is for success after high school.

An older student said, "You should start out strong because it will be easier to be consistent and remain strong than it is to play catch up."

Berger decided to lead her own advisory because she thought that teachers at Banneker were not running the groups in ways that touched on all the issues affecting students. She created her own group to model strong practices, inviting staff to observe her meetings with students. "It's not just an hour of studying or how to navigate the college process or write a résumé," Berger said. "It's an opportunity to work with some students one-on-one for years in an environment that is holistic, peer motivated, and invested."

The advisories create a place for students to share their struggles. Because they are mixed-age groups, older students have a chance to mentor their younger peers. "Not only are they responsible for themselves," Berger said, "but also for someone else. . . . At the end of the day, teenagers would like to hear it from their peers. And it goes beyond advisory. In the halls, you hear students say, 'Hey, man, don't do that. Ms. Berger wouldn't like that.'"

Hearing advice from peers is important, but so is getting support from an adult at the school, particularly in one-on-one conversations during the advisory sessions. "It's a tough love session sometimes," Berger said. "I tell them, 'Don't think that because I am your advisor that I am going to nurture some behaviors that are totally inappropriate.' I have to give them guidance so that they understand, 'I appreciate what you have done, but you have to do better.'"

In one meeting, she reminded a student of what his peers had said during the group meeting. "You have to make some changes," she told him. She asked if he had followed up with a teacher for help as he had promised he would. When he admitted he hadn't, she reminded him not to be ashamed about seeking help and pointed out how this action related to his long-term goals: "When you see someone have that scholarship and you know you should have gotten it, you're the one who's going to be disappointed." Finally, she told him she planned to follow up with both his teacher and his father to check whether he was doing what the teacher asked him to do.

Berger's students appreciated her attention. "It feels awesome to have the principal behind you," he said. "Of course, she's been hard on me, but if your principal is coming to you one-on-one to assess your report card and assess your progress, it shows you that she cares." Added Berger, "I hope students will walk away with self-respect and able to say, 'I am someone of value,' whether it's in the classroom or outside the classroom. Walking away with a positive feeling and a positive contribution is what I see happening from the advisories."

Lever 2: Action 2: Cultural Competency and Diversity

Schools exist within a society in which many students and families, and especially students of color and students in poverty, face persistent barriers of bias and negative assumptions about their potential to succeed. We continue to see evidence of the impact of generations of inequality based on race and wealth, in employment, housing, and education. Even when we have every intention of helping students succeed we, leaders and teachers, can unintentionally recreate these societal biases within the walls of the school, contributing to significant ongoing achievement and opportunity gaps. Because these biases and historical inequities are such a deep part of our broader culture, it takes hard and ongoing work to move past them. But schools can, and must, play an active role in breaking down those barriers both within and outside the school walls.

Table 4.7 outlines the stages of development that principals have gone through to cultivate cultural competency and encourage diversity in their schools.

The first critical step in stage 1 is working together as a staff to understand your own assumptions and potential biases. Effective leaders also tackle this work by exploring their own backgrounds and the power and privilege these confer, particularly in relation to students and families served by the school. They then model this individual exploration for their staff members, and begin to seek out examples of negative assumptions playing out in their work with students and families. Each of us has unintentional biases that inevitably grow out of our life experiences. Even when we have the best intentions, those biases can lead us to reinforce existing power dynamics. Even if we believe we are treating all students equitably, we might not be. Bias, and often unconscious bias, can affect all sorts of school practices: perhaps boys of color are suspended at higher rates than their white peers, or fewer girls than boys are placed in higher-level math classes. Bias can appear in more subtle ways too. Do some of your teachers call on white students more often than students of color? Are they more encouraging of black students than white students? Do they hold certain students to lower expectations for fear of making them feel discouraged by giving them challenging work?

While working to build understanding of their own identity and privilege, school leaders and staff also explore the perspectives and experiences of others, and especially the students and families they serve. What do you and your staff know and understand about your students' experiences? What do you know about the expectations and norms of their communities? What are the assets and strengths of the local

Table 4.7 Lever 2: Relationships: Action 2: Cultural Competency and Diversity

	PRINCIPAL ACTIONS	SCHOOL ACTIONS
Stage 1	Share a focus on bringing equitable practices to the school community and hold cultural competence to be an important part of the school's culture. Provide formal and informal professional development to teachers and staff to improve their understanding of how their own worldviews inform their interpretation of the world. Create opportunities for staff to learn about and experience the community surrounding the school. Address and correct moments of cultural incompetence and challenge.	Teachers seek to understand how other individuals (adults and students) experience the world while not making assumptions about them based on visible characteristics. Data are disaggregated, and existing systems and structures are reviewed to ensure that traditionally underserved and underperforming students are not being treated unfairly.
Stage 2	Lead conversations with staff about inequities and about honoring diversity. Lead teachers through a process to identify students' strengths and assets. Use moments of cultural incompetence as part of ongoing conversations.	The school community values and promotes the cultural values of students and parents. Staff take responsibility for knowing each student's cultural background, assets, and growth areas.
Stage 3	Build staff capacity to lead and create culture-building activities. Mobilize and galvanize the community to interrupt social inequities in the school and beyond.	Pedagogy is culturally and developmentally responsive and relevant. Teachers use culturally competent language and demonstrate knowledge of students' development. Staff consistently interrupt systems and structures that promote inequity within the school. Staff are aware of what to do to be effective in cross-cultural situations. Staff make learning about other cultural groups an ongoing part of the school's curriculum.

community? Cultivating cultural competency requires staff to identify, understand, and eliminate biases and barriers that impede students from succeeding because of their race, class, or sexual orientation.

Cultivating cultural competence requires us to engage in continual reflection on our decisions and change our default assumptions and actions. Schools in stage 1 must work to uncover the patterns and effects of culturally incompetent decisions, not just through studying student outcome gaps and differentials, but also by looking at a wide range of data that can uncover inequitable actions and outcomes: behavior data; attendance data; and data about who gets selected for gifted and honors courses, who is referred to special education, which students are most active and visible in class or in extracurricular activities, and which students receive interventions. It can also extend to thinking about how biases affect school staffing, including hiring and retention patterns, as well as opportunities for staff members to advance, take on leadership roles, and have a meaningful voice in school policies. Successful stage 1 schools are able to identify patterns of unconscious bias and unequal opportunity that negatively affect student outcomes.

In stage 2, principals work with staff to directly address the inequities identified within the school. In this stage, you provide professional development that builds awareness among staff of how their income, educational attainment, race, gender, or sexual orientation influences their actions and attitudes, such as helping white teachers to be aware of their race and how that puts them in a position of power. In many communities, teachers and leaders of color must also explore their own privilege in terms of college completion and income. You hold difficult conversations about how you as a group may at times reinforce barriers that exist for students and families beyond the school walls. You take an asset-based approach to students, recognizing the strengths of diverse individuals and diverse communities. Effective principals consistently unearth and push back on limiting assumptions about student potential based on attributes like race and income.

Schools in stage 2 also explore how issues of diversity and privilege can be addressed within the school's curriculum and instruction. How are your teachers discussing the story of the United States and historical events with their students? How are those class conversations framed? For example, are they asking students to consider who is telling the stories they read and how that narrator's perspective influences how the story is told? Are they exploring mainstream assumptions with their students?[4] Using the lens of diversity in classroom analysis and discussion can encourage honest and thoughtful interactions among peers, and deepen how students think about history and literature. In some cases, it may also bolster student engagement, giving students opportunities to connect their studies to their personal experiences and to acquire the tools and knowledge needed to push for positive change well beyond the walls of their school building.

Culturally competent teachers create classrooms where power is named and students develop the skills they need to navigate dominant power structures while shaping their own experiences.

In stage 3, school leaders, staff, and students are doing the ongoing work of building the skills to reverse continuing inequities not only within the school walls but in the world beyond. The principal and staff continuously review school data to identify and respond to any persistent barriers, and they never stop having conversations about diversity, privilege, and bias. In the words of one school leader, "It's like removing plaque. You never stop going to the dentist."

Students in stage 3 schools learn the skills they need to succeed in the dominant culture while also learning the skills to be change agents within that broader culture. For example, one teacher at Polaris Charter Academy in Chicago led students in an in-depth study of the US Constitution. Living in one of the city's most dangerous neighborhoods, the students wanted to explore the Second Amendment and gun laws and gun violence. Their teacher asked them, "As young people who cannot vote, what do you want to do?" The students created a Day of Peace. In this event, held in several communities on the previous year's most violent day for that neighborhood, students clean up, garden, hold vigils, and share information about violence. One teacher noted that while the students set out to change their community, they ended up changing the way they thought about themselves. "The community was proud of us," one student said. In a related project, Polaris students created a podcast, "Voices of Change," to create discussion about race and stereotypes as they connect to violence. Said one student producer, "It doesn't matter how young you are; if you want to effect positive change, you have to be the one to take up the leadership."

To begin developing cultural competency, start by looking at subgroup achievement data to see where there are gaps along race or class lines, a stage 1 action. This first step will highlight any persistent gaps in student outcomes, but taking action against these achievement gaps will almost always require exploring a much wider range of data and root causes. As one example of such an analysis, imagine a high school where students of color are consistently scoring lower than white students on the ACT. In digging beneath that information, the school leadership team finds that African American students are much less frequently recommended for honors courses, even when they have eighth-grade achievement levels similar to those of their white peers. The data made clear that course placement recommendations made by the middle school teachers were rarely based on demonstrated achievement, but rather on race and the level of motivation students showed in class. School leaders began using data to determine which courses students should be taking. They also used achievement data to create individual learning plans for each student and created summer intervention programs for students who needed extra support.

BUILDING A MORE EQUITABLE SCHOOL BY CREATING REGULAR DIALOGUE AROUND RACE, CLASS, AND SEXUAL IDENTITY: MOVING FROM STAGE 1 TO STAGE 3 FOR CULTURAL COMPETENCY AND DIVERSITY

Acorn Woodland Elementary School, Oakland, California

In his fifth year at Acorn, principal Leroy Gaines saw assumptions about race having a negative impact on his school culture. Gaines began having difficult conversations with his staff and the district on how to improve the culture in ways that would make education for all their students more equitable.

The comfort level needed to have these conversations did not develop overnight. Gaines became principal of Acorn at a time when the neighborhood surrounding the school was changing. Many African Americans were moving out, Latinos were moving in, and the gay and transgendered community in the neighborhood and on his staff was growing. Though at times subtle, there was tension among families, students, and staff around differences in race and sexuality.

Gaines was determined to prevent his students, staff, and families from experiencing the kind of prejudice he lived through as the son of an African American father and Afro-Latina mother growing up in a predominantly white neighborhood: "I know what it means to be the outsider and have a family that doesn't understand how to navigate the institution. I came into education to make sure that that wasn't replicated and that this was something that was addressed."

Acorn's staff was predominantly white, with the exception of a few African American support staff and one Latina teacher, serving a mostly Latino community. In that situation, Gaines said, "issues of race and culture are at the forefront. That's something that you need to talk about. In education, a majority of the issues that we're facing stem [from] these inequalities. Unless we understand that, then I don't know how we could actually get into the work in a deep manner."

Gaines brought in Our Family Coalition, an organization that focuses on a range of diversity issues, to facilitate and support the school's efforts to develop greater cultural competence, a stage 1 action. He wanted the coalition to help the school "work toward justice as opposed to just equality and diversity," Gaines said. "We don't want to just have acceptance and have folks being around each other in the same space. We want to actually move where there's action and that there's a deep empathy for other folks' struggles and a deep commitment to battling those struggles and joining in on the movement. . . . To do that, we needed to understand the struggles of the LGBTQ community. We need to understand the struggles of our black community, of our Latino community, of all these communities that are currently working toward equity. . . . We need to make sure we are accountable and covering the spectrum of inequality." And, he added, the entire school community needed to understand what it means to be an ally—"to understand yourself and the plight of others, but then actually work toward correcting and fixing those things."

With the coalition's support, Gaines devoted significant resources and time to holding professional development sessions dedicated to discussing diversity and issues of justice and equity and rooting out personal biases that his team may not have even realized they possessed, a stage 1 action. "We need to unpack our own prejudices and our misconceptions and understand ourselves before we can actually teach others," Gaines said.

To encourage his staff to open up, he reflected on and shared his own personal story. He explained how hard it was for him to come into a school where African Americans and Latinos, the two communities he comes from, were at odds. He also shared his own learning about LGBTQ issues.

Some of those initial conversations were not easy. He had assumed that his staff shared similar beliefs and definitions of equity. But in the discussions facilitated by Our Family staff, biases were revealed, confronted, and addressed. The staff began to use moments of cultural incompetence as learning opportunities, a stage 2 action. When one teacher said she did not believe in gay marriage, the teachers in the workshop discussed where those beliefs came from and how they might affect the school community. Gaines said he attended and participated in all of the discussions. "Those sessions were really personal," he said. "Even I did not realize how hard it was for LGBTQ people to be in a Latino community, doing social justice work, and not having it be acknowledged that they were dealing with their own struggles."

To address issues of equity in the classrooms, Gaines and his leadership team used elements of the Welcoming Schools curriculum, an antibullying program. The program included reading and discussing age-appropriate books related to diversity and bullying. They started slowly the first year, asking teachers to commit to teaching two or three lessons on the topic over the course of the year. A small number of teachers pushed back, saying they felt it was inappropriate to talk about gay families with students and expressing concern that these conversations would take time away from academics. "I did not try to change their worldviews," Gaines said. Instead, he explained that "part of going to college is understanding differences and having empathy. If we want our kids to be successful, they need to know this."

Gaines dedicated workshop time and used individual conversations with teachers to break down resistance to the cultural competency work, a stage 2 action. Some teachers who were politically aligned with the mission of the program were hesitant to use the curriculum for fear of how parents would react. He explained to teachers that the school has a right and an obligation to cover material around equity. "If you have an issue with a parent, you come to me," he told them.

Gaines also made it easier for teachers to implement the curriculum by working to get parents onboard. The school held monthly family workshops identical to the training teachers received. He says changes are also trickling down to the families. "These are really taboo topics," he said. The workshops, he said, have made it okay to start that dialogue. "You can see that just in the way that our parents carry themselves. We have a number of parents who identify as queer. I like to believe that it's a safe space for that here now."

In the second year of this work, Gaines said, he saw a lot of momentum. Teachers were having more open conversations with each other about race and sexual orientation. He and his staff prioritized hiring more culturally competent staff, asking interview questions like, "What is your definition of educational equity?" (See chapter 5 for more on recruitment.) The school hired more Latino and African American teachers.

A few years after implementing the curriculum, Gaines says he can also see the difference in the students. "Kids understand what diversity is and understand inequalities and understand what their role is in abolishing this and being allies," he said. He has particularly noticed this with the fourth- and fifth-grade student leaders in the way they support the school, carry themselves, and speak with other students. Recently in a fifth-grade class, a student from Cambodia shared with the other students at her table that she could speak three languages. Two classmates then began to speak in an accent they said impersonated a Chinese person. The girl began to cry, accusing them of making fun of her language and her race. A boy at her table told the students to stop and reported to the teacher what had happened. When Gaines was called to the classroom, the girl told him that the boy was her "ally." They have the language to talk about it, Gaines said, adding that he planned to bring all the students involved in the incident together to discuss it, see where the comment was coming from, and discuss why it was wrong. He would then meet with their families.

This history of candid conversations and exploration of cultural competence under Gaines's leadership set the stage for a significant challenge around educational equity; Gaines and his team took on the hard work of dismantling a system that had half of his African American male students isolated in special education classes that were monopolized by behavioral issues, not academic learning.

When the Oakland school district had a number of its special education students bused to Acorn Woodland, the district model gave Gaines one choice: place the high-need special education students in their own class, separated from the rest of the school. So he did that, and several issues around equity quickly emerged. "It was a school within a school," Gaines said. "Students with emotional issues were just thrown into these classrooms. There were no expectations [around academic achievement]; it was just about needing the kids to behave. There were no role models in these classes for responsible behavior, and students were exhibiting problematic outbursts throughout each day. They were not receiving any instruction."

On top of that, in a school that had traditionally worked hard to close the achievement gap between white and African American and Latino students, Gaines began talking with his staff about the fact that almost every seat in the special education class was filled with an African American boy. Given that about half the African American students in the school were in special education, the achievement gap had widened. In these conversations with his teachers and with district staff, Gaines began the hard work of dismantling Acorn's special education class and integrating its students into general education classrooms. The teachers he selected to have those students in their classrooms—some of his strongest teachers—initially pushed back. What kind of support would they have? they wanted to know. How would this change disrupt their classrooms?

"The only way I was able to get the door cracked open for the teachers to talk about it was to discuss the equity issue, the fact that our African American boys were all in this classroom, and that it is their right to be integrated into our general education classrooms," Gaines said.

At the same time, he convinced the district of the importance of integration as an equity issue, and he was able to secure funding for two additional full-time special education teachers to co-teach with general education instructors. "The argument was around providing the type of support that was needed to teach these kids," he said. Acorn became one of two schools in the district to fully integrate special education students into the general education classrooms.

Gaines has begun to disrupt the inequity at Acorn, a stage 3 action. The district has since started exploring how to replicate this model in other Oakland schools.

After a few months of integration, Gaines said he can already see that the special education students are learning and growing. In a few cases, teachers have been able to identify students they believe were misdiagnosed and will be removed from special education status. Other special education students are changing socially. One autistic student who used to struggle to talk to her classmates has made new friends and is often seen joking with them in the school yard. Another autistic student who used to cry every morning before school and had very few words now does not want to leave school at the end of the day. "They are all playing with other kids, and when they're out in the yard, you can't tell who's who," said Gaines. "They have other kids who are modeling what it means to play and to have these relationships."

Inclusion has not been without its challenges, though. Teachers are still figuring out how to manage more extreme behavior issues in their classrooms. To help them with this challenge and prevent them from sending students to his office in droves, Gaines regularly meets one-on-one with the teachers in the integrated classrooms to discuss the underlying causes of the behavior, talk openly about race, and come up with targeted strategies. By addressing these challenges in a way that keeps the students in class, Gaines hopes to be able to improve school culture and help Acorn's highest-need students meet academic goals. "I now have a real comfort with my staff and am more confident about having those conversations."

He feels fortunate to have arrived at a place where he and his staff can devote time to these issues. "A lot of schools are dealing with so many fires that they don't have the bandwidth to deal with that," Gaines said. "We have so few disciplinary incidents that we can put the manpower into this."

Lever 2: Action 3: Student Voice

When students have a voice in how their school is run, they feel more invested in their education.[5] Strong principals come up with innovative and effective ways to incorporate students' perspectives. At Acorn Woodland Elementary School, the principal developed a leadership class that taught older students how to organize and manage school activities like the recycling program and weekly assemblies. In a middle school in Denver, a principal started every faculty meeting with a story about one student's experience at the school, followed by time for each teacher to reflect on what she learned from the story and how it might influence her work. Sharing the students' perspective each week enabled the principal to lead change at a school where the culture had become toxic.

Your teachers, with the right professional development as needed, can teach students to use their voice respectfully and effectively, while teachers learn to feel comfortable stepping back and letting students speak.

Table 4.8 lists some of the practices school leaders have put in place to enable student leadership at their schools.

Table 4.8 Lever 2: Relationships: Action 3: Student Voice

	PRINCIPAL ACTIONS	SCHOOL ACTIONS
Stage 1	Create systems and processes to gather student input and build opportunities for student voice.	Students have opportunities to contribute ideas for school improvement. Students use their voice to express their feelings and ideas in ways that are appropriate in the school settings.
Stage 2	Create structures and developmental opportunities for children to show leadership voice (e.g., student council, student peer review board). Build the capacity for staff to support student leadership.	Students know how to respectfully challenge adults and others in a way that allows their voices to be heard. Students are frequently recognized for their contributions to the school community. Students have multiple opportunities to contribute to school practices and decision making about their learning experiences. Students identify and challenge injustices within the school and in the community (e.g., advocating on behalf of others). Students are invited to express their feelings and ideas about how to improve their experiences in school and attain their goals.
Stage 3	Create opportunities for students of all ages to manage projects and make decisions.	Students analyze data to inform and lead change. Students take a systems approach to address injustices in the school and the larger community.

ENABLING A STUDENT-RUN TOWN TO FLOURISH: MOVING FROM STAGE 1 TO STAGE 2 FOR STUDENT VOICE

Powell Bilingual Elementary School, Washington, DC

There is a small town within Powell. Pantherville, as students have named it, is of, by, and for the students.

"We really wanted to make sure that students were owning their learning, not only in the classroom but in the hallways, at recess, at lunchtime," principal Janeece Docal said. "We wanted to make sure students love learning and love coming to school." Pantherville emerged from the efforts of Powell's staff to draw out this level of student investment. During her first year as principal at Powell, Docal and her staff asked students what role they wanted to play in managing the school, a stage 1 action. She then quickly moved to create structures and opportunities for students to have leadership roles at the school, a stage 2 action, by supporting students in creating Pantherville. Some of her teachers participated in trainings held by MicroSociety, an organization that helps educators around the world use society building as a strategy for learning.

Complete with its own elected mayor and city council, jobs, and currency (Panther Bucks), Pantherville has roles for prekindergartners through fifth graders. After students voted on the name, staff helped students identify appropriate jobs and create the applications students would use to apply for those jobs. A panel of staff and students interviewed applicants for jobs ranging from classroom-based responsibilities to schoolwide positions such as the food manager, who delivers breakfast in the mornings, and post office managers. Some students were trained in peer mediation by the school counselors and in cooperative learning games by an outside organization, PlayWorks, so that they could work as Peace Keepers. Among other things, Peace Keepers help out at recess, teaching students how to be kind to and considerate of one another and to live by the school's core values, which the students also had a hand in writing, along with Pantherville's constitution. Thanks to the work of the Peace Keepers, Docal said, the school has very little bullying.

Pantherville also had an elected government. After a campaign season of posters and speeches, student government officials were elected on Election

Day in November, on the same day their parents were voting for city officials on the machines set up at Powell. Student voters got an "I Voted" sticker. The mayor of Washington, DC, and the local council member came to the school to swear in the elected student officers.

Students who did good work earned Panther Bucks, which they could later trade in at the school store, at book fairs, and as admission to school events. To take the economics lesson further, some homeroom teachers charged "rent" and fees for extra supplies like pencils and erasers (though, Docal emphasizes, no student was penalized for not having Panther Bucks).

Docal attributes the school's low rates of suspension and truancy and high attendance in part to the responsibility students took on through Pantherville. "Pantherville is a real society; everything is authentic," Docal said. "You are a citizen and you have your core values that you follow." When school officials were looking to modernize the school building, members of the Pantherville student council visited the District of Columbia City Council. Not only did they ask questions about the work of the council, but they also explained why the Powell school building needed improvements and what that would mean for their education. Said Docal, "I do think that their visit had a very large impact in the actual realization of our modernization and expansion that's happening right now. They're going to have a beautiful school, and I think the students can take ownership in that."

Students also had a voice in the work they did inside the school building. The school's portfolio projects (detailed in chapter 3) confer student ownership over their school work. In addition to creating their individual projects, students work as a whole class to create museums for their projects complete with scheduled visiting hours for other students in the school. As part of their study on community, for example, the pre-K students created a pizzeria and invited the second graders to visit and get a presentation on the project. When an older grade studied the civil rights movement, the students put on a performance for students from other grades, portraying historical figures from the time period.

"Student leadership is important because the students are contributing to their learning and owning their learning and they are more articulate. They are more passionate and contributing citizens to the community," Docal said.

Principal's Tool 4.6: Activities to Diagnose and Support the Involvement of Student Voice

LEVER 3: FAMILY AND COMMUNITY ENGAGEMENT

It is well documented that when parents invest time in supporting their children's learning, those children do better in school and are more likely to continue their education.[6] Schools can play a critical role in encouraging this involvement by making families feel welcome in the school and the classrooms and by creating purposeful ways for parents to get involved in school academics. When schools actively engage families in supporting their child's learning at home, their children learn more.[7] Remember how staff at Leadership Public Schools Hayward treated families as invaluable partners in meeting the school's mission to prepare every student to be successful in college? Creating effective partnerships meant understanding and valuing what parents bring to their children's education. To reap the potential benefits of that partnership, LPS Hayward staff had to learn about the parents' own experiences and attitudes toward schooling and then build on those experiences by offering tools and information that would help parents support their children's efforts to attend and complete college.

As we saw earlier in this chapter, when schools teach students that with hard work they can accomplish anything, higher student achievement follows. Students need to receive that message from their parents too. Research has found that students' perceptions of how their parents view their abilities affect students' academic performance.[8] Schools can engage parents in workshops and activities that explain the core values of hard work, optimism, and high expectations and why they are so important for their child's education and future. Parents then have the language to reinforce these messages at home.

So what do effective family engagement programs look like? As we saw earlier in the chapter, they have to be culturally sensitive, convenient, and relevant for parents. For instance, schools can provide information and activities in parents' languages and also show respect for all cultures, ethnicities, family structures, economic backgrounds, and work schedules. In addition, school leaders benefit when they recognize that parents can be an asset. When Tatiana Epanchin-Troyan became principal of Monarch Academy, a charter school in Oakland, California, she discovered that some parents were keeping their children at home because they were afraid to have them walk past the drug dealers and prostitutes loitering near the school. She brought five parents with her to a meeting with the police chief. After that meeting, police presence around the school increased, and so did student attendance. Parents also worked with the principal to convince the city to install a three-way stop sign at the intersection behind the school to reduce traffic.

Lever 3: Action 1: Involving Family and Community

New Leaders' research has found that principals were able to deliver improvements in student learning when they took the family engagement actions listed table 4.9.

Table 4.9 Lever 3: Family and Community Engagement: Action 1: Involving Family and Community

	PRINCIPAL ACTIONS	SCHOOL ACTIONS
Stage 1	Create a flexible engagement strategy that values multiple types of family and community interactions. Develop and implement short- and long-term plans for family and community engagement tailored to the school and community context. Identify two or three schoolwide practices to engage families based on an analysis of the community's need.	The leadership team builds awareness of biases about what family is and what family engagement means. At least one person, in addition to the principal, is designated as a lead in family and community engagement work. Systems are in place that engage families on a daily, weekly, and monthly basis about their child's performance (both positive and negative).
Stage 2	Train the staff on how to engage with families and community members respectfully and effectively. Create multiple opportunities for engagement to ensure that interactions do not feel hierarchical to families or community members. Track and analyze whether all families are engaging in positive two-way exchanges.	Families are actively involved in key moments of student learning. Multiple communication strategies with families are integrated into teacher roles and responsibilities. Family and community engagement data are reviewed regularly, and plans are adapted as needed.
Stage 3	Gather and evaluate data from families and community members about the quality of engagement. Provide ongoing and relevant training and supports for community members and families to support and foster high levels of engagement.	Families are viewed by all faculty and staff as critical partners in each student's academic and personal development. Staff members take collective responsibility to engage families and the community.

↑ ENGAGING FAMILIES AND REDUCING
TEACHER TURNOVER IN A BUDGET CRUNCH:
MOVING FROM STAGE 1 TO STAGE 3 FOR
INVOLVING FAMILY AND COMMUNITY

Acorn Woodland Elementary School, Oakland, California

Earlier in the chapter, we saw how this school's principal, Leroy Gaines, worked with families and staff to develop a more culturally competent school. Gaines also saw families as critical partners in increasing the depth of classroom instruction at Acorn. His students could pass a standardized multiple choice test, he said, but they were not reading at high levels and many Acorn graduates were struggling in middle school. As part of the solution, he turned to parents. "I never considered parents as powerful in helping us achieve our ultimate goal until I got here," he said.

The school already had a strong, long-time family coordinator in place, an important stage 1 action. "She knows the families; she knows all of their kids," Gaines said. He expanded her role, making her responsible for creating clear and sustained systems that would "enable the school to continue the process of developing parents," he said. The family coordinator created a system of parent leaders, paid positions for which parents apply. She created monthly half-day trainings for the parent leaders in which they learn "what our big rocks are," Gaines said, and strategies for how they can support children in the classroom. They work closely with teachers to provide academic support and even to develop classroom goals. On a recent day in a second-grade classroom, a parent leader organized and administered a test on high-frequency words, freeing up the certified teacher to focus on other priorities, such as providing one-on-one support to struggling students.

This program has enabled strong parent-teacher relationships, said Gaines. Teachers see parents as critical partners in their work, a stage 3 action. And the program has made parents committed to helping not only their own children but all the students in a classroom. "This is bigger than having parent coordinators photocopy," Gaines said. "Parents have come in and are now playing a role of keeper of quality. They are that common thread. We have family members who have had four different children attend Acorn; they have had kids here since the inception of the school. They have helped build the school and have a strong vested interest in making it a great school. Parents hold us accountable for results."

In addition to serving as parent leaders, parents can get involved at Acorn in a number of other ways. Every family is expected to give four hours of volunteer work a month. They can sit on the School Site Council, which oversees the school plan and budget. The school has an advisory committee for English language learners; a group focusing on the support of African American families; and opportunities for parents to help out in the cafeteria, recess yard, and office.

Principal's Tool 4.7: Guide for Family Engagement: Reflection on the Current State

NEXT STEPS

Developing a strong school culture is as important as cultivating strong academics. Many have argued that both are needed to sustain improvements in student achievement. After reading this chapter, you have probably begun to reflect on your own school and practices. Does your school have a clear vision and mission, and do the values in those statements permeate every aspect of the school? Do you have a system of behavioral expectations that is clear and well known by all students and teachers? Is your curriculum designed and taught in such a way that students of all backgrounds feel empowered to talk about, manage, and challenge the power dynamics that are a reality not only at your school but also in their communities and in society at large? We urge you to return to the text and tools in this chapter as much as you need to tackle this ever-present and ever-important work.

 WATCH SCHOOL CULTURE VIDEO: In this chapter's companion video, you'll learn about great work being done at schools across the country in the category of school culture. To access the video, go to www.wiley.com/go/newleaders.

Principal's Tools for School Culture

Principal's Tool 4.1: Activity: Creating and Sharing a School Vision

Principal's Tool 4.2: How Visible Is the School Vision at Your School?

Principal's Tool 4.3: Reflection Questions on Behavioral Expectations

Principal's Tool 4.4: Behavioral Expectations Self-Study

Principal's Tool 4.5: Reflection Questions on Student Efficacy

Principal's Tool 4.6: Activities to Diagnose and Support the Inclusion of Student Voice

Principal's Tool 4.7: Guide for Family Engagement: Reflection on the Current State

Talent Management

OVER THE DECADE SHE SERVED AS PRINCIPAL OF THE DUAL LANGUAGE MIDDLE School in New York City, Claudia Aguirre regularly reminded her teachers: "We have only thirty months to prepare our students for high school." This sense of urgency shaped Aguirre's approach to teacher development. She knew that without great teaching in every classroom and a shared ownership for student learning among all educators in the building, her students, most of whom lived in poverty and arrived several years below grade level, would not make the rapid progress necessary to catch up with their peers and graduate ready for high school–level work.

With that in mind, Aguirre made improving instruction her top priority. She observed teachers regularly and gave them immediate feedback during weekly one-on-one sessions where they also discussed lesson plans and occasionally reviewed classroom videos. To monitor progress, all teachers maintained an individual improvement plan, which they kept in their portfolio along with samples of their work from year to year, with feedback notes from walk-throughs and classroom visits, curriculum maps and scope and sequence documents, goals, and detailed weekly plans.

Aguirre developed an unusually robust culture of teacher collaboration. Grade and content-area teams met daily, and Aguirre herself met with all teachers twice a week. Faculty worked together to establish a schoolwide learning agenda. Because the school's greatest instructional challenge was improving students' reading and writing skills among the 38 percent of students who were English learners, Aguirre made sure every teacher made significant professional development around advanced literacy strategies regardless of their content area. One staff meeting each month was dedicated to literacy instruction, one to skillful instruction, and one to meeting pressing needs as they arose.

Aguirre's efforts paid off. When she started at the school, she said, the school was known as a "dumping ground" for low-performing students. Five years into her tenure, student proficiency in ELA rose by 40 percent, to 61 percent; math proficiency jumped by 65 percent, to 91 percent; and no student scored "below basic" in either subject on the state exams.

There is ample research showing the power of even one great teacher to boost student learning, but one talented teacher is not sufficient to compensate for the disadvantages of poverty, which leave many students lagging years behind.[1] Principals have a multiplying effect, with the potential to seed great teaching across an entire school, reaching many more students, more consistently, so they catch up to their peers. And even students who are thriving academically deserve access to great teaching in every classroom, which principals are uniquely positioned to deliver by managing, supporting, and developing their staff. As former Los Angeles schools superintendent John Deasy once told a group of aspiring principals, "You are responsible for who teaches our children, because children don't get to make that choice."[2]

As we visited top-performing schools and sought to identify the factors contributing to their success, we found that their leaders tended to be excellent talent managers, with a sharp focus on recruiting, supporting, and retaining strong teachers. These leaders were highly skilled at helping all teachers to grow, creating a culture of collaboration, continuous improvement, and shared leadership that fostered deep commitment to the school and its goals for student learning. The levers they use to achieve this are described in the Transformational Leadership Framework (TLF) talent management category and are undertaken in concert with levers falling under the categories of culture and learning and teaching.

So what are the key levers that have helped schools improve the teaching quality of their staff? Most public discourse in recent years has focused on evaluation as the primary means for getting better teachers in front of our children. But improving teaching requires much more than that. The TLF outlines four key levers around talent management that school leaders use to directly contribute to student learning:

Lever 1: Recruitment and onboarding: *Schools recruit, select, assign, and onboard staff efficiently and effectively.* The most effective school leaders recruit for and hire educators who believe in their school's vision and in their students' ability to learn, who are willing to learn and grow themselves, and who have key foundational pedagogical skills. In addition, they provide regular, targeted support to both novice and veteran teachers from the beginning of the year.

Lever 2: Instructional leadership team: *Schools develop a team that includes teacher leaders capable of supporting instructional improvement among their colleagues.* Strong teacher leaders are crucial for making sustained gains in student achievement, whether they serve on a schoolwide team or lead in other ways, like coaching. Building instructional leadership teams and identifying and developing teacher leaders who can bring the vision of the school to life and help other teachers grow creates a culture of continuous learning among staff members.

Lever 3: Performance monitoring and evaluation: *School leaders monitor and manage individual staff performance.* Both school leaders and teacher leaders can play a key role in monitoring and developing all the teachers in the school by providing them with regular, accurate, actionable feedback.

Lever 4: Professional learning and collaboration: *Schools establish professional learning structures that drive instructional improvement.* The most powerful professional learning happens inside schools and is directly connected to what's happening in classrooms.

WHY MANAGING TALENT MATTERS

Spending time and energy to develop a strong school staff is perhaps the best investment a school leader can make. A strong staff pays off not only in terms of student learning but also by making the job of the principal more manageable. The responsibilities of principals have mushroomed in recent years, with a renewed focus on instructional leadership to meet rigorous academic standards alongside the administrative duties principals have long said distract them from focusing adequate time on instructional priorities. With 75 percent of principals reporting that the job has become too complex, strong schools need thriving leadership teams to effectively manage vastly expanded school leadership responsibilities.[3]

By developing a strong talent management system, the successful principals we observed were able to develop and deploy a team of instructional leaders so that all teachers share the challenge of improving instruction across the building. Developing teacher leaders also helped reduce staff turnover, even in schools with inadequate funding, low student achievement, and an unhealthy culture, where teacher attrition tends to be particularly high. Research has found that more than half of all teachers who leave the profession do so because they lack advancement opportunities,[4] and in fact, principals told us that creating leadership opportunities enticed their best teachers to stay longer at the school.

TALENT MANAGEMENT CATEGORY MAP

Lever 1: Recruitment and Onboarding

Schools recruit, select, assign, and onboard staff efficiently and effectively.

Actions

- **Action 1: Recruitment:** Identify effective and aligned staff candidates.
- **Action 2: Selection and Hiring:** Implement rigorous screening and hiring procedures.
- **Action 3: Staff Assignment:** Implement processes for strategic staff assignment.
- **Action 4: Induction:** Develop systems to introduce new staff to school expectations, processes, and procedures.

Lever 2: Instructional Leadership Team

Schools develop a well-aligned team comprising an instructional leadership team and teacher leaders who support effective instructional practices.

Actions

- **Action 1: Instructional Leadership Team Roles, Expectations, and Supports:** Identify, develop, and support instructional leadership team members.
- **Action 2: Teacher Leadership:** Create ongoing opportunities for teachers to build leadership capacity.

Lever 3: Performance Monitoring and Evaluation

School leaders monitor and manage individual staff performance.

Actions

- **Action 1: Performance Expectations:** Set expectations for all staff members that define what standards and actions will be assessed.
- **Action 2: Observation and Actionable Feedback:** Gather evidence of practice through frequent observations and provide concrete feedback.
- **Action 3: Monitoring Implementation:** Assess where changes in practice are occurring and where additional supports are needed.
- **Action 4: Performance Evaluation:** At the end of the year, review all evidence to assess individual performance.

Lever 4: Professional Learning and Collaboration

Schools establish professional learning structures that drive instructional improvement.

Actions

- **Action 1: Ongoing Professional Learning:** Provide job-embedded opportunities to learn and practice new skills.
- **Action 2: Collaborative Teacher Team Structures:** Establish structures that facilitate collaborative teacher planning and learning.

LEVER 1: RECRUITMENT AND ONBOARDING

Every job opening at a school offers an opportunity. The hiring process is a chance to fill that position with someone who will help bring the school closer to achieving its mission and vision. By being strategic about the qualities and skills they look for in job candidates for particular positions, what classes they assign new teachers to, and the kind of support they give new teachers as they are adjusting to their school, the principals we researched have been better able to meet the learning needs of all of their students. They have treated the hiring and onboarding process as a means to continuously improve their school's culture and academics. In fact, a number of school leaders described the hiring process as the most important part of their job. Said Eric Westendorf of E. L. Haynes Public Charter School in Washington, DC, "We know that when we get it right, it makes a big difference for kids, and when we get it wrong, it takes a lot of time trying to address the problem."

Our research indicates that the most important actions associated with recruiting and onboarding staff are the processes of recruitment, selection, and hiring; how new staff are assigned to positions within the school; and the system for induction into the school community.

WORKING WITH SCHOOL-LEVEL HIRING CONSTRAINTS

We urge you to read this section even if you have limited decision-making power around staffing at your school. While we strongly believe that schools are most successful at putting together an effective staff when principals oversee that process, we recognize that in many districts, large parts of the hiring process, and at times even final decisions around hiring or staff transfer, occur at the central-system level rather than at the school level. However, even when central staff set the hiring criteria, manage the process, or determine the candidate pool, we have seen many school leaders find ways to influence the process to ensure that they get the best possible teachers for their school. After all, district staff oversee a lot of schools, each with different student populations and needs, and therefore they might not be familiar with all the particulars of any one school. They also work on one central time line when it comes to hiring, which might not align with the distinct needs of your school.

In some cases, principals have partnered with their central office human resources team by identifying additional candidates to be interviewed beyond the standard pool or by creating a more robust interview process. In others, school leaders are strategic about how new teachers are assigned and inducted into the school community. We have also seen principals volunteer to serve as part of the district hiring teams, advocating for more local school staff involvement in the process and using their knowledge of teacher contracts and certification policies to establish specific role definitions and needs to shape the hiring and selection process even if it happens centrally.

Because the work of recruiting, selecting, and hiring teachers is so intertwined and relies on the same underlying criteria, we will look at the practices in both of these actions together. Tables 5.1 and 5.2 show the stages of development for each of these actions.

Lever 1: Action 1: Recruitment

Table 5.1 Lever 1: Recruitment and Onboarding: Action 1: Recruitment

	PRINCIPAL ACTIONS	SCHOOL ACTIONS
Stage 1	Assess and expand recruiting sources beyond the traditional district candidate pool by reaching out to partner programs, universities, and other available venues. Hire as early as possible when vacancies are known. Develop materials that present the school as an attractive place to work.	Recruitment efforts cast a wide net for candidates outside of traditional venues.
Stage 2	Recruit for diverse expertise; build networks with traditional and nontraditional teacher sources by reaching out to local universities, partnering with human resources, and asking teachers to tap into their networks. Engage leadership team members in networking to potential staff members at every opportunity.	The school maintains an ongoing, active recruitment network outside standard district resources. Leadership team members identify many sources for high-quality recruits. School branding materials and a website are easily accessible and inspire the right staff to apply by sharing key messages about the vision and mission of the school and its hiring processes.
Stage 3	Identify vacancies early by working with the leadership team to identify staff who are likely to transition. Partner with the central human resources team to identify talent for hard-to-fill vacancies.	Teachers routinely attend hiring fairs and events and tap their own networks to recruit staff.

Table 5.2 Lever 1: Recruitment and Onboarding: Action 2: Selection and Hiring

	PRINCIPAL ACTIONS	SCHOOL ACTIONS
Stage 1	Develop clear selection criteria and a consistent process for selection, including how all decisions will be made. Select teachers who have demonstrated content knowledge, share a belief in the potential of all students, and are willing to learn and develop. Implement application and interview protocols to rigorously screen prospective teachers for the belief that all students can reach college and for commitment to student learning, not just to teaching their content area.	Clear selection criteria, protocols, and hiring and induction processes are in place. An appropriate number of staff members are certified according to state and district guidelines, including for English language learners and special education services.
Stage 2	Include demonstration lessons and formal interviews with teachers, families, and students (where appropriate) as part of the staff selection process. Organize ongoing professional development for all staff participating in hiring teachers in order to develop a common vision of the skills and behaviors of a strong candidate. Develop leadership team members' capacity to manage the selection process.	Multiple staff members participate in multiple aspects of the hiring and selection process and are part of the hiring team. Selected candidates demonstrate a willingness to explore and deepen their understandings of students' cultures.
Stage 3	Set expectations with leadership team members for how responsibilities will be divided, and task them with leading the hiring and selection process.	The selection process is managed by the leadership team and includes the input of the other key stakeholders (e.g., students, family members, and other members of the community). Multiple stakeholders, including students and community members, have the opportunity to participate in the hiring process.

CREATING A VISION FOR THE RECRUITING AND HIRING PROCESS: MOVING FROM STAGE 1 TO STAGE 3 FOR SELECTION AND HIRING

Brooklyn Latin School, Brooklyn, New York

When describing his school's philosophy on hiring, Jason Griffiths, former principal of Brooklyn Latin School, said, "People are at the heart of our organization. While we recognize the importance of providing our students with the most up-to-date books, materials, technology, and resources, our success hinges on the people within our walls. We at the Brooklyn Latin School believe that the most important thing that we can do in order to help our students achieve success is to hire the right people. This is why we spend a great deal of our time and energy in finding the best teacher leaders and support staff we can find." Griffiths believes the school's meticulous hiring process contributed to the success of this selective high school, where, within its first three years, it became one of the most sought after and consistently high-performing schools in New York City.

Griffiths and his team established four guidelines that governed and set the tone for the hiring process at Brooklyn Latin:

1. Hiring is the school's number one priority every year. As a result, we have a strong school, faculty, and staff.
2. Be prepared to work harder than anyone else to find and hire the best teachers in the hiring pool.
3. The school leader should constantly build the capacity of those around him or her by increasing their roles in the hiring process.
4. Be open to change in the process when a step/question is not yielding the data needed.

As the founding principal of the school, which is modeled on Boston Latin School and accepts students from across New York City based on their performance on a specialized high school standardized test, Griffiths and his staff created a hiring process that made clear how selection would be made and who would make it, important stage 1 actions. Within this process, they also implemented stage 2 actions, including demonstration lessons and interviews with stakeholders outside of the principal. There are many ways to design this process. Exhibit 5.1 shows Brooklyn Latin's approach.

EXHIBIT 5.1: BROOKLYN LATIN SCHOOL HIRING PROCESS

1. Identify websites and organizations for job postings.
2. Identify teacher recruiting fairs worth attending.
3. Write detailed job description that tells the story of the culture of the school.
4. Review resumes and cover letters looking closely at candidate writing with leadership team and department representatives.
5. Conduct phone interviews with promising candidates along with leadership team and department representatives.
6. Invite promising candidates to a model lesson where they have interaction with the school leader, faculty, staff, and students. Conduct interview after model lesson.
7. Invite candidates back to school for 2–3 hour visit/interview.
8. Check references.
9. Make offer and prepare for Induction/Personal Improvement process.

Identifying the Right Candidates

Before Griffiths even began the recruiting process, he and his staff wrote job descriptions that described the culture of his school and conveyed the skills and qualities they were looking for in a candidate, a stage 1 action. They then used those criteria as a guide as they screened résumés, interviewed, and hired.

A big part of creating the criteria for an open position is considering the needs of students and the skill gaps on staff. The following questions can serve as a guide as you do this work with your staff:

1. What are our goals for the next few years for the grade level or department and school?
2. What skills, experiences, and pedagogical and content knowledge does our staff lack that the grade level or department and school need to reach current and future goals?
3. Are any teams really struggling?
4. Do the students most in need of support have access to strong teachers?
5. Are the strongest teachers serving in leadership roles?
6. Which teams are demonstrating strong collaborative cultures, and which teams could benefit from change?

These questions help determine where both new and returning teachers are needed throughout the building. We have seen strong principals make the sometimes difficult decision to reassign a teacher to a different grade level or subject area when the teacher's skills were needed there. (See the section on staff assignment in this chapter for more on this topic.)

Once you identify your school's needs, you can consider the criteria you will use to both recruit for and fill job openings. Even if your district has fixed hiring criteria and personnel policies, you can influence the process by recommending more stringent or detailed criteria that will help you find the best match for your school.

Once the principals in our study identified the gaps in their staff, they used some general criteria to find teachers who not only had the core pedagogical skills and content knowledge they were looking for, but also had characteristics that would help the school fulfill its mission:

- Shows a genuine connection to and interest in students
- Deeply committed to the belief that every student is capable of academic success
- Focused on improving student achievement, with a strong sense of responsibility to do so
- Interested in continuously learning and improving their own work
- Capable of working in teams
- Has leadership potential[5]

As we discussed in detail in chapter 4, forging a school culture that cultivates persistence and love of learning among students and adults alike is often critical to a school's success. Believing in their own potential to succeed academically is a precondition for students to excel, and students need the support of teachers and classmates who believe in their capacity to achieve at a high level. Later in this chapter, we outline the importance of teachers working in teams and being open to regularly learning.

Exhibit 5.2 from Brooklyn Latin's teacher job description illustrates the detail with which you and your staff can consider writing your own job descriptions.

Recruitment Timing and Resources

Timing and recruitment resources are critical to identifying, and ultimately securing, the strongest candidates to work in your school. Once you develop materials that accurately and effectively reflect your school and the types of educators you are looking for, an important stage 1 action, consider using a broad range of recruitment resources, from local universities and alternative teacher certification programs to a variety of employment websites.

EXHIBIT 5.2: BROOKLYN LATIN SCHOOL TEACHER EXPECTATIONS

KEY STAFF CHARACTERISTICS	BROOKLYN LATIN EXPECTATIONS
Shows a genuine connection to and interest in students	The teachers will work together with the counselor for the welfare of the student (case studies, advisory, guidance workshops).
	Teachers monitor progress of students and report to the community when concerns arise.
	Teachers work with the students in community service projects.
Deeply committed to the belief that every student is capable of academic success	Teachers believe in the students and will have the highest expectations.
	Teachers will work with students with vast and varied learning differences.
Focused on improving student achievement, with a strong sense of responsibility to do so	Teachers create and use rubrics if applicable and appropriate to the assessment.
	Teachers use standards-based grading.
Capable of working in teams	Teachers formally and informally work together to plan lessons, UBD, Unit.
	Teachers are a part of a large community: teachers, parents, and students.
	We are a team and often participate in group work as a staff, not just teachers of the same discipline.

The timing of your recruitment efforts is also critical. The most effective leaders identify vacancies early, a stage 3 action. At E. L. Haynes Public Charter School in Washington, DC, for example, the leadership team begins the recruitment and hiring cycle in January with a meeting to assess staffing needs and review the effectiveness of the previous year's recruitment and hiring practices.

Your leadership team can help you identify teachers who might be considering leaving so that you can plan strategically to fill those vacancies or even persuade a strong teacher to stay. Several school leaders we studied emphasized the importance of creating a trusting environment in which teachers feel comfortable speaking with you openly about how their year is going, whether they are interested in other positions within the school, or are considering leaving. To ensure your strong teachers know that they are valued, principals can hold "stay conversations" with them right after Thanksgiving, explaining to them how important they are to the school, asking them what their concerns and interests are and if they have thoughts of leaving the school, and if so, what you can do to convince them to stay.[6]

Even if you do not know of any anticipated vacancies, we have seen benefits to building a pool of potential teacher candidates in the early spring, just in case. As one principal who learned the hard way told us, "In July, all the good ones were gone."

The criteria created for the open positions serve to inform not only applicants but also give current staff members the tools to convey consistent messages around the school's vision and mission, the strength of culture, and the beliefs and values that drive their work. We have seen school leaders effectively incorporate teachers into the recruiting process, a stage 2 action for recruiting, by having them reach out to their own personal and professional networks and to speak on behalf of the school at job fairs. Candidates value the perspectives of current teachers to get insight into what it's like to work at the school.

Interviewing

You will hire the best teachers for your school if your interview process is thorough and purposeful. Many principals have told us they have been able to identify stronger candidates with a multistep interview process, since not all important qualities can be detected in a single interview. For example, you might be able to determine in an interview how a teacher might approach working with at-risk students or whether he can plan challenging lessons. However, it would be difficult to ascertain in a conversation what his teaching style is and how he interacts with and engages students. You'll likely be better able to assess that skill by requiring applicants to teach a mini-lesson, a stage 2 action.

Just as important as determining whether you think the applicant is the right fit for your school is giving the candidate a chance to decide for himself whether he feels right at the school. Giving him tours of the school and providing ample opportunity for him to speak with staff and ask questions will help him get a sense of the school and where, if at all, he might fit in.

At Brooklyn Latin, Griffiths and his team put a lot of thought into what questions he and his staff asked candidates from the first conversation, keeping in mind the kind of person they wanted teaching their students. They were looking for how well each candidate understood the mission and vision of Brooklyn Latin, the level and types of work they believed teachers needed to put in to educate children, and the candidate's expectations for students. When interviewing teachers, Brooklyn Latin looked at the following dimensions (with sample questions listed under each dimension) on this phone interview protocol:

- Alignment to mission and vision

  - Why do you want to teach at the Brooklyn Latin School?

- Work ethic

  - Tell us about the last nonclassroom activity in which you partici-
    pated at your school.

- Intellectualism, content knowledge and instructional capacity

  - What was the most recent book that you read? Did you like the
    book? Why or why not?

  - What is your favorite topic to teach in your subject area?

  - After a model lesson: Tell us what you think went well in your
    lesson.

- Ability to work with others

  - Tell us about your least successful relationship at work

- Ability to serve as a role model and develop relationships with students

  - Tell us about a time when you did not properly handle conflict with
    a colleague.

  - Give an example of a time when you were able to build a relation-
    ship with a student whom others had difficulty reaching

- Reflective nature

  - How might your co-workers describe you?

Lever 1: Action 3: Staff Assignment

Once the right people are hired, where should you place both new and returning teachers to maximize the impact of your staff? Our research found that effective principals
think carefully about each teacher team, as well as how skills and expertise are distributed throughout the building to ensure the best teachers are working with the most
students, or at least with the students in most need. For example, rather than keeping
a teacher in the same grade out of habit or tradition, strong principals who determine
that a teacher's skills are needed in a different grade will have those sometimes difficult conversations, explaining where her skills are needed and that it could be a growth
opportunity for both the students and the teacher. When those conversations are handled delicately and the teacher is given adequate support, she can successfully make
that transition.

When Liz Kirby started as principal at Kenwood Academy in Chicago, she found that
most of her strong teachers were teaching junior- and senior-year honors courses. Students who were struggling, and thus were not in the honors classes, lacked access to the

school's best teachers. By explaining to those teachers where they were needed most, Kirby was able to inspire them to teach in the school's ninth-grade academy. Those teachers had a significant impact in helping students in the academy transition to high school and remain on track to graduate.

Table 5.3 identifies the stages of development for staff assignment.

Lever 1: Action 4: Induction

An effective induction process reinforces the school mission, vision, and values. It introduces new staff to the instructional strategies and behavioral expectations that

Table 5.3 Lever 1: Recruitment and Onboarding: Action 3: Staff Assignment

	PRINCIPAL ACTIONS	SCHOOL ACTION
Stage 1	Assess staff skills, and place teachers in grade levels and content areas on the basis of their skills, qualifications, and demonstrated effectiveness.	Strengths, not tenure or other considerations, are used to determine teacher placement. Strongest teachers are placed with lowest-performing students and in grades that have proven to have long-term impact on student success and retention.
Stage 2	Identify, from among the current staff, effective teachers who have demonstrated high leadership potential, and recruit them to grade-level and department leadership. Balance grade and content teams to ensure that more experienced and effective teachers are mentoring and supporting less experienced teachers.	Grade-level and content-area teams have strong leadership. Teams comprise staff with a mix of experience, strengths, and tenure at the school.
Stage 3	Assess needs and strategically deploy people based on skill and need, even if that means moving teachers from grades they have taught in the past Formally leverage the strongest teachers to build the capacity of others. Develop contingency plans for open positions that include providing additional supports to remaining teachers and strategies to support long-term substitutes.	Highly effective teachers are asked to formally develop and support teachers on their teams who are not as strong. Long-term substitutes or staff who are taking on additional responsibilities to provide coverage when there is a vacancy are supported while being held to high standards.

are used throughout the school, stage 1 actions from learning and teaching and from school culture, respectively.

Some schools design the summer induction process as a start to the professional learning work that will continue throughout the year. This process ensures that new and returning teachers alike start the year aware of the school's expectations and with the opportunity to develop supportive and collaborative relationships with colleagues.

 Potential Pitfalls

While new teachers need support, too much support coming from several different directions can create confusion. We have seen districts or schools require that instructional coaches, mentors, and grade team leaders all work with new teachers. Sometimes teachers receive conflicting advice from different people or spend too much time being advised. While ideally the district staff would think through how they want to rationalize all this support, in the absence of that, principals can step in to coordinate the support and make sure the guidance each one gives is consistent.

Table 5.4 Lever 1: Recruitment and Onboarding: Action 4: Induction

	PRINCIPAL ACTIONS	SCHOOL ACTIONS
Stage 1	Create induction processes for new staff at the time of placement in order to share expectations, the school's culture, processes, and procedures.	The school has intensive induction and mentoring processes for new staff.
Stage 2	At the start of every school year, lead returning staff through some parts of the induction process to remind them of the school's key goals and expectations for improving student achievement. Partner with the leadership team to plan and revise induction activities based on their effectiveness in past years.	The induction system is ongoing and touches all staff throughout the school year to maintain a common vision for the school. Induction activities are viewed as positive culture-building moments.
Stage 3	Assess the impact of induction activities to improve on the induction process and ensure that induction has a positive effect on staff performance and feelings about the school.	Multiple staff members have a role in leading induction activities for new and returning staff. Interim staff members participate in a modified induction process to ensure that all adults share similar expectations.

CREATING ACTIVITIES THAT INTRODUCE NEW TEACHERS TO EFFECTIVE INSTRUCTION: MOVING TO STAGE 2 FOR INDUCTION

Boston Collegiate Charter School, Boston, Massachusetts

Under school executive director Kathleen Sullivan, the staff at Boston Collegiate Charter School spent several years developing and perfecting school policies and practices, which they detailed in the school handbook presented to teachers at the beginning of every year. However, despite having expectations written down and circulated, the school leadership team found that even some veteran teachers struggled to understand and meet these expectations consistently.

To improve the induction process, a stage 2 action, the leadership team created a series of videos of strong teachers demonstrating what the school's expectations should and should not look like in practice. During the school's annual boot camp, a two-week induction and orientation program that all new and returning Boston Collegiate teachers were required to attend just before the beginning of each school year, they watched and discussed the videos. The purpose of the boot camp, said former executive director Sullivan, was to give new teachers a chance to learn from successful veteran teachers before the school year starts and reinforce the school's expectations for returning teachers as well. "We want to be able to be frank about what is happening so that we collectively as a school can get better," Sullivan said.

The video series was used in an activity called "What do you see? What would you do?" During this activity, teachers watch two to five minutes of film and take notes on what they observe. As a group, they then discussed what they saw and brainstormed what they would do if they were the teacher in that classroom. "The overarching goal of the activity is to set common instructional and cultural expectations at our school and to fine-tune each teacher's eye so that they are able to see all of the details that go into keeping high academic and cultural expectations at our school," said Eileen Callahan, the school's former dean of curriculum.

In one session, a teacher pointed out that a couple of students were talking during the lesson, one student turned around six times, another student kept tapping his pen on his desk, and there was a lot of paper shuffling. Another teacher noted that the teacher in the video seemed to call only on students who raised their hands to answer questions. Working in pairs, teachers then discussed whether the way the teacher responded to these classroom situations was good practice, and if not, what she could have done differently. Suggestions included giving the student who turned around so much a consequence, calling on all students to get everyone involved in discussion, and arranging desks differently and circulating throughout the room as strategies to bolster student engagement.

"What's critical is that by the end, the 'What do we do?' is consistent," Sullivan said. "Every teacher in the room is in agreement with what we do, and there is an opportunity for the principal to say what we should do."

From these discussions, teachers then created goals for themselves for the year. The new teachers seemed to value this exercise. "Coming in as a new teacher, it's great to have a core group of teachers that you are working with to tackle these kinds of issues and reflect upon that, and also to see what the protocol of the school is," said one new seventh-grade teacher. "During boot camp you go through that practice so you feel a little more confident going into that classroom on the first day."

The school saw consistent improvement in student achievement, which Sullivan attributes in part to this work around teacher development. During Sullivan's last four years at the school, student English language arts proficiency rose by 17 percent, with 86 percent of students performing at the proficient or advanced level. Math proficiency increased by 8 percent.

> Principal's Tool 5.1: Reflection Questions and Tools for Staff Hiring

LEVER 2: INSTRUCTIONAL LEADERSHIP TEAM

As we emphasize throughout this book, schools are most effective when they are run by strong teams of educators. The field at large has focused too much on the principal as the only instructional leader. In one of the most extensive studies of school leadership to date, a group of researchers examining 180 schools over five years found that collective leadership has a stronger influence on student learning "than any individual source of leadership."[7] School leaders have the greatest effect on student learning when they identify strong teachers with diverse backgrounds and expertise and develop them into a high-functioning community of instructional leaders.

Our own research confirmed that finding, and the critical actions within this lever revolve around building thriving instructional leadership teams and strong teacher leaders. As we discuss in this section, creating an instructional leadership team (ILT) is an effective place to start this work, but teacher leadership needs to spread far beyond the team, finding its way into department meetings, collegial conversations in the cafeteria, and, of course, classrooms. All the successful schools in our research had multiple high-quality instructional leaders helping to elevate teaching across the buildings in which they worked.

Lever 2: Action 1: Instructional Leadership Team Roles, Expectations, and Supports

Consider what you and your team could accomplish together if you distributed instructional responsibilities across your staff. A good first step to doing this is to create a strong ILT. This team is distinct from the often mandated school leadership team, usually comprising the principal, parents, and teachers charged with helping to develop and implement school policies. Instead, an ILT is made up of educators who take an active role in supporting and improving instruction across all classrooms.

As you can see from table 5.5, you can move through the stages of development of this lever by first defining the roles and responsibilities of the ILT members and making sure their skills meet the needs of the school, stage 1 actions. In stage 2, principals are building the capacity of the ILT members to conduct classroom observations and give their colleagues quality feedback. With those practices in place, a school leader can give ILT members ownership over other projects and initiatives, including managing grade teams and departments.

Who Should Sit on the ILT?

Putting together a team of teachers who can support your efforts to improve instruction at your school is a critical stage 1 action. Research has found a team size of eight to ten members is ideal (too many people will make it hard to schedule meetings and make decisions). The team should draw on the diverse strengths of the faculty, including educators with expertise in different content areas, background teaching different grade levels, and experience across a range of roles of both administrators and teachers.

What are the qualities of an ideal ILT member? Teacher leaders need to be great teachers, but great teaching does not automatically translate into effective leadership. Instructional leaders need the adult and personal leadership skills to be able to improve the practice of other educators through observation, candid feedback, coaching, and leading meetings. They should be able to serve as a trusted and respected resource for their colleagues. The following list offers a guide as you consider which teachers you want on your team:[8]

Table 5.5 Lever 2: Instructional Leadership Team: Action 1: Instructional Leadership Team Roles, Expectations, and Supports

	PRINCIPAL ACTIONS	SCHOOL ACTIONS
Stage 1	Define the roles and responsibilities for the instructional leadership team: supporting and leading teacher team meetings, leading data-driven instruction cycles, conducting teacher observations, providing feedback, and completing final evaluations.	Instructional leadership team roles and responsibilities are clear and transparent.
	Assess the alignment of the current instructional leadership team members to the school's vision, mission, approach to instruction, and culture, and take immediate steps to remove or replace any members who are unwilling or unable to carry out the current expectations.	Identified instructional leadership team members have an individualized development plan based on their strength and growth areas.
	Model effective team meeting protocols and processes for looking at student outcomes and planning responsive strategies.	Instructional leadership team members take part in regular learning walks during which they are looking for the implementation of specific practices.
	Create monitoring systems to track the work of instructional leadership team members and their teams, looking at consistency and quality of implementation.	Instructional leadership team meetings focus on student work and formative data.
	Ensure that the processes and roles of the instructional leadership team are clear to all members of the staff.	Staff understand the roles and responsibilities of the instructional leadership team.
Stage 2	Design year-long professional learning for the instructional leadership team members to build consistency in their assessment of teacher practice.	The instructional leadership team consistently models and enforces schoolwide philosophy, core values, responsibility, and efficacy.
	Build capacity of instructional leadership team members to conduct observations and provide effective feedback.	Instructional leadership team members conduct observations and provide effective coaching and feedback.
	Develop reporting systems so that instructional leadership team members can share feedback, input, and concerns of the teams they are leading.	Instructional leadership team members have clear and consistent ways in which to share the concerns, challenges, and successes of the teams they are leading.
	Create clarity around decision making, especially letting staff know when a decision will be yours or made by consensus.	Instructional leadership team members use consistent protocols and processes to lead their departmental or grade-level teams.
	Develop a succession plan for essential roles on the instructional leadership team.	

Table 5.5 (*continued*)

	PRINCIPAL ACTIONS	SCHOOL ACTIONS
Stage 3	Build systems for distributed leadership through which members of the instructional leadership team manage specific initiatives and grade-level teams or departments.	Instructional leadership is provided by multiple instructional leadership team members using consistent protocols and processes and a relentless focus on data.
	Expand the roles of the instructional leadership team to include teacher evaluation (when policy allows).	Instructional leadership team members successfully lead autonomous projects.
	Provide instructional leadership team members opportunities for additional autonomy to manage projects and teams.	

Key Traits and Skills to Select For and Develop in ILT Members

- Shared vision and a belief that all students and teachers can succeed
- Excellent instructional skills
- A willingness and ability to provide teachers with honest and candid feedback
- Commitment to ongoing learning and reflection, for themselves and others
- Openness to new leadership strategies and new ideas
- Strong interpersonal skills
- Skills and informal authority to implement change
- Coaching and feedback skills around instruction and instructional improvement
- Strong knowledge of teaching and learning
- Meeting facilitation skills
- Willingness to collaborate with a team

Strong school leaders not only look for these skills among their teachers, but actively cultivate them by providing opportunities for teachers to build key leadership skills incrementally. We have seen effective principals regularly offer ILT members frequent feedback, coaching, and professional development to support their work as teacher leaders.

We recognize that creating a strong team is not easy. One elementary school principal had great success identifying teacher leaders to make up her ILT when she started at the school. But when a few of her ILT members left the school a few years later, she had to change her approach to developing leaders within her staff.

Principal Tatiana Epanchin-Troyan of Monarch Academy in Oakland, California, had several strong educators in the building, but most of them did not see themselves as leaders. "I had to backtrack and say, 'Okay, we have to build our capacity and our belief around what it is to be a part of a leadership team.'" Although she saw leadership qualities in them, she said, "I had to help each of them harness the leader within." Epanchin-Troyan worked with each of the team members individually to help them develop their leadership voices. She attended team meetings and modeled how to facilitate the meeting for each new ILT member. She then began to gradually transition leadership of the teacher team meetings to each member. She co-planned the meetings with the ILT member who would be leading the meeting that week and began to join meetings as a participant rather than a facilitator. She also continued to meet with each member to coach them on the feedback and support they were providing to teachers. Over the course of the school year, Epanchin-Troyan saw her team members build confidence and begin to take ownership of the ILT work that they had hesitated to take on earlier that year. The team then helped Epanchin-Troyan maintain a strong focus on data cycles to improve instruction. The school saw some important successes: the proportion of students meeting adequate yearly progress in ELA rose from 13 percent when she arrived at the school to 45 percent six years later; math achievement quadrupled in that same period.

Getting the Team Started and Focusing the Work of the ILT

Principals facilitate their ILT meetings in ways that model the kinds of protocols, focus on instruction, use of data, and decision making they want to see in all the teacher team meetings. They are building skills in their ILT members to lead teacher teams by modeling these approaches.

Based on our research and experience working with principals in schools, we developed guiding questions to help leaders establish and structure an effective ILT:

1. *Purpose:* How will you use the ILT? What will be the primary responsibilities of the ILT?

2. *Goals:* How will the ILT participate in school diagnosis and goal setting? Does the ILT understand the school's data and needs? Does the ILT have goals that align to the school's needs?

3. *Data collection and use:* Are the data the ILT is collecting aligned with SMART goals, and how frequently are those data collected? Are the data collected in a structured, efficient way? Are they transparent and user friendly? Are they being used to analyze and change systems, structures, and processes at the school? Are all teams collecting and using data related to SMART goals to change daily practice?

4. *Data review:* How does the ILT use and discuss school-level data? How is it analyzing data? How are its members expected to use the data discussed at the team meeting with teacher teams or teachers they supervise?

5. *Coaching:* How do ILT members learn to coach adults? How is this coaching monitored and supported? Are coaching conversations focused on school goals? Do teachers leave coaching conversations with clear next steps? What impact do these coaching conversations have on instruction? How do you know?

6. *Staff culture:* Are feedback loops in place that incorporate teacher voice? How are non-ILT voices included in decision making?

7. *ILT meetings:* Do ILT meetings have a clear purpose? How are decisions made in the meeting?

Supporting ILT members as Classroom Observers and Meeting Facilitators

By clearly defining the roles of the ILT members, a stage 1 action, you will enable them to take on concrete responsibilities and begin their work quickly. We have found two crucial functions of the ILT to be observing their colleagues in their classrooms and leading teacher team meetings.

Each time a teacher receives feedback on her practice, she can use that guidance to adjust her instruction, improve the way she is implementing teaching strategies, and ensure that her lessons are appropriately challenging for students. Offering frequent observations and feedback is therefore much more valuable than relying solely on formal evaluations that happen once or twice a year. Of course, unless you oversee a very small school, there are not enough hours in a week to get to every classroom and give effective feedback, let alone handle all of your other responsibilities. The members of the ILT are critical partners in observing classrooms and giving teachers ongoing feedback to drive continuous growth, stage 2 actions. You might also find that your team members benefit in surprising ways from taking on this responsibility. By watching their peers and giving feedback, they often improve their own instruction as well.

Each member of the ILT is also usually responsible for supporting a small group of teachers and for coaching them one-on-one. Typically each ILT member leads a grade-level or subject-area team, for which he or she facilitates instructional planning, monitors the consistency of instruction, and provides coaching.

To make sure each ILT member is using the same criteria to assess teachers, you can offer training and support on what to look for in classrooms and how to look for it, and how to then give teachers trusted, accurate feedback that they are able to internalize and apply. As we discussed in detail in chapter 3, we have seen schools make real improvement in student learning when the staff have agreed-on definitions of rigor and high-quality instruction. Some leaders make sure everyone is on the same page by going into classrooms with ILT members and comparing notes on what they saw and what feedback they would give the teachers. They discuss the quality of the lesson, what they thought students took away from the lesson, and what they would prioritize for this teacher to work on over the next several days. At Monarch Academy, for example, principal Epanchin-Troyan met with her team once a week, and once a month those meetings focused on professional development for the team. As part of that work, they would read and discuss relevant articles and work on honing their leadership skills.

As we discuss in chapter 6, principals have seen benefits to scheduling regular meeting times for the ILT (ideally twice a week for at least an hour). Sometimes teams have to do some creative and flexible scheduling to achieve this, such as meeting before or after school if district and union rules, and team member willingness, allow. Some teams also schedule a retreat once or twice a year to have uninterrupted concentrated time to look at data and create action plans.

Lever 2: Action 2: Teacher Leadership

Let's look beyond the ILT because teacher leadership needs to spread far beyond the walls of the ILT meeting room for the greatest impact. You might have teachers who want to provide coaching in their field or mentor new teachers. By spreading leadership throughout the building, school leaders in our research saw improvements in instruction and student learning. They were thoughtful about the types of leader roles and career pathways they created, as well as the skills and values they looked for in teacher leaders, both stage 1 practices. We saw school leaders inspire effective teachers to stay at the school by giving them leadership roles, a stage 2 action, and encouraging teachers to continue to build their expertise, stage 3.

Effective leaders work with their ILT to think through what those leadership roles and responsibilities could look like and create detailed job descriptions for them. All too often, teacher leader roles are vaguely defined or not defined at all, creating confusion around who is ready to become a leader, how they should spend their time, what success looks like, and what support and resources they require to be successful on the job. For example, an instructional coach could have responsibilities as varied as overseeing interim assessments and reporting or leading small groups of student interventions. It is therefore essential that teacher leader position descriptions be clear. If you determine that a teacher could help improve the after-school program by both coordinating the program and mentoring after-school instructors, those responsibilities should be outlined explicitly to ensure that teacher accomplishes what you envisioned.

If a leadership role is assigned by the district and that person reports to the district, principals need to understand what the leader's responsibilities and expectations are

Table 5.6 Lever 2: Instructional Leadership Team: Action 2: Teacher Leadership

	PRINCIPAL ACTIONS	SCHOOL ACTIONS
Stage 1	Name and describe career pathways that teachers and noninstructional staff can pursue in their current roles and, more broadly, within the school and the district. Provide leadership opportunities and support for leadership roles for highly skilled staff who demonstrate a commitment to the school vision and priorities. Select effective teachers who share values, beliefs, and commitment for key positions on the instructional leadership team.	Teachers begin to participate in regular development opportunities to build their leadership capacity. Teachers begin to facilitate professional development for others to gain leadership experience. Aligned and skilled teachers are identified and developed as leaders in their classrooms, in their grade-level teams, or on the instructional leadership team.
Stage 2	Identify mid-level and high-performing teachers for development and leadership opportunities. Track retention rates of effective teachers to identify trends and patterns. Inspire effective teachers to stay in their roles by providing positive feedback for high-quality work and selecting them for school-level leadership opportunities.	Teachers are encouraged to create new leadership opportunities if they see a gap or an area for development. All teachers have opportunities to stretch their leadership skills with supports and parameters appropriate to their current level of expertise. High-performing teachers are given multiple opportunities to develop and demonstrate their own leadership. Teachers regularly design and lead professional learning activities as part of their leadership development.
Stage 3	Encourage teachers to participate in high-quality self-reflection and action research activities (e.g., National Board certification, advanced degree programs) that continue to build their expertise.	Staff members proactively assume leadership roles. To the greatest extent possible, retention of teachers and recommendations for leadership are determined on the basis of demonstrated effectiveness as measured by student learning. Highest-skilled and fully aligned teachers receive substantial leadership opportunities and are supported in taking on these roles (even to the point of leaving the school to become leaders in other schools if necessary for their continued development). Structures are in place to support teacher retention by creating opportunities for growth and development.

and, whenever possible, create structures to give feedback and advocate for what the school specifically needs.

New Leaders' research identified the stages of development around developing teacher leaders that are listed in table 5.6.

Supporting Leadership Roles

Once teacher leader positions are identified and defined, you can work with the appointed leaders to analyze data and establish team- and school-level goals related to each leader's role.

Your leaders will also need support and training, which can take many forms. It could be part of your school's internal professional development or be provided by the district or through an external provider (e.g., an institution of higher education or a nonprofit organization).

Research indicates that adults learn best when they have regular opportunities to practice new concepts and skills in real-life settings.[9] For example, the 70-20-10 leadership development model (70 percent of learning comes from challenging work-based assignments, 20 percent from coaches or mentors, and 10 percent from formal course work or training) has been used effectively across a variety of sectors for many years.[10] Moreover, New Leaders' experience confirms that leadership responsibilities should be built up incrementally and deliberately over time, scaffolding opportunities so teachers' skills and responsibilities grow in tandem.[11]

School-based teacher leadership development should include the following characteristics of effective job-embedded professional development:

- Driven by data analyses of school, teacher, and student needs
- Multiple opportunities for teacher leaders to learn, practice, receive feedback, and reflect on leadership concepts and skills
- Time, space, and other school structures that promote peer collaboration (e.g., leadership retreats and leadership team meetings)
- Strong session facilitation, including by school leaders or teacher leaders

▼ Potential Pitfalls

It can be easy to assume that all teachers who are effective in the classroom will automatically be effective teacher leaders. That is not the case. Teacher leaders need sustained training and support to learn how to coach other adults. Teachers should not be expected to rely solely on their classroom experience to guide them in their new leadership role. Being a teacher leader means more than modeling instructional practices for individual teachers. It is about applying key leadership skills and strategies to achieve even better outcomes for many more students.[12] At the same time, one-off or one-size-fits-all training sessions are not the solution.[13] Some 96 percent of principals say their on-the-job experiences, including working directly with peers, are more valuable than classroom-based preparation programs.[14] The school leader needs to plan for the time it will take to train and support teacher leaders.

GIVING TEACHERS A MEANINGFUL VOICE IN SHAPING INSTRUCTION: MOVING FROM STAGE 0 TO STAGE 3 FOR TEACHER LEADERSHIP

Expeditionary Learning School for Community Leaders, Brooklyn, New York

When David O'Hara became principal at Leaders in 2011, the school had a 37 percent graduation rate. During his first year as principal, more than half of the staff left the school. Under the previous principal, he said, "The staff was disenfranchised.... For teachers, there are a few factors that are really important: autonomy, voice, and people being challenged."

To develop and retain a strong staff moving forward, O'Hara prioritized creating a school based on collaboration and democratic decision making. Once a football and track coach, O'Hara knew well the benefits of teamwork. Distributing leadership across the staff, he believed, would not only spread out the workload but also create challenging and exciting growth opportunities for teachers that he hoped would entice them to stay at Leaders and play integral roles in helping the school improve. "That means involving staff and students in decision making and providing everyone at our school with real opportunities to be leaders," he said.

That's not to say that he did not try to make some big decisions on his own early on, particularly as he focused on improving school instruction. Before creating leadership opportunities for teachers, he and his administrative team made sure a solid instructional program was in place. He explained that he "needed to know we were all working together on a strong shared instructional foundation" before gradually releasing instructional leadership responsibilities to teachers.

As part of that effort, O'Hara designed a comprehensive, independent reading program for the school: "I did it all by myself, so there was not a lot of investment by others, and it fizzled out. It was tough to know I put all this work and time into this and it just didn't work out." This experience reinforced his commitment to creating a school culture where teachers had a meaningful voice in instruction and curriculum planning.

Since then, O'Hara has overseen the development of a range of differentiated teacher leader positions that meet school and individual teacher needs. He regularly identifies teachers who are ready to lead in some capacity, a stage 2 action in the TLF; they have classroom expertise, strong student results, and leadership potential. He said he would not put a teacher in a leadership position without first having evidence that he or she had acclimated to the school's community and its mission and vision.

At times O'Hara has put friendly pressure on teachers with expertise and potential to step up. And sometimes that's all they've needed. "David gave me that push of encouragement I needed to take on a leadership role," said the school's social studies department facilitator. O'Hara recognizes the importance of giving positive feedback to his teachers. The weekly staff meetings usually start with recognizing staff members who have been doing incredible work, and sometimes they include conversations around how to give positive feedback to one another because, says O'Hara, "feeling respected as a teacher is so important."

O'Hara's efforts have led to a broad range of leaders spread throughout the school. One-third of the teaching staff sit on the school's ILT, and teachers lead grade-level and content-area teams and coteach classes. Leadership roles can also be informal. One science teacher said that while he does not have a formal leadership position, he considers himself a leader in the school because he regularly opens up his classroom to his peers.

O'Hara supports this work by delivering leadership training before and during the school year. In addition to holding a three-day retreat over the summer, the leadership team meets biweekly. Among other things, they discuss real-life and simulated leadership challenges, brainstorm solutions, and read about and discuss leadership concepts and strategies. A few years into his tenure at Leaders, O'Hara also instituted classroom intervisitations. These give every teacher in the school a leadership role of observing and giving feedback to colleagues. In an effort to encourage teachers to reflect on their work as teachers and leaders, an important stage 3 action, teachers compile the feedback from colleagues into a portfolio that they present to the staff at the end of the year. With these portfolios, they reflect on what they have learned and where they have met their goals for the year or fallen short.

To further his staff's development, O'Hara has also connected teachers to leadership programs outside the school, such as the NYC Outward Bound network with which the school is affiliated. O'Hara has devoted significant time and resources to developing teachers as leaders. Through those efforts, he explained, he was able to forge "a really strong school culture of high expectations and high support at the same time."

These changes did not always come easily: some teachers acknowledged that they were initially nervous about having other teachers in their classrooms. "But it's a reinforcing cycle," said Kevin Mears, a tenth-grade team leader. "The feedback I received was so valuable that I wanted it to keep happening." They also said they felt energized by the dynamic leadership structure at their school and the room that the structure gives them to grow.

Most important, O'Hara's commitment to building the capacity of other leaders in his school has yielded tremendous improvements in student achievement. Although just two seniors were on track to graduate when O'Hara arrived at the school, he ultimately saw more than half that class, 56 percent, graduate on time. Since then, graduation rates have risen rapidly, reaching a remarkable 84 percent in 2014, with 100 percent of those graduates accepted to college. Although 90 percent of Leaders' graduates are the first in their families to go to college, the portion who go on to complete college is 22 percent higher than the city average.

To better understand how O'Hara's work reflects the actions in the TLF, table 5.7 outlines what O'Hara and his staff did, the data they used to support their work, and what their next steps should be to continue to make improvements.

Table 5.7 TLF Analysis of Expeditionary Learning School for Community Leaders

TLF ACTION	ARTIFACTS	EVIDENCE	TLF STAGE AND LEVER	NEXT STEPS/ STRATEGIES
Talent management, instructional leadership team	Exit interviews with departing teachers	Teacher retention rate low during new principal's first year; departing teachers say they felt disenfranchised, lacked autonomy and voice.	Stage 0: Teacher leadership	Name and describe career pathways that teachers and noninstructional staff can pursue in their current roles. Provide leadership opportunities and support for leadership roles for highly skilled staff who demonstrate a commitment to the school vision and priorities.

(*continued*)

Table 5.7 (*continued*)

TLF ACTION	ARTIFACTS	EVIDENCE	TLF STAGE AND LEVER	NEXT STEPS/ STRATEGIES
		With positive feedback, encouraged effective teachers to take on leadership roles.	Stage 2: Teacher leadership	Encourage teachers to participate in high-quality self-reflection activities.
	Training sessions over the summer and during the year	Offers leadership training to ILT members before and during the school year.	Stage 2: ILT roles	Expand ILT member roles to manage new initiatives.
	Teacher portfolios of feedback from throughout the year; portfolio presentations to staff at end of year; reflections on whether they have met goals	Encourages teachers to self-reflect on their work.	Stage 3: Teacher leadership	
	Teacher registration in Outward Bound and other training	Encourages teachers to seek out professional development opportunities outside of the school.	Stage 3: Teacher leadership	

LEVER 3: PERFORMANCE MONITORING AND EVALUATION

While there has been some controversy surrounding the design and implementation of new evaluation systems for teachers in recent years, most educators would agree with the importance of frequent feedback and identification of specific strengths and growth areas as a means for improving their instructional practice. Like any other professionals, teachers will improve their practice only if they are given constructive feedback from other educators who are familiar with the subject and context in which they are teaching. Frequent observations and actionable feedback are the key to doing this well.

Formal evaluations once or twice a year are not enough. To make sure that feedback is effective, we train principals to set clear performance expectations and give teachers ample support as they use that feedback to change their practice.

This lever on performance management and evaluation focuses on performance expectations, observation and actionable feedback, monitoring implementation, and performance evaluation. In this section, we illustrate how other principals have set clear expectations that are regularly reinforced for the staff, given feedback in ways that enable teachers to improve their practice, monitor how instructional strategies are being implemented in all classrooms, and use multiple points of data for formal evaluations so that they are seen as cumulative moments of feedback, not just a snapshot.

Lever 3: Action 1: Performance Expectations

Imagine after observing a teacher a couple of times over the course of the school year, you call him into your office for his evaluation. "Well," you say, "the two times I was in your class this year, you called on the same few students, the kinds of questions you asked did not push the students to think critically, and your students did not do well on their achievement tests."

"Wow," the teacher responds. "I wish you had told me these things as you saw them. The school year is over, so there's nothing more I can do for these students."

Strong principals use every opportunity to remind staff of their expectations throughout the year in onboarding activities, staff meetings, and informal conversations.

We have seen many principals spend time reviewing the district or state rubric with their leadership teams and their full staff, discussing aspects of the rubric and evaluation process to create a school-level vision of quality instruction and a rationale for the evaluation process and its benefits. This work helped them make sure all the teachers were on the same page from day one. Everyone knew how and when their work would be assessed, and the expectations were aligned to state standards and to schoolwide and individual student goals and priorities, so there was a direct connection to daily instruction. (For a detailed look at setting goals, targets and priorities, see chapter 2). Some schools also set expectations related to school culture, and assess teachers on them. At Sci Academy in New Orleans, for example, teachers are evaluated not only on academic goals but also on how they are living the school's core values.

Table 5.8 identifies the stages of development for establishing performance expectations.

Table 5.8 Lever 3: Performance Monitoring and Evaluation: Action 1: Performance Expectations

	PRINCIPAL ACTIONS	SCHOOL ACTIONS
Stage 1	Set and share performance expectations aligned to schoolwide goals and school priorities for each staff member. Ensure that each staff member is aware of the standards and metrics against which his or her performance will be assessed. Explore and build the common language of the teacher evaluation system by exploring the concepts and rubrics at the school level. Share all key components of the performance management cycle, including individual goal and target setting, formal observations, mid-year reviews, and final summative evaluations.	Performance expectations are clear, and they match the job responsibilities and design. The performance management schedule, calendar, and sequence are transparent.
Stage 2	Differentiate targets for each grade and subject area based on historical performance data for that grade, as well as for the incoming cohort of students.	The performance management system includes team and individual goals for each staff member that align to the schoolwide goals and priorities.
Stage 3	Individualize the performance management system for each staff member, including: • Individual student achievement targets • Individual performance goals • System for consistent monitoring and follow-up on improvement	Every adult in the school is aligned to high achievement goals and understands his or her specific role.

Lever 3: Action 2: Observation and Actionable Feedback

Having put clear expectations in place, you and your leadership team can use them to guide classroom observations and shape actionable feedback you provide for every teacher. We have consistently seen teachers get the most out of their principal's feedback when it is given frequently and with enough concrete detail that they can make immediate changes in their classroom practices.

Informal feedback is meant to maintain a consistent dialogue about the teacher's practice. When it is done regularly, we have found that ongoing feedback to be more

Table 5.9 Lever 3: Performance Monitoring and Evaluation: Action 2: Observation and Actionable Feedback

	PRINCIPAL ACTIONS	SCHOOL ACTIONS
Stage 1	Create an observation protocol for walk-throughs, which are done frequently with schoolwide foci. Find creative ways (sticky notes, e-mail) to give feedback on progress with nonnegotiable instructional practices, including discussions of specific student work and data.	The instructional leadership team begins conducting staff observations. Teachers receive concrete and actionable feedback within forty-eight hours of an observation or walk-through. All staff are observed, at least briefly, on a weekly basis, with a focus on schoolwide-consistent routines and schoolwide priorities for improvement. Every classroom is visited for five to ten minutes at least two to three times each week as part of ongoing learning walks.
Stage 2	Create systems and schedules for conducting frequent, brief, and differentiated observations by members of the instructional leadership team on the basis of teacher need. Provide regular feedback and/or have systems in place so that staff receive feedback from a member of the instructional leadership team. Use analyses of student learning outcomes to update observation protocols.	An expanded group of school leaders engages in observations and provides feedback based on a consistent protocol and set of expectations. Instructional leaders review lesson plans for evidence of corrective instruction and spiraling. Instructional leadership team members provide frequent observations and feedback to staff on instructional practices and handling of student conduct concerns, with follow-up to ensure improvement.
Stage 3	Expand observation protocol and practice to include consistent schoolwide expectations, individual teacher development areas, and study of specific student subgroups as identified by data. Implement a system for offering consistent support and follow-up to gauge improvement that includes formal and informal feedback from members of the leadership team, master teachers, and other school leaders. Feedback is based on school goals, schoolwide nonnegotiable goals, and teacher-generated goals.	The observation protocol and practice include consistent schoolwide expectations, individual teacher development areas, and study of specific student subgroups as identified by data. All new teachers and teachers with specific development needs are mentored by highly skilled peers. Peers are able to provide ongoing feedback to one another on learning walks and interclassroom visits.

powerful than formal evaluations because it allows you to normalize what could be difficult conversations and creates opportunities to make frequent, explicit connections to mission and values. Principals in schools that made significant increases in student learning in our study observed teachers much more often than did their counterparts in comparison schools, and they ensured that teachers, particularly those with key areas in need of improvement, were receiving actionable formative feedback. These principals went well beyond what was required by formal evaluations, providing more frequent, deeper feedback that helped teachers continuously improve their practice.

Table 5.9 identifies the stages of development for making observations and giving actionable feedback.

Classroom-level observations can illuminate trends across your school. For example, if you go into ten classrooms and notice that eight teachers are trying to cover too much material in each lesson, then you might decide that a number of teachers need support around more effective planning. In this way, you can use these observations to inform schoolwide professional development.

For observations to work, teachers need to trust and respect the people giving them feedback, and they need to feel comfortable opening up their classrooms. We have also seen that when teachers help develop the observation process, they are more open to participating.

 REDESIGNING THE OBSERVATION SYSTEM TO SUPPORT AND RETAIN TEACHERS: MOVING FROM STAGE 1 TO STAGE 3 FOR OBSERVATION AND ACTIONABLE FEEDBACK

Boston Collegiate Charter School, Boston, Massachusetts

In response to a high rate of teacher turnover, leaders at Boston Collegiate Charter School redesigned its classroom observation system to better support, and in turn retain, new and developing teachers. The teachers asked that the leadership team move from a system of infrequent, full-length observations to shorter (five to ten minutes each) but more frequent ones, accompanied by immediate written feedback on a standard observation form, a stage 2 action. As a result, new teachers, under former school director Kathleen Sullivan, received feedback weekly or even daily if needed. Second- and third-year teachers who were still struggling to meet expectations, or those who request additional support, continued to receive weekly observations and coaching support, a stage 3 action. Coaches differentiated support for teachers based on their needs, such as instructional rigor, pacing and differentiation, and small group work. During their observations, coaches focused on an agreed-on area of need or an area the teacher requests feedback on, and they used a mix of facilitative and instructive coaching strategies to match the developmental needs of the teacher.

Teachers reported great satisfaction with the level and type of feedback they were receiving. One math teacher who was more accustomed to lecturing asked for dean of curriculum Eileen Callahan's support with how he was using small groups in his classroom. "She really pushed me to teach outside my comfort zone," he said. During one lesson, he asked Callahan to watch how students transitioned into small groups and whether they began working right away and stayed on task in their groups. After a couple of weekly meetings with the teacher, Callahan said she saw great progress in his class and was able to shift their conversations from how to transition effectively into small group work to how to increase the rigor of instruction. "My weekly meetings have been successful because he has taken the lead with putting students in small groups," Callahan said. "It is great to be able to say the transition went well. I think it will help his confidence in terms of experimenting with small groups and keeping it as a part of his weekly repertoire and to have students work more collaboratively and apply their knowledge in different ways."

After each observation, Callahan had the teacher complete a written reflection assessing the lesson, which she and Callahan would discuss. Together they would choose a particular area to focus on in a peer feedback session. The new teacher would then present a video of her lesson to a few teachers, who would ask clarifying questions, identify areas of strength, and make specific suggestions for improvement. This peer feedback helped Callahan target her support of both the new teachers and the teacher observers based on how they responded to the videos, while also giving first-year teachers many opportunities to see teaching in action and to analyze what works.

Boston Collegiate has seen successes. During Sullivan's last four years at the school, student proficiency in reading jumped 17 percent, to 86 percent, and rose by 8 percent in math.

↓ Potential Pitfalls

At turnaround schools, principals' view of what good teaching looks like tends to bend toward where the school's average teacher is. This perspective will only get a school to mediocre, not great. It is therefore critical to always keep in mind what excellent teaching is. You can do this by taking your staff to visit strong schools and observe particular practices you would like to implement.

Observing for Details

If you tell a teacher that her lesson was not rigorous enough, any professional will ask you what you mean by that. "Can you give specific examples?" she might ask. We have found principals and teachers get the most out of classroom observations when the observer focuses on taking detailed notes during the class and waits until after the lesson to analyze what he is seeing. To most effectively capture the scene and collect evidence that you can later present to the teacher, we recommend scripting all of your classroom observations, taking down direct quotes and detailed descriptions of these aspects of the observation:

- Types of questions asked (open-ended, interpretive, recall, evaluative)
- Which students respond; who is and is not engaged
- Academic language used
- What the students do
- What the teacher says

There are many good references available about how to conduct observations. To name a few, we recommend Kim Marshall for material on making frequent observations, Jon Saphier on scripting, and Paul Bambrick-Santoyo for useful tools on charting and tracking frequency of observations.[15]

Lever 3: Actions 3 and 4: Monitoring Implementation and Performance Evaluation

When you and your teacher leaders observe instruction, a lot of what you are looking for is how teachers are implementing instructional strategies and the curriculum. As we noted in chapter 2 on diagnosis, it's most effective to have a system for regularly monitoring teaching practices and revising them as needed.

Classroom observations can't be left to chance. As leaders, we need to pay attention to the details of how we structure observations in our schools. You can start by planning a careful schedule identifying which leaders in your building will observe which teachers. As you think about scheduling, make sure there is frequency while also considering which leaders are the best match for observing specific teachers. Among other things, you can take into account particular skills, subject matter expertise, and whether it would be more helpful for teachers to get feedback on their practice from consistent or differing voices. Schools in stage 3 involve members of their ILT in the evaluation process. To capture different aspects of a teacher's instruction, consider observing teachers at different times of the day rather than always observing the beginning or end of a teacher's class. You'll need to think about how to plan your time so that you can do this work (for more on time management, see chapter 6).

Also consider how you can differentiate your observations, for example, observing new or developing teachers more often than your strongest instructors. Effective principals are particularly mindful of how they monitor and evaluate teachers who are consistently not meeting expectations. This means making frequent observations of those teachers and working to clarify and support their needs for improvement. Part of the challenge in this work is distinguishing between issues of skill and issues of will, and being able to help teachers develop both. Good teaching requires pedagogical and content knowledge and an ability to help students learn the subject (skill), as well as motivation and passion to hone your own skills so that you can help every student achieve success.[16]

When evaluating educators, principals in our study used multiple measures, including student achievement data, to make judgments about teacher performance. For lower-performing staff, school leaders gathered as much information as possible to confirm that they were accurately assessing performance. In our trainings, we encourage aspiring principals to take particular care when evaluating teachers who are eligible for tenure. To ensure that schools maintain the strongest faculty possible, it's critical that school leaders hold a high bar for those teachers. If teachers don't improve even after getting targeted support, strong leaders take actions to convince a teacher that he is not the right fit for the school, or remove the staff member.

Tables 5.10 and 5.11 identify the stages of development that principals in our study followed for monitoring implementation and evaluating staff.

Principal's Tool 5.2: Identifying Teacher Skill and Will to Develop

---

Principal's Tool 5.3: Instructional Leadership Team Reflection Questions on Teacher Observation and Supervision

---

LEVER 4: PROFESSIONAL LEARNING AND COLLABORATION

We have heard some variation of the same story from lots of school leaders tasked with turning around a school: their teachers spend much of the school day behind closed classroom doors, and there are no regularly scheduled meetings for teachers to discuss instruction. In one case, classrooms for the same grade level were located in different parts of the building, making it even harder for those teachers to collaborate.

Table 5.10 Lever 3: Performance Monitoring and Evaluation: Action 3: Monitoring Implementation

	PRINCIPAL ACTIONS	SCHOOL ACTIONS
Stage 1	Ensure consistent implementation of nonnegotiable instructional strategies by comparing lesson plans to what is occurring in classrooms. Become a constant presence in the classrooms of staff identified as not aligned with school's core values and/or unskilled and unwilling or unable to develop, and develop a plan to counsel out or remove them through existing formal processes. Once expectations are established, conduct a staff inventory that determines staff member skill (certifications, tenure, commendations) and will to improve, as well as any disciplinary actions. Conduct a series of preliminary observations and conversations with each staff member to assess his or her strengths and weaknesses to determine the most effective supports.	Nonaligned or poorly performing staff are closely monitored through additional reviews of work and observations. Staff who are identified as less skilled are provided with ongoing support and are prioritized for more frequent observation. Nonaligned staff are identified, and if they do not make improvements, they are counseled out or, where necessary, removed through existing formal processes.
Stage 2	Hold teachers accountable for student learning, including displaying student work during classroom observations and referencing student data during teacher debriefing. Support struggling teachers with specific improvement plans that focus on what steps they will take to improve their performance. Prioritize support for teachers with clear development needs, including full lesson observations and peer mentoring. Use teacher assessment data and student performance data to determine teacher development activities. Assign instructional leadership team members to work with specific sets of teachers on the basis of their skills and areas of growth.	Leadership team members monitor teachers through observations and review of data and student work. Struggling staff are put on specific performance improvement plans that address their specific needs. Each teacher is involved in differentiated support activities that match his or her areas of growth.

Table 5.10 (*continued*)

	PRINCIPAL ACTIONS	SCHOOL ACTIONS
Stage 3	Track and monitor staff review data to ensure that monitoring is occurring and that individual staff interventions are effective.	Staff demonstrate consistent high-quality practices for instruction and student and staff culture. Developing staff are taking rapid action to close the gap between current practice and expectations for quality practice.

Table 5.11 Lever 3: Performance Monitoring and Evaluation: Action 4: Performance Evaluation

	PRINCIPAL ACTIONS	SCHOOL ACTIONS
Stage 1	Compile multiple data sources to assess teacher practice. Have a second reviewer analyze evidence for teachers approaching tenure.	A performance management system is in place, and end-of-year ratings are based on documented evidence from multiple sources. Tenure decisions are reviewed to ensure that the teacher meets expectations for teaching skill belief in student potential, alignment to school core values, and willingness to learn and develop.
Stage 2	Model for leadership team members who participate in evaluation how to assess multiple data points to come to a practice rating that is based on evidence rather than judgments. Identify and move out the severely mediocre and poor teachers.	Staff have ongoing conversations with members of the leadership team about their performance. Underperforming staff are put on improvement plans with appropriate supports. Staff who are voluntarily transitioning from the school are invited to participate in an exit interview to improve retention.
Stage 3	Use effective processes for managing underperforming staff, including learning specific district-approved practices for human resources management (e.g., specific union regulations and time lines).	Summative evaluation is seen as a cumulative moment of feedback rather than a snapshot because staff receive frequent feedback about their performance and are given ample notice and opportunity to improve as needed.

Professional learning is a critical piece of the school improvement process. Raising student achievement requires improving classroom instruction, which requires teachers to understand what they are doing well and where they can improve. In fact, actively leading teacher learning and development has twice the positive effect on student achievement than working toward teacher quality in any other way, including establishing goals and expectations.[17]

The most effective professional learning for teachers happens inside schools. Just as students learn more when they talk to each other, students learn more when their teachers talk to each other. Regular collegial conversation about instruction and trust in colleagues is a key indicator of high achievement for students.[18]

Michael Barber's research in school districts around the world found that high-performing principals spend significant time working with people in their school, coaching teachers and interacting with parents and students.[19] As school leadership expert Michael Fullan has written, "The principal's role is to lead the school's teachers in a process of learning to improve their teaching, while learning alongside them about what works and what doesn't. . . . Groups of teachers, working together over time, will produce greater learning in more students."[20]

As outlined in this lever, effective principals ensure that ongoing professional learning and collaborative teacher team structures are in place at their schools.

We have found from our time in schools that you can't have one of these practices without the other. Teacher collaboration is critical to supporting the development of every teacher in your school and to supporting your own work as the building's instructional leader.

Lever 4: Action 1: Ongoing Professional Learning

Knowing what you know about your teachers, what opportunities could you create that will best help them be better instructors? We have seen the best learning moments tie directly to the day-to-day work of the team and include content and approaches that are immediately applicable.

Our research found that as effective principals move thorough the stages of creating a system of ongoing professional learning, outlined in table 5.12, they differentiate, matching up people who are good with classroom management with those who are not, for example. They maintain a year-long professional development calendar and have improvement plans for each teacher, particularly those who are underperforming.

Designing Learning Opportunities That Make Sense

You and your staff will likely get the most out of professional development sessions if they are directly connected to school needs and goals. That requires knowing the

Table 5.12 Lever 4: Professional Learning and Collaboration: Action 1: Ongoing Professional Learning

	PRINCIPAL ACTIONS	SCHOOL ACTIONS
Stage 1	Design a comprehensive professional learning plan and calendar aligned to school goals and trends observed in learning walks. Directly engage in development sessions as leader/facilitator or active participant; set clear expectations for implementation of presented practices and strategies, and monitor their implementation and use. Identify classrooms and schools that demonstrate strong instructional programs and results; target them for staff visits and reflection.	The school has a clear professional learning calendar of topics aligned to established school expectations. Professional development for all staff focuses on schoolwide instructional nonnegotiable goals; aligned, rigorous curriculum mapping; and consistent implementation of instructional strategies. The professional learning plan includes cycles of lesson observations, large group training sessions, teacher-team meetings, and coaching and mentoring for individual staff. Teachers participate in regular development opportunities that seek to build their capacity.
Stage 2	Develop a clear plan for adult learning across the school that aligns areas for whole-school improvement, teacher team areas of focus, and individual development priorities. Create structures for job-embedded collaborative learning: professional learning communities, protected time for grade-level and content-area planning, and protocols for systematic examination of practice.	Teacher-driven professional development focuses on student learning challenges and progress toward student achievement goals; it occurs during the school day and includes teacher-team meetings and peer visits. All new teachers and all teachers with specific development needs are mentored by highly skilled peers.
Stage 3	Structure professional learning around compelling student data. Provide individual teachers and teacher teams access to new research and other developmental resources geared to identified development needs. Create individual development plans and focus areas for each teacher.	Professional development is job embedded and directly relates to the school's goals, occurs during the school day, and supports quick improvements in practice. Staff share a collective awareness of individual skills and growth areas; they self-direct professional development based on student achievement outcomes.

strengths and challenges of each teacher and your instructional team as a whole. All professional learning should grow out of what is seen during classroom observations, addressing identified development areas to improve individual teacher practice, as well as broader priorities to help the entire school reach its goals. If you send teachers to external professional development sessions, consider how those workshops directly connect to your students' learning needs. It can be helpful to ask attending teachers to present what they learned to the full staff.

In stage 1, a whole school learning plan is in place with a calendar that is tied to the school's priorities. Too often principals delegate too much of the professional development process; they have either other members of the staff or consultants lead sessions. But we have found that school leaders who get the best results are directly involved in professional development and are part of the planning, making sure it is aligned to the teacher and school needs and actively participating in the sessions. In stage 2, the leader brings professional learning to life, making sure there are plans for both individual teachers and for teams and that the collaborative learning is job embedded. Finally, for stage 3, we have seen principals use student data to design and evaluate professional learning opportunities and create plans for each individual teacher.

Lever 4: Action 2: Collaborative Teacher Team Structures

Chances are your school already has some form of teacher team structure in place. If your school does not have such structures, then we suggest you return to the lever in this chapter on ILTs for some guidance on how to get that team started as a first step toward creating a culture of teacher collaboration. In this section, we focus on how to make sure collaborative team structures are effective.

Schools that use teacher teams to improve instruction have practices in place to make sure those teams are having high-quality conversations. The goals and expectations of the teams are clear, a stage 1 action, and have a laser focus on improving student learning. Teams of teachers are using part of their regularly scheduled meetings to examine data for the purpose of determining why some students are not mastering the material (stage 2). Once they have become accustomed to doing that work, the teams are able to shift some of their discussions from examining schoolwide instructional strategies and classroom materials to being able to discuss individual student work (stage 3). Part of the secret to these teams' success is having a strong educator who is adept at facilitating team meetings and supporting the team's work. (For more on selecting teachers to take on this leadership role, return to the section on lever 2 in this chapter.)

Table 5.13 presents the stages of development we saw principals pass through as they created and maintained effective collaborative teacher teams.

Table 5.13 Lever 4: Professional Learning and Collaboration: Action 2: Collaborative Teacher Team Structures

	PRINCIPAL ACTIONS	SCHOOL ACTIONS
Stage 1	Create teacher teams (if not already in place) and protocols focused on student outcomes, student data, and student work. Articulate clear expectations for common planning time; model the process and the unwavering focus on student learning.	Instructional strategies, instructional consistency, instructional development of staff, and definitions of rigor are discussed at teacher team meetings. Teacher teams use protocols and processes designed to guide collaboration. Grade-level and content-area teams have common weekly planning times with clear outcomes focused on student learning and not just student behaviors. Teacher teams build common assessments.
Stage 2	Implement protocols in team meetings for frequent group analysis of data in pursuit of root causes. Observe teacher team meetings, and provide feedback on their processes to help them develop as a team.	Intervention teachers collaborate closely with all other classroom teachers to ensure effective planning and instruction to implement individualized education programs. Instructional leadership team members lead effective teacher team meetings focused on student learning data and student work. Time to review individual student learning data is built into the schedule of collaborative team meetings.
Stage 3	Provide individual teachers and teacher teams access to new research and other developmental resources geared to identified development needs.	Instructional leadership team members serve as instructional leaders in the school, leading effective teacher team meetings focused on student learning data and student work. Teacher team discussions are clearly focused on individual student learning progress and student work, not just general standards and strategies. It is common practice for teams to share best practices and problem-solve together, and teams leverage the individual differences and strengths of each member of the team.

Alfred Nobel Elementary School, Chicago, Illinois

When Manuel Adrianzén became principal of Nobel, he immediately recognized that his staff was not working together to improve teaching and learning. He saw "a lot of isolation from classroom to classroom. If teachers collaborated, it was basically around things that did not focus on achievement or children," he said. Grade-level teams were meeting, he said, "But they were talking about field trips, discipline, or parents not being supportive."

While he describes himself as the school's lead learner, when it comes to building the capacity of the teachers, he still knew that he needed a thriving team to be successful. "I can't do this on my own," Adrianzén explained.

To address that challenge, he assembled an ILT with one teacher from each grade level, along with some bilingual and special education instructors. The team, he hoped, would play a central role in developing a system for ongoing professional learning and collaboration at Nobel. Together, he and the team designed professional learning cycles.

During each cycle, Adrianzén and the ILT examine data and, based on these data, set an instructional goal and identify strategies to meet it, a stage 1 action. Cycles last anywhere from six weeks, the length of time they spent learning how best to use workshops in class, to a year for improving practices around guided reading. Within each cycle, teachers (not only members of the ILT) conduct peer observations and, at the culmination of the cycle, more extensive learning walks to see how teachers across the school are implementing strategies and where support is still needed so that all students in every grade level are making gains.

"The professional learning cycle scales to address the development of our teachers," Adrianzén said. For example, he created a schedule of grade-level meetings, assessments, and peer observations, a stage 1 action. For each cycle, the ILT presents to the full staff the goals, strategies, and supporting materials, also a stage 1 action.

The grade-level teams reflect on the learning cycles during their weekly meetings, when teachers discuss relevant readings and instructional videos, examine student work, and exchange ideas on how implementation is going and what they could improve on. This job-embedded collaborative learning is an important stage 2 action.

In a recent grade-level meeting, teachers read a text about using a promising practice, the workshop model, in their current cycle. "We had deep conversations about this part called the 'think aloud,' where the teacher really lets the students in to that expert thinking, where the teacher communicates possible pitfalls and really gets to talk about the steps that lead to the learning," said instructional coach Joseph Oberts. By having those conversations, teachers were then better able to implement the practice in their classes. And they recognize that the conversation is not over after that first meeting. In the next grade-level team meetings, teachers discussed how the lessons went and planned adjustments as needed for the following week.

Because each grade team is led by an ILT member, the ILT serves as a liaison between the teachers and instructional coaches and the administration. During the ILT meetings, members discuss teachers' concerns regarding the learning cycle. "Then we create an action plan or adjust our cycle to ensure that all the voices are heard throughout the school," said Adrianzén. The school has the stage 2 action in place of focusing on both the whole school and teacher team levels for professional development. In some cases the specific needs of teacher teams result in change in the schoolwide focus areas, and in other cases, these discussions give the ILT clarity on the supports that particular teacher teams need.

Peer observations are also an important part of the learning cycle. During a recent cycle, Adrianzén explained, "We gathered data that basically let us know that children were sitting for forty minutes listening to the teacher lecture them about the skill and strategy or the concept that they were trying to teach that day or that week." In that case, he said, the next round of professional development focused on teaching mini-lessons and how to intentionally set expectations and learning objectives.

Said one instructional coach, "Peer observation gives us data within grade levels for each teacher to communicate her needs. By looking into each other's classroom, they realized there might be holes and gaps, that there might not be a common understanding. That's when they try to address those."

After each observation, observers share feedback with the teacher. Adrianzén recognizes that this collaborative practice is giving teachers the tools to improve their instruction: "When the powerful practice is not being effective in one or two classrooms, we decide as a team how we're going to provide the feedback to that teacher. We support that individual and make sure that practice is happening during the next walk-through."

At the end of the learning cycle, the ILT conducts a series of learning walks during which they look for the implementation of specific practices. During those walks, one person is responsible for observing the teacher and collecting data on instruction. A second teacher examines the classroom environment, looking for charts and other tools visible in the classroom. A third teacher collects the data throughout the school building to ensure that there is alignment, a stage 2 action. "That gives us schoolwide data on whether we've been successful in implementing the teaching practices that we decided on, or whether we need to go back and readjust, or whether we might need to give support to specific teachers or a specific grade level while we move to the next cycle," said an instructional coach.

"Once we gather those data, we determine whether our powerful practice has been effective," Adrianzén said. "We analyze the data. We try to find trends across the school." Professional learning is structured around multiple sources of student data, a stage 3 action.

At that point, the ILT decides whether the school is ready to move on to another learning cycle. Do particular grade levels or teachers need more support? An instructional leader explained, "Sometimes the adjustment might be we need two more weeks to work on this component of a skill."

These ongoing cycles of professional learning at Nobel Elementary illustrate how Adrianzén has pulled several talent management levers by developing the leadership capacity of his staff through a highly functioning ILT that has consistent protocols for observation and feedback within an environment that promotes ongoing professional learning. These actions all work together to transform the school's culture in a systematic way, yielding steady achievement gains among the school's high-need students. Over the past few years, reading proficiency rose from 25 to 40 percent, and math proficiency increased by 32 percent, to 59 percent.

Principal's Tool 5.4: Reflection Questions on Professional Learning

NEXT STEPS

As you think about this work of managing talent in your school, leadership expert Jim Collins offers some sage words: "If your school or organization or company cannot be great without you as its leader, it is not yet a great enterprise."[21] You can see from the stories in this chapter that successful principals tackle staffing, professional development, developing teacher leaders, and fostering a culture of professional collaboration in strategic steps.

You can achieve similar success if you follow the examples laid out in this chapter. If you have struggled with staffing, consider adopting some of the strategies that Brooklyn Latin uses to find the right teachers for its students. If you are struggling with retention or staff investment in your school improvement strategy, look to Boston Collegiate or Leaders to address those challenges. As you do that work, the guiding questions and tools we provide in this chapter can guide your work in developing a thriving ILT, bolster the impact of your classroom observation processes, and establish consistent expectations for staff to help accelerate student learning.

 WATCH TALENT MANAGEMENT VIDEO: In this chapter's companion video, you'll learn about great work being done at schools across the country in the category of talent management. To access the video, go to www.wiley.com/go/newleaders.

 Principal's Tools for Talent Management

Principal's Tool 5.1: Reflection Questions and Tools for Staff Hiring
Principal's Tool 5.2: Identifying Teacher Skill and Will to Develop
Principal's Tool 5.3: Instructional Leadership Team Reflection Questions on Teacher Observation and Supervision
Principal's Tool 5.4: Reflection Questions on Professional Learning

Planning and Operations

IF YOU THINK OF YOUR SCHOOL AS A HUMAN BODY, PLANNING AND OPERATIONS is the skeleton that holds together and organizes the meat and muscle of instructional practices and school culture. School operations are critical but often invisible components of school success and improvement. These systems, from bell schedules to budgets, structure how learning time is managed and how funding and school facilities are organized to best support student achievement. When implemented effectively, these structures give staff members the right tools, processes, and resources to move toward schoolwide goals and to determine if and how to adjust strategies to meet those goals. Granted, this is not exciting stuff, but it is critical.

Research has found that when school leaders are strong in organizational management, student test scores rise and teachers and parents say they are happier with the school.[1] Even when school leaders devote significant time to becoming instructional leaders, if they don't also take the time to ensure that resources are targeted where they are most needed, teachers have the time and structures they need to improve, and the school is safe, the school is much less likely to see gains in student learning.[2]

We know that the most important areas of operation are those that help us manage time, set and implement goals, prioritize budget, maintain facilities, and develop external relationships. For example, by developing a comprehensive calendar, you can create time for teachers to collaborate on lesson planning and teaching strategies. Data systems enable you to collect, share, and analyze evidence of student learning in order to better target instruction. Budgets allow you and your staff to use your financial and human resources in ways that directly contribute to improving student outcomes and other schoolwide goals. Facility maintenance systems help keep a school safe and

 **PLANNING AND OPERATIONS CATEGORY MAP**

Lever 1: Goal Setting and Action Planning

Tracking of clear and focused school goals and adjusting strategy based on progress

Actions

- **Action 1: Goal Setting and Action Planning:** Create clear goals and identify priorities, then create action plans and strategies to attain goals and establish milestones to monitor progress toward goals.

Lever 2: Time Management

Aligning use of time to make progress toward and attain schoolwide goals

Actions

- **Action 1: Time and Schedule Review:** Assess how time is allocated and used.
- **Action 2: Master Schedule:** Use schedule to maximize instructional time and access to rigorous content.

Lever 3: Budget

Aligning budget, external partnerships, and facilities to the strategic plan

Actions

- **Action 1: Budget and Resources:** Create a budget and plan to manage resources.
- **Action 2: External Partnerships:** Create external partnerships that support the schoolwide goals and priority areas.
- **Action 3: Facilities:** Manage the facilities to ensure that students are safe and that the school is set up to facilitate learning.

Lever 4: Community and District Relations

Managing district context and school system relations to ensure a focus on learning

Actions

- **Action 1: Stakeholder Communications and Engagement:** Build and manage systems for stakeholder, family, and community engagement.
- **Action 2: District Relationships:** Build and manage district relationships.

comfortable so that staff and students can focus on learning. External partnerships that are directly aligned with school goals can expand your school's ability to meet your students' needs.

Many of these operations are interconnected. How a principal allocates his staff's time and how he allocates his budget are closely connected. Staff is the biggest driver of the budget, the most expensive item. School leaders must therefore think deeply about how to maximize those dollars by carefully aligning staff assignments and staff time with school goals.

By aligning all time and resources to clear strategic plans, principals have found they can most effectively focus talent, tools, and dollars on the school's intended goals and priorities,[3] and they can better manage forces that might seem outside their control, such as spending mandates, government regulations, and union contracts.

New Leaders' years of research and experience training and supporting principals have revealed that schools with sustained improvement in student learning have four key systems in place for planning and operations:

Lever 1. Goal setting and action planning: *Tracking of clear and focused school goals and adjusting strategy based on progress.* Principals have greatest success in their schools when they diagnose the state of their schools, identify priorities and strategies to address areas in need of improvement, develop an action plan, and monitor and adjust plans as needed. Because this important work cuts across all categories, chapter 2 is devoted to it. We recommend you read that chapter before delving into the work of assessing the other operations and systems detailed in this chapter.

Lever 2. Time management: *Aligning use of time to make progress toward and attain schoolwide goals.* You can put systems in place to use time effectively, through master schedules and daily, weekly, monthly, and annual calendars that are shared across the community in order to make effective plans. Consider how and where you spend your own time, designating time every day to observe instruction, participate in teacher team meetings, and address family concerns.

Lever 3. Budget: *Aligning budget, external partnerships, and facilities to the strategic plan.* Effective leaders align their budgets to their school's instructional needs and make sure the school building is in a condition that is most conducive to learning. They also build partnerships with external stakeholders who are able to provide additional resources and capacity to the school's goals.

Lever 4. Community and district relations: *Managing district context and school system relations to ensure a focus on learning.* Work closely with district leaders to ensure that goals set at the school level also support the district's priorities. When school leaders understand the workings of their school systems, are aware of the challenges their districts face, and are able to collaborate with district staff, they are better able to improve student learning.[4]

Together these practices undergird a structure that allows schools to create a consistent and high-quality learning environment for students and staff.

LEVER 1: GOAL SETTING AND ACTION PLANNING

Creating both multiyear and annual strategic plans are key actions to support change and growth within a school. To maximize student learning, principals need to collect and analyze a range of data, including an examination of the actions school leaders and their staff are taking, and, working with their staff and communities, set, prioritize, and publicize goals. Effective school leaders then develop and implement action plans that will enable schools to make progress toward the goals.

To underscore the significance of this lever, we devoted chapter 2 to it, and we suggest reading it if you have not already done so. Once you have done the work of diagnosing, goal setting, and action planning, you will be ready to begin to consider how you can align your school's schedules, budgets, and external relationships to your goals and priorities.

LEVER 2: TIME MANAGEMENT

We all wish there were more hours in the day to do all that needs to get done: to observe one more teacher and give her thoughtful feedback or talk to the parent who's worried about his son's math skills. We are unable to turn back the clock, but there are systems and practices you can put in place to help you make targeted use of the time you do have. Too often, out of habit or tradition, schools plan their schedules and calendars in patterns that mirror previous years without accounting for changes they've made to curriculum, expectations, and student performance. Untargeted use of time can stand in the way of school improvement. Consider the priorities and goals you have set for your school. If you do not make time for them in all of your calendars and schedules, they will never get the attention they need from you, your staff, and your students. "The key is not to prioritize what's on your schedule, but to schedule your priorities," leadership expert Stephen Covey once noted.[5]

Principals whose schools have seen sustained improvement in student learning regularly assess both how they have been planning to spend their time, and how they are actually spending their time. They have systems in place to determine whether school plans and school actions are aligned, why there is some misalignment, and how to adjust schedules and calendars to better meet their goals.

As your school's leader, you are in the best position to ensure that the schedules of everyone in your building—students, teachers, administrators, and the principal—are built around school priorities. Time is carved into detailed annual calendars, as well as monthly, weekly, and daily student, teacher, and principal schedules. When we refer to *calendars* in this chapter, we mean annual calendars that map out each month of the school year, capturing student and family events, as well as instructional activities like interim assessment cycles and professional development. *Schedules* outline the weekly and daily planned classes, prep periods, and lunch schedule. A well-developed schedule plans for collaborative teacher time, intervention blocks when teachers can offer students intervention services, and times when each grade level will have lunch and recess, and it indicates which staff members will take time to supervise those periods.

We recommend you do most, if not all, of this planning well ahead of time. Principals have found it most helpful when they plan schedules long before the start of the school year and revisit and revise them as needed.

Strategic leaders also help teachers use classroom time effectively by planning lessons from bell to bell and creating time inside and out of the classroom to meet the differentiated needs of all students.[6] Well-planned lessons increase student learning time, a point often emphasized by teaching experts like Doug Lemov and confirmed by our own experience and research.[7] Picking up five minutes at the beginning or end of every class adds up to ninety hours of additional instructional time over the course of the school year.

When a school's time management system is well aligned, it should be easy to glean from any of the school's calendars or schedules what the school's priorities are.

How do effective principals do all this work, and do it well? Based on New Leaders' research and experience supporting school leaders, we have found the school actions around time management set out in tables 6.1 and 6.2 have enabled principals to most effectively improve student learning. To highlight the need to reflect on how time is being used and encourage leaders to reflect on their assumptions on how time should be used we separated the work as two basic actions: time and schedule review (table 6.1) and the master schedule (table 6.2).

Coordinating with an Annual Calendar

Like all other school structures, the annual calendar will be more effective if it is directly linked to the school's action plan and is also organized around district calendars. For families and students, the calendar outlines days off, celebrations, and other events

Table 6.1 Lever 2: Time Management: Action 1: Time and Schedule Review

	PRINCIPAL ACTIONS	SCHOOL ACTIONS
Stage 1	Review the existing schedule to assess how time is used and any areas where additional time may be available. Assess the speed and efficiency of transition times to identify instructional time that can be recaptured through improvement of processes. Gather data on frequency of interruptions to class time. Review your personal schedule to assess priority of time use for classroom observation, teacher team meetings, and family communication.	Staff members are asked to reflect on the effectiveness of the calendar and weekly schedule. Insights and recommendations from the schedule and calendar review processes are publicly shared.
Stage 2	Ensure that time blocks, rotating days, and house or community structures are serving student needs and do not focus on the needs of adults. Work with members of the leadership team to implement a classroom observation schedule that supports new and struggling teachers. Delegate tasks and responsibilities such as being initial point of contact for student discipline issues and parent questions to others to maintain a focus on instructional leadership.[8]	Leadership team members lead components of the schedule assessment based on their areas of responsibility. Leadership team members conduct frequent classroom observations for new and struggling teachers. School staff know and access first points of contact besides the principal for a range of key needs and requests.
Stage 3	Use student learning data and teacher input to identify needs that are not being met with the current schedule.	Staff members find and improve inefficiencies in their classrooms and make suggestions that support schoolwide improvements.

that will affect them. A separate calendar for staff outlines key benchmarks linked to the schoolwide goals, professional learning sessions, interim and summative assessments, as well as other key meetings for team members. It also includes specific dates for data analysis and action cycles for the school leadership team and teacher teams and established dates for communications with parents.

How school leaders design their calendars can vary. For example, the staff at Alfred Nobel Elementary School in Chicago keep a calendar for all schoolwide and parent events, which they make available to teachers and the public through the school's

Table 6.2 Lever 2: Time Management: Action 2: Master Schedule

	PRINCIPAL ACTIONS	SCHOOL ACTIONS
Stage 1	Create a daily and weekly schedule aligned to strategic priorities and focused on student needs: • Establish multiple times per week for collaborative teacher planning time. • Develop clear class intervention schedules and credit recovery schedules. • Ensure that the schedule meets district and state requirements for English language learners and special education instruction. Create extra time in the school day for core subjects; students not yet achieving at grade level receive additional instruction time (e.g., create two literacy periods—one to teach at grade level and one to teach developing skills for those not on grade level). Establish a calendar of all professional development, assessments, and key decision points for student interventions based on assessment results. Create a personal schedule that builds in time for teacher observations.	The school has a detailed and consistent schedule of teacher team meetings, leadership team meetings, class schedules, and intervention activities, including staff and students involved in each. Class time for learning and teaching is maximized, with few to no interruptions. Staff have a calendar of major assessments and professional development activities that include cycles of lesson observations, coaching, and mentoring. The calendar is not paper based, and updates and edits are instantly shared on a platform or system accessible to families.
Stage 2	Create with members of the leadership team a master calendar that includes key dates for data-driven instruction, student intervention, major professional opportunities, and talent reviews. Create opportunities for all students to have access to arts and physical education. Create a personal schedule that builds in time for teacher observations and protects your ability to be present during arrival and dismissal times. High school: Develop a schedule that allows all students access to college preparatory and advanced courses.	Leadership team members manage and make public a detailed daily and weekly schedule of classes, curriculum focus (such as literacy blocks), student interventions, teacher team meetings, and professional development sessions. The master schedule accounts for student course requests, takes graduation requirements and credit accumulation into account, and creates a daily and weekly schedule for staff professional learning aligned to strategic priorities. Staff help develop the detailed calendar for the semester and a tentative calendar for the school year prior to its start.

Table 6.2 (*continued*)

	PRINCIPAL ACTIONS	SCHOOL ACTIONS
Stage 3	Use student learning data and teacher input to adjust the schedule as needed to maximize time spent on learning and ensure that all students are given ample time to make up any missed course work.	The master schedule comprises individualized student schedules that include accommodations for myriad different student needs, including extra time in a subject and smaller class size.
	On the basis of frequent reviews of student-level data, continually adjust the school calendar and schedule to match shifting priorities and needs.	The schedule supports student development in areas beyond the school day.

website. A separate administration calendar includes staff meetings, district meetings, and teacher observation schedules. The testing calendar includes district and state testing windows for the entire school year. Instructional coaches also keep their own calendars for observations and coaching sessions with teachers.

Regardless of the calendar structure you and your staff choose, it is critical that you stick to it once it is set, and make sure that all affected stakeholders are informed when changes are made.

Creating Student Master Schedules

Effective schools maintain weekly, monthly, and daily schedules that give staff, students, and families a clear picture of the weeks ahead and list all key activities for each week. The schedule is an opportunity for the administration to ensure that all students have access to challenging course work that pushes them to advance in each subject area and creates time and space to review student work and progress.

Effective principals first create a master weekly schedule that lays out course schedules, lunch and recess time, and transition time between classes. There are several different kinds of daily course schedules schools use to support high-quality instruction. Several studies provide conflicting evidence on the impact of scheduling on student performance.[9] Given the variability in the research, the type of schedule that works best for you depends on your school's context. There are a number of factors to consider when creating a master schedule: the grade levels you serve, your students' learning and behavioral needs, the skill of your teaching staff, contractual constraints, and district and state mandates about the number of permitted instructional hours. The master weekly schedule then becomes the basis for teacher, student, and principal schedules.

To illustrate effective scheduling work, consider the story of a high school principal who used the school's schedule as a vehicle for improving student performance.

When Glynis Jordan became principal of Bladensburg High School in Prince George's County, Maryland, in 2008, she spent her first weeks on the job, in the heat of summer, examining test scores, student and teacher attendance data, classroom observations from the previous year, and graduation, college acceptance, and suspension rates. She also called on teachers to meet with her (voluntarily, since it was summer) to discuss their perceptions of the school.

After doing some analysis on her own, she spoke with the assistant principals and then the department chairs, critical stage 1 actions for schedule review. She knew she needed input from other school staff to create a well-informed schedule and, eventually, to be able to hand off some responsibility for schedule revisions to other staff, a stage 2 practice. The previous year, 72 percent of students were proficient in reading, and 68 percent were proficient in math. Through her examination of all the data, Jordan realized the school had not been creating enough opportunities for students to get intervention or extension services or to recover credits so that they could graduate. Staff feedback also made clear that teachers, particularly those in the core tested subjects, were not collaborating enough and did not have enough job-embedded professional development.

Her immediate solution was to overhaul the master schedule to ensure it better served students' learning needs and the improvement priorities that Jordan and her staff had identified, a stage 1 action in master planning.

With the first day of school just weeks away, Jordan and her staff chose the block schedule shown in exhibit 6.1, which aligned well to their four strategic priority areas: intervention, acceleration options, credit recovery, and teacher collaboration. From that master schedule, Jordan and her master scheduler and assistant principal created weekly student and teacher schedules like the ones in exhibit 6.2.

EXHIBIT 6.1: BLOCK SCHEDULE AT BLADENSBURG HIGH SCHOOL

BLADENSBURG HIGH SCHOOL

Sample Master Schedule

A Day - M/W/F		B Day - T/R	
Period 1 8:30 to 9:45		Period 2 8:30 to 9:45	
Transition 9:45 to 9:52		Transition 9:45 to 9:52	
Period 3 9:52 to 11:07		Period 4 9:52 to 11:07	
Transition 11:07 to 11:14		Transition 11:07 to 11:14	
Period 5 11:14 to 1:05 • Lunch A – 11:15 to 11:45 • Lunch B – 11:55 to 12:25 • Lunch C – 12:35 to 1:05	Seminar for targeted students before or after 30 minute lunch	Period 6 11:14 to 1:05 • Lunch A – 11:15 to 11:45 • Lunch B – 11:55 to 12:25 • Lunch C – 12:35 to 1:05	Seminar for targeted students before or after 30 minute lunch
Transition 1:05 to 1:12		Transition 1:05 to 1:12	
Period 7 1:12 to 2:12		Period 8 1:12 to 2:12	
Transition 2:12 to 2:19		Transition 2:12 to 2:19	
Period 9 2:19 to 3:35		Period 10 2:19 to 3:35	

EXHIBIT 6.2: SAMPLE SCHEDULE FOR AN ELEVENTH-GRADE STUDENT AND A TEACHER

Semester 1

A Day	B Day
English 11	English 11
Geometry	Geometry
World History	Art 2
Speech Communications	Environmental Science

Semester 2

A Day	B Day
English 12	English 12
Algebra 2	Algebra 2
World History	Art 2
Drama	Environmental Science

Sample Teacher Schedule

A Day - M/W/F		B Day - T/R	
Period 1 8:30 to 9:45	Geometry	Period 2 8:30 to 9:45	Algebra II
Transition 9:45 to 9:52		Transition 9:45 to 9:52	
Period 3 9:52 to 11:07	Algebra I	period 4 9:52 to 11:07	Math Team Meeting
Transition 11:07 to 11:14		Transition 11:07 to 11:14	
Period 5 11:15 to 11:45 11:55 to 12:25 12:35 to 1:05	Lunch Geometry Help Seminar	Period 6 11:15 to 11:45 11:55 to 12:25 12:35 to 1:05	Lunch Algebra Help Math Club
Transition 1:05 to 1:12		Transition 1:05 to 1:12	
1:12 to 2:12	Tier 2* Algebra (*intervention and support)	1:12 to 2:12	Tier 2 Geometry
Transition 2:12 to 2:19		Transition 2:12 to 2:19	
Period 9 2:19 to 3:35	Planning	Period 10 2:19 to 3:35	Tier 2 Algebra II

In addition to ensuring consistency, this schedule, by decreasing the number of times students switched classes from seven to four, increased class time and reduced truancy, hallway incidents, and the amount of time administrators spent monitoring hallways. The new schedule also allowed for common planning time for vertical teams, subject area teams, and instructional leaders. That consistent schedule also enabled Jordan to meet with entire teams when needed. Since only a few teachers were experienced in teaching high-quality lessons on the block schedule, which had longer class periods than teachers were accustomed to, Jordan created professional development opportunities to support teachers' adjustment to the new schedule.

How Jordan and her staff structured English and math instruction within the schedule offers a strong example of how to align schedules to student needs, a critical stage 1 action. Based on assessments, Jordan saw that her students needed extra support in algebra. So every ninth grader (except those in the honors class) took algebra on A days and algebra support on B days. In other words, they had algebra every day. The support classes (labeled "Tier 2" in the sample teacher schedule) pulled in math coaches and had the teachers rotating depending on their areas of strength in algebra. If students struggled to grasp a concept after being taught by one teacher, they would be taught the same concept a different way by a different teacher during the support class. "There was no reteaching," Jordan said. The consistent schedule, which had teachers teaching six out of the eight blocks each day, enabled teachers to rotate in and out.

Jordan also saw that after a strong performance in English coming out of eighth grade, the ninth graders, based on interim assessments, were not continuing to advance. She attributed this to the fact that the eighth-grade curriculum was more difficult than that for ninth grade. Her students were not being challenged, she said. Since she lacked the authority to change the district-mandated curriculum, Jordan again turned to the schedule. In the first semester, every ninth grader took English 9 every day, and in the second semester, every ninth grader took tenth-grade English every day. That pushed the students and allowed them in tenth grade to take specialized classes like grammar or speech or to continue in the English sequence and, in some cases, graduate early.

Bladensburg staff also aligned the master schedule with the school's goal of preparing all students for college and careers by creating time in the day for seniors to take college courses or have internships. The schedule design enabled 30 percent of seniors to spend half of each day in college or internships during Jordan's first year and 70 percent by the third year, giving them a jump-start on college free of cost. With so many students off campus on those afternoons, teachers could devote that time to working with students needing extra support.

With the schedule in place, students immediately showed results: The school made adequate yearly progress for the first time at the end of Jordan's first year, with 73 percent proficient in reading and 74 percent proficient in math; students' SAT scores jumped by 86 points. By the end of Jordan's third year, proficiency rates had risen to 81 percent in reading and 86 percent in math. The percentage of students in credit recovery also fell, from 30 percent to 20 percent, and nearly all of those remaining recovery students had transferred to Bladensburg their senior year, having heard about the school's work supporting students in meeting graduation requirements.

With a leadership team and process in place for creating a master schedule and a strong system for collecting and using data, the staff at Bladensburg were able to take the stage 3 action of regularly adjusting the schedule to match shifting priorities and student needs. The process for designing a master schedule for the following year began in December. Jordan, her lead assistant principal, and her master scheduler first examined recent data. Among other systems, they had created a data room whose walls were papered with index cards for each student. The cards were color-coded for special education needs, attendance problems, over age, English language learner, and proficiency in the tested subjects. This system informed student, teacher, and master schedules; accounting for student course requests, graduation requirements, and credit recovery needs are important stage 3 actions. In one meeting, staff noted a student card that showed this student was academically advanced but had a yellow dot for poor attendance. "Your problem is you're bored," Jordan said of the student. So they redid this student's schedule, placing him in more advanced classes.

Using the wall and other data, the leadership team discussed how the master schedule needed to change the next year. Jordan shared those key priorities with her assistant principals, core content coordinators, and department chairs. Each department chair then met with his teachers to get input on what worked and what didn't work, and what they wanted to teach the next year. "If there was a change, the department chair had to be able to justify it," Jordan said.

One change that staff agreed on for Jordan's second year was no longer allowing students to take the same course twice. If a student failed algebra 1, for example, he would have to take some other variation of an algebra course, for example, an algebra/geometry split, or go to summer school, which cost students up to $300. After this change, Jordan said, "A lot of student failures stopped because students had the responsibility of repeating that course over the summer, and paying for summer school, or waiting for another creative opportunity, which would not come until the next year."

After several reviews and revisions by staff, the schedule was tested in mid-June (a district mandate). By then, said Jordan, the schedule was nearly final and reflected the school's instructional priorities: increased rigor to prepare all students for college, intervention services and credit recovery for students who needed extra support, and time for teachers to collaborate and in turn work together as a professional learning community.

Priorities That Create Common Scheduling Challenges

While every school has its own set of priorities, a few issues arose in New Leaders' research that presented particular scheduling challenges: creating time for teacher collaboration and student intervention and maximizing learning time by limiting interference caused by class transitions and lunch and recess.

Fostering Teacher Collaboration in the Master Schedule. Imagine that to bring to life the concepts he has been teaching in his eleventh-grade math class, one teacher holds a bridge-building competition in his class. His students spend hours working in small groups to design their bridges, applying the math they have learned to their creations. Meanwhile, the teachers in the other eleventh-grade math sections draw on more traditional, and at times bland, methods of teaching the material, using work-sheets and lecturing on math concepts. At the end of the unit, all of the bridge builders do noticeably better on their assessments than the majority of the rest of the eleventh graders.

Now imagine what all of the eleventh graders could have learned during that unit if all of the math teachers had worked together to determine what teaching methods were more effective than others, and perhaps had created a grade-wide bridge-building contest. While we discussed the importance of teacher collaboration and common planning time in detail in chapters 3 and 5, here we look at the role the schedule plays in making a collaborative teaching culture possible. With the school schedule, you can create moments of ongoing learning and growth for the adults in your building by scheduling peer observations and feedback sessions and targeted in-school professional development. We've seen teacher teams be most effective when they meet at least once a week, and ideally more.

Schools that have not yet reached stage 1 tend to have a weekly schedule that does not include regular time for teacher collaboration. As a result, teacher preparation periods in those schools are spent in isolation, with individual teachers either reviewing student work or creating lessons without other members of their grade-level teams.

If you are in a smaller school with one class per grade, consider how your teachers can work in vertical team groups and be matched with teachers from other schools with similar profiles in the district. These cross-school meetings might be less frequent, but they will give the teachers opportunities to meet with other teachers at the same grade level.

Transitions. Instructional time is often wasted at the start and end of class periods: a teacher hands out papers at the start of class; students trickle in on their way back from lunch; and when an assignment is complete, students sit waiting for the bell to ring, books away and backpacks on desktops.

Thinking through transitions is closely connected with the lesson planning issues addressed in learning and teaching, but here in the context of planning and operations, the focus is on assessing the current state of transitions and creating clear expectations about how long different transitions should take.

Start and end of day. How students flow into the school building in the morning can set the tone for the rest of the day. School leaders benefit from examining how students and families are greeted as they enter the building and how quickly students are able to transition into academic content.

In-class transitions. Transitions are important within classrooms too. For elementary students, whose core subjects are usually led by one teacher, a transition does not always mean moving to another setting. It can be as simple as closing one text and opening another. When you are assessing how time is used, consider whether there are common transition practices used across classrooms. How do the teachers indicate that the time for one content area is over and another is beginning? Are schedules posted? In middle and high schools, are teachers teaching up to the bell in their classes, or is it common to see students ready to leave class before the period has ended?

Lunch and recess. Transitioning from lunch and recess back to the classroom can present challenges. After running around at recess, students need time to cool down with a quiet activity; otherwise the energy of the school yard can come into the classroom in a disruptive way.

Scheduling Your Own Time

A principal's own daily and weekly schedules are as important to align with school goals as are the master and weekly schedules. As with any other senior leader, time is your most precious commodity, and where you spend it speaks volumes about your priorities. However, we know from many conversations and coaching sessions with principals that it can feel nearly impossible to stay in control of your own schedule. Between the daily surprises of student, teacher, and parent concerns and the unexpected expectations and e-mails from the district office, setting and maintaining priorities for your own time is a huge challenge. However, we have seen effective leaders find creative ways to protect their time. Some leaders spend every Sunday reviewing monthly and annual targets, and creating a schedule for the upcoming week that allocates time to take next steps in all key areas. This weekly process has helped keep school leaders focused on school goals. From those schedules, principals can create daily "to-do" lists with space to note weekly goals. Others have specific structures in place for how surprises and urgent needs are handled first by other staff at the school. In one particularly festive example, one of our principals, a native of New Orleans, wore Mardi Gras beads every day during her time dedicated to classroom observation and feedback, a clear sign to staff that they should hold off from interrupting her with concerns that could wait but also a clear sign of the priority she put on instructional improvement.

While this is not an exact science, and these figures will vary depending on your school's needs and priorities, exhibit 6.3 offers a consolidated example of how a sample of the principals in our research allocated their time.

EXHIBIT 6.3: PRINCIPAL TIME ALLOCATION EXAMPLE

Instruction: 60%

   Teacher conferences: 18%

   Classroom observations: 18%

   Teacher team meetings: 12%

   ILT meetings: 6%

   Response to Intervention meetings to review student progress and determine next steps: 3%

   Case manager meetings to discuss IEPs: 3%

Culture: 30%

   Student culture building (morning greeting, lunch duty, transitions, etc.): 15%

   Administration meetings to review discipline data, attendance, teacher issues, upcoming events, adjustment to hallway transitions, etc.: 9%

   Family engagement: 6%

Operations: 10% (all small percentages, but often bunched into specific times of the year)

   Strategic planning: 5%

   Budgeting: 2%

   Scheduling: 2%

   Facilities: 1%

Principal's Tool 6.1: A Process for Analyzing and Optimizing Your Own Time

Deep Dive: An Analysis of Time Spent on Student Discipline Issues

Imagine, after conducting his time analysis, an elementary school principal discovers that he is spending 35 percent of his time on student discipline issues. While he knew that teachers had flagged student behavior issues in meetings, he was surprised to find how much of his time it was eating up. He realized that daily student behavioral problems were pulling him away from deeper work around instruction.

To figure out how he could spend less time on discipline, he first wanted to better understand what his discipline work entailed each week. As suggested in principal's tool 6.1, he first created several subcategories of time use and analyzed what portion of his time focused on discipline issues over the previous two weeks he spent on each subcategory. Based on his first analysis, he saw the following breakdown of time:

- Meetings with individual students about infractions: 35 percent

- Monitoring hallways and lunches: 25 percent

- Conversations with parents or guardians about student infractions: 15 percent

- Time meeting with grade-level teams focused on behavior issues: 10 percent

- Meetings with teachers about student behavior: 15 percent

He immediately realized that he was spending a large portion of his time as school leader dealing with individual student situations and monitoring nonclassroom time. Did he need to spend so much time sitting with students in detention, and why wasn't he spending more time working with teachers and teacher teams to problem-solve around behavioral challenges?

He began by asking two critical questions: To whom can I delegate some of this discipline work? and Are there systems that could be put in place to reduce student discipline problems?

He discussed his findings with his assistant principal, and they met with the school's leadership team to discuss how to better distribute the day-to-day work of handling student discipline infractions. They also sought to begin to create a system for shifting the school culture to make students more responsible for their behavior and to make teachers more responsible for handling discipline issues as they arise in the classrooms rather than sending students to the principal's office for each incident. These changes allowed him to spend much less time on individual student issues and much more time on instruction. In fact, he reduced the portion of time he spent on discipline to only 25 percent, and most of that time he was working with families and teachers on broader preventative and responsive approaches to students struggling with behavior issues.

LEVER 3: BUDGET

When a school leader discusses the challenges he's facing, the conversation almost inevitably turns to money because the school budget underlies so many of the decisions a school leader can make. It starts with staff, the biggest piece of any school's budget. Say, for example, that recent assessments at a high school reveal that the tenth graders' math proficiency is dropping. Is there money in the budget to hire another math teacher to offer more differentiated instruction in targeted math classes where students are struggling? Or can the principal rearrange math teacher schedules to create more time for math support? When another principal loses funding for an assistant principal, can he find another staff member to pick up the school operations work?

The level of budget control that a school leader has varies greatly from district to district, state to state. With that in mind, we are structuring this section for leaders who have some level of autonomy to determine how their dollars are spent. An important note is that school leaders often have more budgetary flexibility than they realize, so you are encouraged to read this section even if you believe you have very little discretionary budget at the school level. As you will see, effective principals have found creative ways to design budgets that maximize their ability to meet school goals while following district and state budget rules that at first glance appeared restrictive. They have done this by examining how all staffing and other financial resources are aligned to the school's strategic plan. They connect the budget to staff assignment decisions discussed in chapter 5. They think about how time is translated into dollars and look at whether the way staff members are spending their time each day is maximizing the school's ability to support student learning. This lever also extends to aligning external partnerships and facilities with the school's goals of improving teacher effectiveness and student achievement. Your school's action plan (see chapter 2 for detail on how to create one) should serve as a guide for determining what partnerships outside the school will best help your school meet its goals and what systems you should have in place to ensure the condition of the school building offers student and staff safety and in turn maximizes learning.

Lever 3: Action 1: Budget and Resources

Table 6.3 outlines the stages of development we found around budgeting.

Table 6.3 Lever 3: Budget: Action 1: Budget and Resources

	PRINCIPAL ACTIONS	SCHOOL ACTION
Stage 1	Conduct a comprehensive review of all current resources (financial, staff, in-kind, supplemental, external partners/programs/resources) and, wherever possible, shift existing resources to align to strategic priorities. Identify key partners in the school and the system to support the budgeting process.	School resources are reallocated to support strategic priorities.
Stage 2	Forecast new resources and materials needed two to three years out based on the strategic plan (e.g., robust classroom libraries to increase students' literacy skills) and begin purchasing and planning for these needs.	Staff forecast resources they will need, accounting for materials they can reuse, to support strategic priorities.
Stage 3	Effectively leverage all potential resource sources through an ongoing, active approach to budget and resource management.	New resources and external partnerships are adequate to fund professional development and student intervention time and skills.

BUDGETING STRATEGICALLY TO IMPROVE A SCHOOL: MOVING INTO STAGE 1 FOR BUDGET AND RESOURCES

Sullivan High School, Chicago, Illinois

At the end of his first year as principal of Sullivan High School in Chicago, at the time the lowest-performing school on the city's North Side, Chad Adams turned down a $1.2 million federal school improvement grant. Many might see this as a strange move for the principal of a struggling school that had been on academic probation for a decade. After all, he had seen the wonders that that same grant had done for the school he had worked in previously, at Harper High School: it had been able to create a student intervention system by using the grant to hire school social workers and psychologists and more security guards to help control the violence. Over time, attendance increased by 20 percent and there were fewer fights in school. The passing rate rose too: in the first semester of the first year of the grant, only 53 percent of tenth graders had passed their core courses; by the end of the second semester, the passing rate for those students rose to 76 percent.

With those improvements, however, came the US Department of Education's decision to end the grant. Adams, then an assistant principal, worked with the school's business manager to determine how to reconfigure the budget without that money and without losing sight of the school goals of maintaining safety and improving academic performance. They focused on the staff. "Programs and supplies can only get you so far. You have to get into the meat, and the meat is staffing," he said. "We started playing with things and thinking about school safety and school goals, looking at where we are, where we are trending up or down. If we moved someone out, who would take on their responsibilities? It was like a game of chess."

With the school goals and organizational chart in front of them, they hypothetically removed each staff member one at a time, then small groups of staff, and they discussed the effect each move would have on the school. In the end they cut twenty-seven staff members: sports coaches, a handful of security guards, the student intervention team (counselors, heads of security, and community partnerships), and Adams, one of two assistant principals. All that was left, he said, were the academic departments and the instructional leadership team. The next year, attendance dropped, college enrollment went down, and student misconduct increased.

Adams learned never to rely on such a large sum that was not sustainable. "It allowed me to think outside the box," he said. When creating the Sullivan budget, he asked himself, "Based on who is in the building and with our current funding, how do I hit the social-emotional side and the academic side?"

He first worked with his staff on the stage 1 action of shifting resources to align with strategic priorities, creating a detailed organizational chart, the document he points to as the heart of his work at Sullivan. "That organization chart helps us drive the work," he said. It distributes leadership and assigns roles, responsibilities, and goals to each staff member, and it makes clear who is responsible for supervising each staff person (see chapter 5). "It helps us know what goals we are targeting in on," he added.

In his first year, he and his staff also created a core sequence, something the school lacked and, Adams noted, was critical for budgeting. The sequence laid out what classes students would take from freshman year to graduation. "There were too many offerings before and not enough of what the kids need," he said.

He also determined that they needed to improve school culture. All of this then allowed him to budget effectively and creatively. His philosophy: "You have to trim fat to get flexibility elsewhere."

He saw that the school had too many social studies offerings, so he removed one of his social studies teachers from the classroom and made him director of culture and climate; that teacher stayed on the social studies budget line and was paid overtime to compensate for his new responsibilities.

Adams replaced both assistant principals with just one. To compensate for that, he shifted one of his five science teachers out of the classroom and into the role of operations manager, for which this teacher already had the skills to manage scheduling and school programming. Identifying a key partner to support the budgeting process is an important stage 1 action for budgeting. To make this change work within his budget, Adams wanted to keep him on the science teacher budget line. However, under the Chicago Public Schools contract, teachers are thirty-eight-week employees. Adams asked the district for permission to make him a fifty-two-week employee to avoid paying him overtime. The district granted clearance.

He examined what each employee did all day and decided to let some administrative assistants go, instead relying on Google calendar to manage his schedule. This allowed him to hire more teachers.

While all these staffing changes, and especially those resulting in staff being let go, were incredibly tough for Adams and his team, they succeeded in focusing their staff spending in ways that reflected their core sequence, organizational chart, and priorities. After Adam's first year at Sullivan, the district increased its rating of the school based on that year's achievement data and academic growth. Attendance increased by 5 percent, and the portion of students meeting or exceeding expected growth on the ACT Educational Planning and Assessment System grew from 3 percent to 43 percent.

Adams sees more areas for improvement. For starters, the school is not offering enough electives, he said, and some classes are too big. He has begun to address that within their budget by having some students do course work online, freeing up teachers to teach other courses.

This next case offers a less extreme budgeting situation. Rather than having to triage as Adams did, school leaders examined how to shift resources to better meet their students' learning needs.

ALIGNING SPENDING WITH SCHOOL NEEDS: MOVING INTO STAGE 3 FOR BUDGET AND RESOURCES

Healy Elementary School, Chicago, Illinois

When Alfonso Carmona became principal at Healy Elementary in Chicago, his problem, he says, was not a lack of money. With fourteen hundred students, the size of the budget was decent. The priorities were just all off. The school was spending $130,000 for two full-time employees to make copies and for the supplies and equipment needed to make all those copies. Another $40,000 went to workbooks. Meanwhile, the classrooms had no computers or other digital technology. "Money was being used on resources that were not really impacting student performance," he said. "The priorities were not set."

He quickly identified several resource misalignments, a stage 1 action, cutting the budget for copies, letting those staff members go, and eliminating kindergarten aide positions that were no longer needed. He and his instructional leadership team (ILT) then created a new budgeting process. He made teachers critical partners in determining school needs, made negotiating with vendors for the best price and services a regular part of doing business, and planned the budget two to three years in advance. The result was that in late February of a recent school year, the school still had more than $500,000 to spend, and with budget cuts anticipated across the city for the next year, Carmona was not concerned. In his first two years, student reading and math proficiency rose slightly to 86 percent and 92 percent respectively. "I believe the growth has been there because of how we structure our budget," he said.

To get clear understanding of supply needs, Carmona and his ILT created a process for soliciting teacher input into the budget process, a stage 2 action. Each spring, the ILT uses an online Google document to circulate two wish lists to teachers for the following school year: one for instructional materials and the other for equipment. Carmona said, "I ask teachers, 'What can I give you to improve performance of your students? How can I remove any obstacles that you have to be sure every one of your students performs at a high level?'"

Carmona and his team carefully review the requests, comparing them to prior year supplies and, for new or questionable items, asking teachers to explain how they plan to use the supplies to improve student learning. For materials that can last more than a year, teachers need to explain how the item can be used for the next two to three years.

Then Carmona became more strategic about purchases. "We started purchasing only the stuff that was needed," he said, noting that on purchases alone, the school saved $120,000 his first year. He closed the full-time purchasing staff position when that person retired and split the job with his assistant principal. For each needed purchase, they called the vendors on the district's approved list, got quotes, and chose the company whose price was low and whose service made sense for the school. "A savings of two dollars an item when you are buying one for every student in a school with fourteen hundred students adds up to significant savings," he said.

Carmona's first survey of teachers after coming to Healy identified technology as a top classroom need. He set a long-term goal of having a laptop for every student. He called each of the district-approved computer vendors and told them how much he had to spend (in fact, he told them a little less than what he actually had) and specifically what he was looking for. Each company placed a bid, and the vendor he chose provided laptops for less than half what the district's largest computer vendor was charging. Carmona also hired a consultant to maintain the computer equipment in the school for an entire year. The consultant cost the school $15,000 for the first two years, compared to the $180,000 the school was paying for a technology coordinator. Four years later, through gradual accumulation, the school is just one year away from having a computer for each student.

Carmona also changed the professional development allocation. Rather than continuing to give each teacher up to $200 to sign up for whatever workshop she wanted to take, without any monitoring, he restricted that budget line to $1,500 per year. Now the school invites facilitators to the school to train several teachers at a time on skills and topics Carmona and his team have identified as staff needs.

All of these savings have enabled the school to staff three reading interventionists and one math interventionist (stage 3 actions). It has also been able to purchase nine hundred technology devices (iPads, Chromebooks, laptops, and desktop computers) over four years, an investment of more than $1 million.

Taking advantage of a fund of money in Chicago that rolls over each year, Carmona has been able to work toward larger projects as well. Identifying a need to renovate and upgrade the auditorium, Carmona called the district's "fanciest" vendor, who sketched out the scope of work and gave a quote.

Carmona took that proposal as the standard to guide the scope of the work needed. He then asked other vendors for additional quotes, ultimately finding a company able to do the work for less than half the price of the first vendor.

As for the impending budget cuts, Carmona explains he is not concerned because he has already planned out spending for the next three years, a stage 2 action. "I always save some money to protect my most crucial positions," he said. As for equipment and curricular materials, "I already have things paid for the next two or three years." For example, a couple of years ago, he had extra money in the budget, so he renewed the school's license to use its preferred reading and math software for three more years for consistency in the classrooms. As of February, supplies for the next year had already been paid for, and he has been able to set aside a cushion of $200 per student should cuts be made in the district's per pupil allocations.

Part of that longer-term planning, he adds, is his decision to invest only in items the school can continue to afford. Using his math and reading interventionists as one example, he said, "If I can't sustain that investment for three years, it makes no sense to make that investment."

> Principal's Tool 6.2: Reflection Questions on Budgeting

Lever 3: Action 2: External Partnerships

External partnerships that are aligned to your school's vision and goals can help move your school closer to achieving its mission. They can provide not only programmatic support for the work you are doing, whether it is related to school culture or instruction, but also significant fiscal investment. Whatever the nature of the partnership, you will find the collaboration most effective if you monitor and manage the work to make sure it is helping you meet your school's goals. Too often we have seen schools open their doors to willing volunteers without carefully considering how those volunteers will contribute to the school's mission.

In cases where a partner's work is not directly in service of your goals, you can work with the partner to modify the approach. If that is not possible, you can graciously dissolve the partnership, leaving a door open for collaboration in the future.

To decide whether to maintain, restructure, or end a partnership with a community member, consider developing a process for determining how those partnerships align, or misalign, with current school goals and for taking action when there is misalignment.

Table 6.4 Lever 3: Budget: Action 2: External Partnerships

	PRINCIPAL ACTIONS	SCHOOL ACTION
Stage 1	Review existing community partnerships to assess their current impact on the school. Introduce partners to the school's priority areas to ensure alignment between partner and school. If partners are unable to adapt to a focus on high-priority areas, reframe, eliminate, or replace the partnership.	Criteria are established to review and identify partnerships, including alignment to the strategic priorities and identified student support needs of the school.
Stage 2	With the leadership team, actively seek and cultivate external partners to fill gaps or enhance and extend programming, all in support of schoolwide goals.	External partners and programs are aligned with the school's key goals around student achievement and social-emotional development. Partners are clear that their work aligns to the school's goals.
Stage 3	Collaborate with external partners to create explicit links to the schoolwide goals.	External partners and programs have demonstrated impact on the school's progress toward achieving key goals. External partners are fully invested in the school's success.

Table 6.4 shows the stages of development around developing and maintaining effective external partnerships.

Principal's Tool 6.3: Reflection Questions on External Partner Alignment

Lever 3: Action 3: Facilities

The upkeep of a building sends a message to students and families about the school. Does it feel like a serious place for learning? When a school leader oversees a clean and orderly school, she is showing her staff and students that she respects them, values the important work that goes on within the school walls, and has high expectations for every aspect of the school.

Even when aspects of a school building, such as age or shoddy construction, are beyond the control of a principal, she can work with the maintenance staff and the central office to ensure that systems are in place to maintain the building. Effective school leaders have also leaned on the school's values to inspire other members of the

Table 6.5 Lever 3: Budget: Action 3: Facilities

	PRINCIPAL ACTIONS	SCHOOL ACTIONS
Stage 1	Conduct a facilities survey prior to the start of school; assess and prioritize immediately needed repairs and desired improvements. Create systems to maintain the building's safety and cleanliness. Develop a crisis management plan that ensures that all students and staff are safe in the event of an emergency.	School buildings are clean and safe; all basic facilities (bathrooms, windows, sinks, locks) are in working order; there are no broken windows or other safety hazards. The school participates in regular safety drills. The school participates in regular crisis management drills, and all staff are familiar with procedures.
Stage 2	Identify a few ways to creatively use and manipulate space to support academic priorities and initiatives.	The physical plant supports major academic priorities and initiatives (e.g., reading nooks, improved library, enhanced computer lab, comfortable staff lounge and meeting areas).
Stage 3	Continually assess the ways in which space is used to maximize learning.	The entire physical plant (common spaces, classrooms, hallways, resource rooms) visually and materially supports and advances schoolwide goals and initiatives.

community—students, teachers and families—to take responsibility for maintaining a clean and orderly environment.

As part of the work of aligning all aspects of the school with the ultimate goal of improving student achievement, leaders also consider how they can use the spaces within the building to facilitate and support learning. Some schools might create a reading nook under a staircase where small groups of students can work. Other schools might move classes around to cluster around grade levels or subject areas. The TLF stages of development around facilities are outlined in table 6.5.

 CLEANING UP A SCHOOL BUILDING TO BOOST MORALE: MOVING TO STAGE 1 FOR FACILITIES

Airways Middle School, Memphis, Tennessee

When Sharron Griffin became principal of Airways, the school was known throughout the community as a place afflicted by violence and other behavior problems where little learning took place. She decided that to increase student learning, she first needed to create a space that was conducive to that learning. She conducted a survey of the physical condition of the school, a stage 1 action in the TLF, and quantified the ways in which the building was a mess. The roof leaked in a number of places, paint was peeling, and the hallways were drab, dirty, and littered with trash. By improving the physical facility, she hoped she and her staff could demonstrate the school's commitment to the students and signal a broader vision for change. While 93 percent of her students lived in poverty,[10] she said, "I wanted them to be educated in what they would consider to be luxury. I knew that needed to start with creating an environment that looked conducive to learning."

Before making any changes, she brought her plan to the students, telling them that she believed in their potential but that she needed them to respect the space and do their part to help maintain it. She had the roof repaired and installed an Airways Middle School sign outside the building. Noting the sense of pride the sign created among the students, she said, "That's the best eighteen hundred dollars I ever spent."

When the district did not respond to repair requests quickly enough for Griffin, she rallied the staff with a sense of purpose, telling them, "I can't do this alone." They bought paint and replacement light bulbs themselves and repainted their classrooms after school and on weekends. They hung motivational posters and bulletin boards in the hallways and displayed student work.

From these initial efforts grew a schoolwide system that quickly won its custodial staff two district-wide awards for building maintenance.[11] More important, once these systems for creating a positive learning environment were in place, Griffin and her staff could focus on improving instruction. From her second to third year, the portion of students proficient or advanced in math according to yearly progress calculations rose from 77 percent to 84 percent and in reading and writing from 71 percent to 85 percent. Students with disabilities who were proficient and advanced in math rose from 34 percent to 49 percent.

Once a school like Airways improves its physical condition, school leaders can take stage 2 actions using the physical plant to support major academic priorities and initiatives. When Michelle Pierre-Farid was principal of Tyler Elementary, she did this by regrouping classrooms. When she started at the school, classrooms were not grouped by grade level, which she took as a sign that teachers were not communicating with each other. "I figured they did not work or collaborate together since they didn't see the need to be near each other," she said. Before the school year started, she rearranged classrooms to put grade-level teachers together, displacing staff that had been in the same rooms for years. She also cleared off bulletin boards that were outdated and lacking in student work so that teachers could start fresh. An unused classroom where materials had been stored was converted into a teacher resource room, and classrooms were repainted with teachers' colors of choice. "I called this 'housekeeping'—people noticed the changes when they came into the building," she said. "Then came the rationale—collaboration for the support of kids."

Safety and Evacuation

Schools are not immune to the crises that occasionally hit towns across America, whether natural disasters or acts of violence. A strong safety and crisis management plan clearly outlines what students and staff should do in an emergency—whether and how they should evacuate—and is regularly updated. Consider whom in the school system you should work with, as well as police and fire, to follow district policies on safety specifics.

At the start of the school year, leaders should create or revise the school safety and security plan, including plans to budget for and hire safety officers. Once the plan is drafted, information should be reviewed with the entire staff so that every adult is clear on the expectations and the procedures for fire drills and other emergencies. Each classroom should have evacuation plans that clearly mark exits, show how to line students up, and instruct in how to secure the classrooms. Additionally, drills should be included in the schoolwide calendar and practiced by the school community so that everyone knows how to be safe.

As a part of the plan, leaders should form a committee that will help to implement and monitor the plan. Depending on the building's layout, principals and other adults may identify areas that need to be monitored at transition times.

LEVER 4: COMMUNITY AND DISTRICT RELATIONS

Schools do not exist in a vacuum. They live within districts and communities whose central office staff and community members have their own interests and concerns about how their local school is doing. The political interests of various local stakeholders have direct implications for how principals should lead their schools.[12] By taking time to understand the interests and concerns of families and community members and the reasons behind those interests, you can build strong allies who can help you improve your school. Effective school leaders have done this by creating systems for regularly communicating with community members, local officials, and families, as well as with district administrators and staff.

Table 6.6 Lever 4: Community and District Relations: Action 1: Stakeholder Communications and Engagement

	PRINCIPAL ACTIONS	SCHOOL ACTIONS
Stage 1	Map community leaders and key political relationships. Share the school vision and strategic plan with community and political leaders to engage their support.	Community leaders and families receive consistent communication about key school events and information. Structures are in place to ensure that all stakeholders have multiple opportunities to engage in a dialogue with members of school leadership. Communications from stakeholders are responded to in a timely manner, with appropriate tone and a tailored message.
Stage 2	Develop an initial plan to communicate with key community leaders and families; the plan should include a communication calendar, key messages, audiences, communication media, a time line for rollout, and staff responsibilities for executing the plan. Incorporate community and family input into the school's plan for improvement and growth. Build staff capacity to develop meaningful relationships with community members and all other stakeholders.	The leadership team drives key messages to internal and external stakeholders. Stakeholders have multiple ways to communicate with all staff in addition to key leadership.
Stage 3	Actively involve community leaders and families in planning for the school. Put structures and processes in place to consistently partner with stakeholders, including staff, families, and students, to inform and adjust strategies.	Community participation is evident in multiple aspects of the school. Stakeholders and community members have multiple ways and opportunities to become involved in the school.

In the first action in this lever, stakeholder communications and engagement, leaders have moved their schools through the stages of development detailed in table 6.6.

Action 1: Stakeholder Communications and Engagement

Family and Community Communication

In chapter 4, we looked at how school leaders have engaged families as critical partners in each student's academic and personal development and what it means for school staff to partner with families.

One important element of engaging families is a consistent pattern of communications and updates from the school to families. A strong family communication plan can help you systematically and regularly share updates about the school, outline the frequency of engagement, and identify which staff are responsible for engagement. This communications plan can be expanded to include other community stakeholders and supporters, leveraging similar updates and outreach to build awareness and support for the school throughout the local community.

BUILDING COMMUNITY BEYOND THE SCHOOL: MOVING TO STAGE 1 FOR STAKEHOLDER COMMUNICATIONS AND ENGAGEMENT

Sheffield High School, Memphis, Tennessee

As the new principal of Sheffield, Jimmy Holland quickly noticed there was little family engagement with the school. Sheffield was on the state's high-priority list, with low achievement ratings in all grades and subjects, as well as below-average attendance levels. Holland wanted to use community resources to improve student academic performance.

Initially the transient nature of the community made this work challenging. Many businesses, community organizations, and churches had moved out in recent years. Holland traveled to institutions in neighboring communities to ask for support and shared the school's vision and strategic plan with community members, a stage 1 action. One church opened its gym to students after school, provided they got a library card first. Holland convinced Walmart to offer job shadowing and other resources to the school even though it no longer had a store in town. Several citywide organizations, including the Rotary Club, also offered support.

Holland and his staff also reached out to families by regularly attending school sporting events and PTA meetings. He tapped into a small base of involved parents to create a leadership council, embarking on the stage 1 work of putting structures in place to ensure that all stakeholders had multiple opportunities to engage in dialogue with the school leadership. The council, with equal numbers of parents and teachers as members, met monthly. Holland asked the council to focus on both neighborhood and school issues, including problems with crime and the reluctance of residents to call the police when suspicious activity occurred. By Holland's third year, the parent-teacher-student association and booster club had become active organizations. To dispel negative perceptions about the school, Holland distributed data about both school performance and community crime statistics to parents and other community members, asking them to be on the lookout for problems and serve as the eyes and the ears of the community.

Sheffield students also became more of a presence in the community. Holland encouraged the creation of service-learning projects, such as helping students with disabilities at the nearby Shriner school during its field day, volunteering in nursing homes, and helping to clean up a rundown neighborhood cemetery. "Kids gave up two days of spring break, and we had an eighty-five-year-old grandmother helping clean up and clear brush," Holland said. Such highly visible activities "put a place in people's hearts for Sheffield," he explained. "You start wanting your kids to go there."

Lever 4: Action 2 : District Relationships

A district's central office can enable your work or hinder it. To foster relations with district staff and secure more targeted support from them, effective principals share their vision and action plans on a regular basis with their supervisors in the central office, along with the reasoning behind those plans. For one thing, this transparency can help you better manage when and how you introduce district initiatives to your school and avoid being pulled into work that does not align with your school's plans for the year.

Table 6.7 Lever 4: Community and District Relations: Action 2: District Relationships

	PRINCIPAL ACTIONS	SCHOOL ACTIONS
Stage 1	Proactively share the school vision and strategic plan with the district/school system manager. Share priority areas for the year, as well as the rationale for each priority area.	School system managers receive consistent communication about key school events and information. Principal supervisors have a clear understanding of the school's areas for growth.
Stage 2	Establish a clear message to the district/system manager around strategic plans; create confidence and a buffer from system management to allow staff to implement strategic plans. Maintain constant contact with the district office to share successes and challenges.	The strategic plan is translated to a district/system process so that it incorporates specific strategies to meet district/system expectations.
Stage 3	Anticipate opportunities where district management can advocate on behalf of the school.	The district/system manager has a clear sense of the school's plans and is a strong advocate for the school.

We found the sets of actions in table 6.7 important for developing and maintaining supportive district relationships.

ALIGNING DISTRICT MANDATES WITH SCHOOL NEEDS: MOVING TO STAGE 1 FOR DISTRICT RELATIONSHIPS

PS 230, Bronx, New York

Sometimes school leaders discover that a district priority conflicts with their school's needs. When she was principal at PS 230, Drema Brown knew that her teachers faced a steep learning curve as their district planned a simultaneous rollout of new curricula and instructional strategies in math, reading, and writing. Brown recognized that her staff was still early in developing consistent approaches to instruction and to team learning, and she knew that tackling all three new curricula at once would be too much for her team, likely resulting in poor implementation for all three. In response, she laid out what she felt was a workable plan for implementing new curricula over several years.

After sharing the school's vision and strategic plan with the district, a stage 1 action, Brown convinced her regional superintendent to let her delay the adoption of the system's new model for teaching reading for one year and instead continue using the reading program the school had started using, with success, a couple of years earlier. Brown did agree that her school would start implementing the district's new writing program, which would allow her to begin introducing the same elements that they would use later when they switched to the district's reading curriculum. The school also agreed to follow the district's implementation scheduled for a new math program. "It was enough that you have a new principal, a new chancellor, a whole system reorganization, and now you're telling them to learn a whole new way of teaching," said Brown.

NEXT STEPS

If, after reading this chapter, you have begun to think about ways to make your school run more efficiently, you now have the tools you need to make that happen. To look for ways for you and your staff to make more targeted use of your time and resources, use the guiding questions and activities in the Principal's Tool Kit around time management and budgeting. While this work can feel overwhelming, we know it is doable. We have seen many principals do this work, taking it one step at a time. The principals in the real-life stories told in this chapter are here to give you guidance and inspiration. Think of them as your personal coaches and come back to their stories and tools as often as you need to.

 WATCH PLANNING AND OPERATIONS VIDEO: In this chapter's companion video, you'll learn about great work being done at schools across the country in the category of planning and operations. To access the video, go to www.wiley.com/go/newleaders.

 Principal's Tools for Planning and Operations

Principal's Tool 6.1: A Process for Analyzing and Optimizing Your Own Time
Principal's Tool 6.2: Reflection Questions on Budgeting
Principal's Tool 6.3: Reflection Questions on External Partner Alignment

Personal Leadership

IMAGINE THAT FOR TWO YEARS, YOU AND YOUR STAFF WORKED DILIGENTLY TO improve instruction at your school. You pored over the state's new set of college and career-readiness standards and introduced an updated curriculum aligned with those standards. To make sure all of your teachers understood and were able to successfully teach from that curriculum, you made time in the schedule for them to regularly work together in teams to plan lessons and identify the most effective instructional strategies and materials. While at times the work was a struggle, after two years of effort, the whole school was in a better place. You could see from interim assessments that students were closer to meeting standards, and teachers were collaborating with each other and with parents in a new way.

Then, to the excitement of you and your staff, you find that for the first time in a few years, your students have made gains on the state tests. However, when you look more closely at the data, you realize that not all students improved: African American students and special education students show no gains at all. In fact, the achievement gap between white and African American students and between general and special education students grew.

What should you do next? There are certainly key technical steps related to learning and teaching and culture and talent management that you can take to address this disappointing disparity. However, this is also a crucial moment for you to demonstrate strong personal leadership. As a leader, the way you respond to this disappointing finding, the way you communicate the news to staff and the broader school community, and how you go about devising and implementing solutions to address it all have an enormous effect on the outcomes you and your team will be able to achieve when responding to this important challenge.

Personal leadership encompasses your values, beliefs, and attitudes, the way you interact with staff, students, and families, and how you approach your work. This chapter makes explicit the personal leadership actions and approaches a leader would use to respond effectively to pivotal moments in a school like the one just described. To lead the school forward in such a situation, you need to consider your own beliefs and how they influence your leadership style. How would you and your staff celebrate the good in the results while also being clear about what needs improving? How would you recognize the hard work your staff has done while noting that the school's instructional strategies have not been equally effective for all students? How would you handle the growing achievement disparity that is revealed by the data? All of these questions are related to personal leadership and come into play in this scenario.

Up to this point, we have outlined specific actions you can take to improve your school. However, *how* you make changes is as important as *what* changes you are making. Research has found that school leaders' values and dispositions affect the quality of education at their schools[1] and contribute heavily to a principal's overall success as a leader.[2] Our personal leadership category summarizes the actions that principals take to bring those values, beliefs, and dispositions to life at their schools.

The actions in this category will push you to think deeply about who you are as a leader. As you work through some of the self-assessment tools provided, you'll reflect on your own deep beliefs about children and education and how best to share those with your school community. You'll explore your own biases or judgments about students and schooling, and you will be transparent in that work so you can serve as a model for others. In the process, you will sharpen your own ability to self-reflect and persevere, demonstrating for your staff and students how to keep growing and improving.

In our study, New Leaders found that there is no single leadership style or personality type that is most effective. It is not about being the boldest or most charismatic leader. In fact, research, including Jim Collins's influential book *Good to Great*, provides ample evidence that charismatic leadership alone is insufficient to move an organization to greatness.[3] This chapter highlights the actions we observed in successful leaders across a wide range of personalities. Many of these actions are often assumed to be innate, such as having strong interpersonal skills. But while you might find that some of these skills and working styles come more easily to you than others, we believe that with the right support, effort, and experience, anyone can develop and adopt these personal leadership qualities.

We've organized these personal leadership actions into five levers:

Lever 1: Belief-based and goal-driven leadership. They demonstrate an unwavering belief in the ability of every child to achieve at high levels, inspire staff to adopt that belief, and set ambitious but achievable goals for all.

Lever 2: Equity-focused leadership. They consistently explore their own biases and assumptions around students, staff, and families from different backgrounds and model this reflective process for the school community. They seek out and give access to a wide range of voices and perspectives to inform their own beliefs and actions.

Lever 3: Interpersonal leadership. They build strong and trusting relationships with multiple stakeholders and always communicate respectfully.

Lever 4: Adaptive leadership. They are able to adapt to changes and help staff, students, and families navigate changes to the school landscape while maintaining focus on the school vision; they inspire changes in values, beliefs, assumptions, and habits of behavior in order to support student success.

Lever 5: Resilient leadership. They demonstrate resolve in the face of adversity, constantly looking for solutions that will move their school closer to its goals. They also reflect on their own actions to ensure that they are continuously learning and improving their work.

The first two levers, belief-based and goal-driven leadership (lever 1) and equity-focused leadership (lever 2), focus on being a leader for social justice. While schools cannot (and should not be expected to) solve all of society's struggles, school leaders do have a significant role to play. They are in a unique position to help young people and their families develop the confidence and belief that with hard work, they can learn and succeed. By leading staff to identify and address issues of bias and inequity within the school, they reduce the barriers to success faced by many students, especially students of color and students in poverty. The rest of the personal leadership characteristics we highlight in this chapter are more general but no less important.

As we emphasize throughout this book, your school's success depends as much on your belief in your own and other adults' ability to learn and grow as it does on that belief for students.[4] This is captured most clearly in lever 5, resilient leadership, and the action focused on ongoing self-reflection and openness to feedback and improvement. While we recognize the challenge of stepping back from the day-to-day intensity of the work, it's crucial to create the time and space for your own self-assessment and to gather input from others to inform your ongoing growth.

A principal's leadership style and approach is present and influential regardless of the level of practices in place within the other TLF categories; thus, the personal leadership category is not divided into stages of development. Effective leaders model these core leadership practices regardless of the school's developmental stage.

In this chapter we give you a set of actions to help you find effective ways to interact positively with and influence your school community to improve student learning. You will meet three principals who have put some of these

 **PERSONAL LEADERSHIP CATEGORY MAP**

Lever 1: Belief-Based and Goal-Driven Leadership

Leader consistently demonstrates belief that every student can achieve at high levels.

Lever 2: Equity-Focused Leadership

Leader continuously dismantles inequitable and exclusionary practices and creates a fully inclusive environment where all children and adults thrive and learn at high levels.

**Lever 3:
Interpersonal
Leadership**

*Leader builds
trusting relationships
and facilitates
engaged communities
of adults and
students dedicated
to reaching
school goals.*

**Lever 4:
Adaptive
Leadership**

*Leader mobilizes
others to resolve
challenges
requiring changes
in values, beliefs,
assumptions, and
habits of behavior.*

**Lever 5:
Resilient
Leadership**

*Leader demonstrates
self-awareness,
ongoing learning,
and resiliency in the
service of continuous
improvement.*

leadership actions in place and as a result have been able to advance school goals. We also offer activities to guide you in determining your current leadership strengths, and which areas of personal leadership you can work on developing, along with concrete guidance about how to make those improvements.

LEVER 1: BELIEF-BASED AND GOAL-DRIVEN LEADERSHIP

You've probably heard it before: A couple of months into the school year, a teacher tells you that some of her students "just don't get it," that they have been "slow" to grasp the material. "I just don't think they will ever be able to do the work," the teacher says with a sigh.

For you, the school leader, this conversation offers an opportunity. How should you handle it? In addition to talking through the instructional needs of those particular students, you could remind her of your school's goals and the importance of holding all students to high expectations. You might tell this teacher that all of the students in the school, even those who are struggling, can achieve at a high level with hard work and the right supports. Consider how you can reinforce these values of equity, possibility, and accountability in all of your encounters with teachers, thus reminding them that their job and yours is to find instructional approaches that enable all students to successfully tackle challenging academic work.

The following list shows the key practices within belief-based and goal-driven leadership:

- Set high but achievable goals for students.
- Focus decisions on student needs, not adult outcomes.
- Create and maintain a schoolwide urgency to improve school outcomes.
- Demonstrate personal commitment to ensuring high academic achievement for all students.
- Inspire a schoolwide sense of positivism and possibility.
- Hold self and others accountable for outcomes.

In thinking about how these practices can be applied across categories, consider what this work would look like when addressing talent management priorities. For instance, you could regularly steer conversations in staff meetings and teacher feedback sessions toward concrete strategies for helping students reach higher expectations and differentiating instruction so all students are appropriately supported and challenged. In learning and teaching, you could assess for instructional rigor whenever you observe classrooms and make that part of the feedback you provide. (For more on what rigorous, high-quality instruction looks like, see chapter 3.)

Of course, it's not enough to simply talk about your beliefs. "The only way to develop a shared mindset is through purposeful and continuous interaction and learning over a period of time," wrote leadership scholar Michael Fullan.[5] While consistent messaging matters, you will communicate your values and priorities most effectively by putting those beliefs into action. You might send teachers who appear to hold low expectations for their students to observe teachers in their building who hold a higher bar for their similarly situated students and successfully enable their students to meet those expectations. Alternatively, you might ask a strong teacher to model a lesson in his classroom to help other teachers see what his students are capable of achieving if challenged. In some cases, modeling a lesson yourself may be the most powerful example.

Principals working to build shared beliefs among their team also use short- and long-term goals to make expectations for teachers and students explicit, and they ensure that these goals are realistic but ambitious enough to help students below grade level get back on track to catch up with their peers. To attain these higher goals, leaders need to match their messages with coaching on effective instruction to help developing teachers shift their pedagogy as well as their thinking.

Your role as school leader is to set a high bar, consistently reinforce the belief that it can be met, and provide coaching and support to bring that vision to life, together. Josie Carbone has been able to do that as principal of Girls Prep in the Bronx, New York.

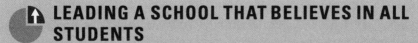

LEADING A SCHOOL THAT BELIEVES IN ALL STUDENTS

Girls Prep Bronx Elementary, Bronx, New York

Principal Josie Carbone does not mince words when she defines her beliefs around education: "I fundamentally believe that all students can achieve at high levels and can be given the tools to think critically, to articulate their thinking clearly, and to be able to engage in some deep-level practices across all content areas."

Since Carbone founded Girls Prep in 2009, those beliefs have shaped every practice she and her staff have put in place. About three-quarters of kindergartners start school below grade level, and 15 percent of all students receive special education services. "As educators, it is our job to figure out what the missing pieces are for students so that we can ensure that we are providing whatever leverage point is needed, whether it's an intervention or an extension, so that all students have access," she said.

In opening the school, Carbone said, "I wanted to be very clear about, 'This is how we talk to kids, this is how we believe in kids, this is what we are going to look like and feel like.'"

Carbone maintains a sense of urgency around student learning and holds all her staff responsible for improving it, key attributes of belief-based and goal-driven leadership. The staff read work by Carol Dweck, and Carbone weaves Dweck's growth mind-set philosophy into staff meetings, conversations, and professional development. Her school's culture is organized around the principles that intelligence can be developed, that children can improve regardless of their starting point, and that to be successful, students must believe these things themselves.

She begins communicating this message as early as the hiring process, asking probing questions—for example: "Identify a time when you realized you had low expectations for a student. What were you doing that displayed low expectations, and how did you shift your mind-set?" Everyone has had low expectations at one time, Carbone said. She is looking for whether a teacher can recognize those moments and then make appropriate changes, diagnosing whether a prospective teacher is reflective and able to act on what she sees in her practice and on constructive feedback from colleagues.

Carbone works with her staff to develop their teaching skills so that when a student is struggling, the teachers identify a skill gap and do not question the student's fundamental abilities. She uses her notes from classroom observations to echo back to teachers what she heard them say in class: "I'll say, 'When you said this, this is what I heard. What was going on there?'" She works with teachers on plans for shifting their expectations and practices to ensure students are continuously supported in progressing toward their academic goals for the year.

Carbone recognizes that she alone cannot inspire staff and create a sense of schoolwide urgency around improving student outcomes, so she has invested a lot of time and effort in developing leadership teams whose members hold the same beliefs and high expectations. "It is critical that we are all aligned in our messaging so that it is not just going to come from me," she said.

To build these consistently high expectations during her first year, Carbone regularly observed classrooms with her leadership team. They noticed, she recounted, that "the experience was not as rich in some classrooms as in others." Among other things, "We realized we did not have a clear enough understanding of what engagement is. We set a schoolwide goal around consistently and intentionally delivering engaging and challenging instruction for all students." Together, she and the staff began to create a definition of *engagement* that staff could use as a benchmark to assess their own and their colleagues' instruction. While that definition is still a work in progress, the staff look for students to be actively engaged by participating and intellectually engaged by being asked challenging questions that push them to analyze, critique, and defend their thinking.

By leading teachers in an analysis of their students' academic engagement and in the level of the academic challenge in their classrooms, Carbone hoped to strengthen teachers' beliefs in what their students could accomplish. As a goal-driven leader, she was putting the needs of the students first and trying to create systems to better hold all of her staff accountable for student learning. She did this by having her instructional leadership team (ILT) and teachers together conduct a set of parallel learning walks to all classrooms, looking for evidence aligned with their definition of engagement. "Getting teachers into one another's classrooms to make teaching public has allowed teachers to both begin to norm practice and also reflect on their own practice and what students experience during their instruction," Carbone said.

The first set of learning walks conducted by grade team leaders in January confirmed that most of the students were not consistently engaged in their classes. Students were well behaved in class, but they were completing assignments easily or not noticing errors and moving on, or completing activities without being asked to explain the key concepts behind them. As part of the school's effort to hold all students to high expectations, Carbone and her team used the learning walk data to devise a series of "quick wins," practices or strategies that teachers could quickly put in place in their classrooms and see results. These "wins" could include giving each student a white board to write their answers on so that everyone is participating, or giving students a couple of minutes to write down questions they have about a task before the task begins. This built on Carbone's effort to inspire a schoolwide sense of optimism by encouraging teachers to set incremental goals that would allow them to prove, over and over, what's possible for students. "Because the goals are bite-sized and incremental, and the strategies are concrete, you see students making progress," Carbone said. "Then a teacher realizes, 'Okay, the student did this; here's the next level.'" As students continued to meet increasingly rigorous goals, teachers' beliefs in students' capabilities rose accordingly.

By late spring, 98 percent of teachers had participated in a learning walk. After just a few months, Carbone said, student engagement had increased. This was clear from the learning walks as well as an analysis of what was happening in classes, what students were saying and doing in class versus what teachers were saying and doing, and whether tasks were open-ended. Students were leading discussions in which they were challenged to build on one another's ideas, provide evidence to back their thinking, and paraphrase one another's ideas to ensure clarity. When students worked in groups in class, teachers gave them task cards to clarify expectations around the types of questions students should discuss with each other and build in extensions that increased the rigor of the assignment. A task card students use as a guide in a math class might say, "How do you know? Why did you choose that strategy? What other way could you have approached the task?" Teachers were using simple methods, too, like cold-calling on students and having them show their answers on individual whiteboards.

Carbone said that she was "seeing teachers do things that I have given them feedback on several times, but now they are hearing this from their colleagues and they are putting changes into practice that were not happening as quickly when it was just me or my literacy coach talking to them." She also saw that the grade team leaders were providing more effective support to their teams.

Carbone understands that belief-based and goal-driven leadership means holding herself and others accountable for students' success. She enacts this accountability through the learning walks, as well as by looking at other forms of data and using the local evaluation framework to guide discussions with teachers.

Carbone is equally committed to her own continuous growth as a leader, so she regularly seeks out feedback and ideas from other principals as well as from coaches, and is transparent with her staff about the details of her efforts to improve. "Even though this is my eighteenth year in education, I am still thinking a lot about what I'm learning and how I'm developing," she said. She and the leadership team members invite input from the rest of the staff, holding drop-in office hours twice a week and surveying the staff twice a year. She invites comments and ideas from parents as well, making herself accessible not only at her drop-in hours but also by standing outside at arrival each day. "I try to listen to parents and see what the lens is that they are seeing their child's education from," she said.

Carbone knew the school was making an important shift when a teacher argued in a grade team meeting that students did not need to learn to write clearly until seventh grade and her colleagues passionately refuted the idea, declaring that Girls Prep students could and should learn that skill now. "Belief is important," Carbone said. "I used to be the one to make that point. Now you are hearing it from people other than me."

LEVER 2: EQUITY-FOCUSED LEADERSHIP

Schools that do not create a strong sense of belonging and connection for some students often find that those students do not learn as well as classmates who feel they are integral members of their school community.[6] Chapter 4 discussed practices that effective leaders put in place to break down cultural barriers to learning. Those principals dismantle inequitable and exclusionary practices and create a school environment in which all children and adults feel safe and can thrive and learn at high levels. To do this work effectively, we have identified a handful of key actions related to personal leadership that principals take to support these priorities.

As you read this section, consider how you handle the power dynamics at work within your school community. Are you able to discuss issues of power and privilege openly with your staff, families, and students, and do your teachers also have the capacity to initiate those conversations? What perspectives inform the school's vision and programs and initiatives? Are you pulling from a diverse set of points of view? Do you capitalize on moments of cultural incompetence and conflict, treating them as learning opportunities for your staff and students?

The following list outlines the key practices in the TLF for equity-focused leadership.

- Demonstrate a commitment to reflect on how your personal biases and privileges affect your actions, and create learning opportunities and a supportive culture for others to do the same.
- Initiate direct conversations about equity and bias to build the school's collective capacity.
- Seek out and engage diverse perspectives to build an effective organization.
- Foster equity and inclusion by consistently addressing the dynamics of power within the community.

The first action for equity-minded leaders is reviewing and addressing their own implicit biases, making that difficult journey visible to staff so it can serve as a model for others. You can start by asking yourself how your race, power, privilege, and experiences have influenced your perceptions of students and of teaching. By definition, privilege is an unearned advantage a person holds over someone else in a particular situation. Even if you are of the same race or ethnicity as most of the families in your school, your advanced education, socioeconomic background, and position as leader of the school creates a certain power dynamic. If you are not aware of and do not seek out ways to acknowledge and minimize the impact of this power difference, it can be challenging to form strong relationships with your staff, your students, and their families (see chapter 4).

To build an equitable organization, you also have to feel comfortable seeking out and engaging a wide range of perspectives and receiving feedback and input from this broader set of voices. You can do that in a way that does not reinforce the existing power dynamic. Are there people in your school community, whether inside or outside the school walls, whose voices are not being heard? What can you do to give them access and to make their perspectives part of decision-making processes? As part of this work, you'll need to maintain an awareness of how issues of power and privilege affect whose input is more influential in the school's decision making. Are there perceived patterns of unequal influence from parents and other community stakeholders? What steps can you take to ensure that differences in race, income, age, or gender don't also reflect differences in access and influence in the school community?

In the cultural competency section of chapter 4, we described how one principal, Leroy Gaines of Acorn Woodland Elementary School in Oakland, California, engaged in this work. Despite challenges along the way, Gaines came to see concrete improvements in the culture of the school and how students, teachers, and families treated one another. In that story, you can see his promising practices around developing a strong school culture, as well as the personal leadership skills he used to do that work effectively.

> Principal's Tool 7.2: Reflection Questions for Considering Your Own Biases, and Those of Your Staff, Related to Diversity at Your School

LEVER 3: INTERPERSONAL LEADERSHIP

For schools to function well, adults have to feel good about their workplace. They must want not only to show up each day but to work hard in the face of challenges. By demonstrating that they believe in and care about their staff's success, school leaders motivate and inspire teachers to improve their instruction. They help teachers achieve success by making it clear what is expected of them and letting them know that their work and input are valued and needed to help shape and improve school practices and policies. They build trust that ensures that their feedback is welcome, internalized, and applied. Effective leaders are able to make lasting improvements at their schools because they have garnered the cooperation and support of their staff and have deeply involved them in setting and carrying out plans for achieving excellence. In fact, much research has found that schools do best when principals and teachers collaborate.[7]

In this section we take a closer look at these interpersonal leadership actions that effective principals take and how those actions contribute to creating a strong school culture:

- Be transparent about expectations with all stakeholders and treat all stakeholders with respect, even those who may not share the same beliefs.

- Create a culture that facilitates the development of trusting relationships around the work.

- Motivate and inspire individuals, and communicate their value to the school.

- Seek multiple perspectives from key stakeholders to predict and plan strategic actions.

- Select appropriate facilitation and leadership strategies when leading groups of people; these should balance appropriate communication strategies for diverse constituents and contexts (e.g., active listening, seeking feedback).

Be Transparent about Expectations and Treat Everyone with Respect

Setting schoolwide goals is critical for making long-term improvements to your school. The interpersonal leadership lever focuses on how you communicate to your staff what those goals are and why they were chosen.

By the time goals are set, many principals have already spent hours and sometimes weeks discussing and revising them with district-level leaders and members of the school leadership team. Too often, however, they neglect to adequately communicate the rationale of the goals and associated expectations to the rest of the staff. If teachers do not know the goals or understand why these specific goals were selected, they will likely have difficulty meeting them; some might even resist them.

Effective leaders remind their staff of the school's vision and goals at every turn, ideally involving a diverse group of teachers and staff in goal setting. Principals may feel that this constant reiteration is repetitive and redundant, but regularly communicating the school's vision and goals demonstrates to staff that expectations will be consistent and helps ensure that every stakeholder is well informed.

Once expectations are clear, successful leaders respond to teachers who are not meeting those expectations in timely and transparent ways. Many leaders make the mistake of not addressing concerns to avoid conflict or tension. We have seen leaders struggle to be candid about performance when they become friends with teachers and we have seen principals be overly harsh when a teacher does not share their beliefs. Both of these extremes limit the leader's effectiveness and their ability to coach and develop teachers' skills. Instead, leaders can focus on identifying and supporting specific improvements in behaviors and practices related to the expectations and goals.

When principals are critical of teachers without attempting to help them improve, they often lose the trust and respect of adults in the building too. The result is that the rest of the staff will fear opening up, and the principal will not be able to establish a culture of open dialogue that is needed to move the school forward.

For example, imagine you have a teacher who is resistant to implementing a new approach to differentiating instruction for struggling students. As we've seen happen at times with principals we have trained, you might infer that this teacher has negative core beliefs about these students and what they can accomplish. Based on those assumptions, you may not invest much time in helping the teacher change practices. But the successful leaders in our research kept the focus on the specific expected behaviors, monitored those expectations, and worked to determine why the teacher is being resistant. Is it because she still does not know how to implement the strategy? Is she afraid of failing? You are likely to have more success if you keep the conversation focused on the behavior, reinforcing the expectation that the work needs to happen while offering additional supports or seeking to identify other challenges the teacher might be facing.[8]

Create a Culture of Trust

As we discussed in chapters 4 and 5, successful schools have strong adult-student relationships as well as authentic structures for adults to learn with and from each other. We found that schools where the students were learning and growing had adults who were learning and growing as well. One key to that adult learning is creating a culture that enables all adults to feel comfortable learning, growing, and trying new things. Teachers need to feel they can take risks and that failure is okay as long as they learn from it and improve. You can create a school climate that gives students and staff the confidence to try new things by showing them that they will not be judged for their mistakes but rather will be supported as they learn to do things better. As noted by researcher Tony Bryk, "Elementary schools with high relational trust were much more likely to demonstrate marked improvements in student learning." And equally important to note for this chapter, Bryk and his colleagues go on to say, "Principals' actions play a key role in developing and sustaining relational trust."[9]

One framework for thinking about building trust comes from Stephen M. Covey in *The Speed of Trust*.[10] Covey discusses two fundamental aspects of trust building: character and competence. By *character* he means maintaining deep consistency between statements and actions and always treating others with respect and dignity; *"Competence"* is about making and meeting commitments, big and small, and consistently getting visible results over time. As you think about the trust you have built with your staff or your school community, you can reflect on both aspects of trust. Do individuals and groups around you believe that you are true to your stated values, and do they see you valuing everyone in the school community? Would they say that when you promise you'll get something done, it gets done?

Of course, there will be difficult conversations along the way. Interpersonal leadership is not about making friends with your staff. You can't brush aside difficult topics for fear of creating conflict or tension. Instead you need to cultivate relationships that will allow you and your staff to support one another and, when necessary, respectfully wrestle with challenging issues that ultimately lead to school improvements.

Use Appropriate Facilitation and Communication Strategies for Every Situation

One particular area for building trust requires being clear about how decisions are being made and how staff can participate in those processes. If staff members are unclear about why they are making changes or how they are supporting a greater vision, they might comply, but they are unlikely to buy in. And issuing directives and relying on the formal authority of the principal role has similar limitations in terms of inspiring compliance but not investment. Not every decision needs to be made by consensus. However, to show respect, you need to be transparent about the process. When decisions are made without a lot of input or discussion, explain why, whether it is due to an urgent time line, the sensitivity of the topic, or because the decision was made at the district or school system level. It is also disrespectful to ask staff for input if a decision has already been made. People want to know that their participation is authentic, and if they perceive that their input is consistently sought but then ignored in decision making, their trust in you will fall.

Beyond clear decision-making processes, you also need to be thoughtful about your approach to communications for a wide range of stakeholders and situations. When sharing major decisions with the school community, keep in mind the important but different questions that may come from students, from staff, and from families and members of the broader community. While the core information will remain the same, the specific talking points and priorities addressed will likely vary across these audiences. The leaders in our research also focused on the best communication vehicles for different messages: What can be shared easily and clearly by e-mail or newsletter? What works best for in-person, large group meetings and discussions? What messages need to be shared in small groups or with individuals? They tailored their approach and planned for communications with these questions in mind.

EARNING TEACHERS' TRUST TO BUILD A BETTER SCHOOL

Powell Bilingual Elementary School, Washington, DC

As we described in the introduction to this book, before Janeece Docal became principal of Powell, the school had been on the city's list of failing schools for a few years. Parents had protested outside the school, pleading for improvements to be made, and a survey showed that only half the parent body was satisfied with the school.

As principal, Docal set out to build trusting relationships with both staff and community members, a critical interpersonal leadership action. She introduced herself to parents, local businesspeople, and clergy. Having taught high school in the neighborhood several years earlier, Docal had already developed relationships with some parents, some of them her former students. "It was really beautiful to be able to serve the community again," she said.

She interviewed as many staff, parents, community members and students as she could about what worked at the school, what needed improvement, and what they envisioned for the school's future. By seeking out multiple points of view to plan strategic actions, she demonstrated strong interpersonal skills. She shared the information she gathered with her staff, and together they developed a clear mission statement and an action plan. By collaborating with the staff she inherited, Docal demonstrated that she valued their input and hoped that this would encourage them to trust her and feel invested in the school goals and vision. "I want teacher leaders to be able to articulate the mission and how we do things better than I can, because I want the school to be theirs," she said. "I'm the vanguard but they're really the ones who will make sure that their peers, that the students, that all of them are moving towards the mission."

Once she made a few immediate changes to the school designed to support student learning, including creating a scope and sequence and curriculum that aligned to the district standards (an action we describe in chapter 3), Docal began developing a strong team of teachers and teacher leaders. She showed teachers she respected them by empowering them with meaningful responsibilities that drew on their strengths. Her academic leadership team started out small, but, she said, "As you grow and you want to develop teacher leadership and the staff gains in experience and trust with you as a leader, more people want to participate." When she started as principal, she felt the staff did not have the capacity to lead the school's curriculum development work. However, thanks to Docal's work engaging teachers in instructional leadership and supporting the school in reaching its goals, six years later her instructional coaches and teacher leaders now manage curriculum development.

"My role is to take a step back," she said. "I'm behind the scenes. I'm asking questions, but I don't want to be the only one leading the meetings or setting the agendas. I'm happy that it's other people. That is the role of the principal too, to push and to be present but not the face."

New and veteran teachers are also invited to participate in the hiring process each year. She believes that involving a range of people in the work of running the school will ultimately make the school stronger. She values different perspectives. "That voice really helps you know the direction in which to go and that will help you also develop trust," she said. "It's uncomfortable, but it's very much the work of the leader."

Docal is also open with her staff about the fact that she struggles with the work just the way they do. "I've learned to show my emotions more," she said. "I'm very even-keeled but I think it's important for staff to know that I'm a human too. Though I'm working really late long hours, they can see, 'Oh, she's tired,' or 'That made her sad,' and to talk about those feelings because they have them too."

Principals with effective interpersonal leadership also make sure they are clear and consistent about expectations. "I think in my heart, there's always this fire of social justice and commitment to education as a civil right that fuels me," Docal said. "The sense that no excuse, make it happen, this passion for all students to have excellence. That will drive me no matter what."

The instructional program at Powell, based on project-based learning (see chapter 3 for more on Powell's curriculum), is designed to hold all students and teachers to consistent expectations. "Whatever is assessed in this class is assessed in that class," Docal said. "There's not just pockets of equity; it's not that this teacher is more rigorous or better. All are trying to achieve the same high level and have high expectations for students." The results of assessments are available for everyone on staff to see, and the teacher teams work together to determine how to improve instruction across classrooms. Staff surveys are also made public and are worked through in open leadership team meetings. This collaboration builds trust among staff members; they are able to show their vulnerabilities to one another, just as Docal models for them, and in turn learn from one another.

Docal built this trust by first listening and responding to her staff's needs. She asked teachers in a survey what kind of support they needed more of. When they told her developing assessments, curriculum, and analyzing student work to design lessons, she and her leadership team created the Curriculum Development Institute (detailed in chapter 3). The institute started with meetings during already set-aside planning periods to discuss curriculum and lesson plans. But the teachers pushed back that this was not enough time. So for the next school year, Docal and her team designed and mapped out sessions in the school calendar for the year and included half-day retreats with classroom coverage so teachers could attend.

Still, Docal said, a small number of teachers were resistant to collaborative and outcomes-oriented work, and they spoke out about feeling micromanaged and distrusted. Docal used every opportunity to explain the rationale for the work and pointed to positive results as they started to emerge. She also rolled out her expectations slowly. She added "contribution to school community in collaboration" to the school's teacher ratings system. At first, teachers could earn an "effective" rating just for showing up to a meeting. "This built confidence and allowed for experimentation and vulnerability without pressure of some measure or perfection," she said. To then get "highly effective," teachers could show evidence of outcomes or having led professional development sessions. Over time, she said, most of the teachers came to enjoy the work and found they were learning from one another.

For Docal, developing trusting relationships is not limited to school staff. She also develops relationships with people in the district office and with law firms and community organizations. The school holds tours every Tuesday for anyone interested in seeing the school. She notes that "leveraging partnerships is critical, especially if you have a tight budget. We make sure that the partners are value-added, that we're value-added to them, and they're value-added to us, and the missions and the messages stay the same." Students also have responsibility in this work, meeting with city council members to advocate for the school's needs.

Docal's strong communication skills have greatly benefited the school. These partners have donated food, provided mental health services, and helped the school secure garden space and remodel playgrounds. In the six years Docal has led Powell, the student population has nearly tripled, creating a need for more space. "By having such an open space and inviting and welcoming everyone in, Powell went up on the needs list," she said. That openness allowed the school to begin to modernize and expand. "A leader needs to leverage partners, have clear communication with central office, and be very inviting and welcoming and hope that that will also spread your message of what you need," she said.

LEVER 4: ADAPTIVE LEADERSHIP

While the TLF is all about changing certain practices at your school to improve student learning, we recognize that this work is not easy and can be daunting for you and your staff. The key question is, How can you make changes that get at the heart of the challenges you face, while minimizing the anxiety that change can cause you, your staff, and your entire school community? And how can you lead your staff and community through changes required by others, such as those from district or state policy? We have found that before launching big changes in practice, a critical first step is building organizational and relational trust, work that falls under the interpersonal leadership lever. You can then go on to reinforce those efforts through adaptive leadership by building on your school's strengths, managing the emotions that come with change, and being willing to step aside and let others lead for the sake of strengthening the school.

Our research found that strong principals enact the following key practices of adaptive leadership:

- Identify root causes and adaptive challenges that need to be resolved.

- Take risks to challenge existing school and district/charter management organization practices, policies, and traditions, including those that you have created, that do not have a positive impact on student achievement.

- Identify and build on the existing school and community strengths that have a positive impact on student achievement.

- Establish and maintain a sustainable level of urgency and ongoing learning needed to tackle adaptive challenges.

- Recognize and manage the emotions of change, including resistance, fear, and loss.

- Be a courageous follower when other leaders in your school step forward.

Identifying Challenges and Their Root Causes

As we discuss in detail in chapters 1 and 2, one of the most important parts of a school leader's job is diagnosing the state of her school. That diagnosis involves recognizing problems when and where they arise, identifying the root cause of the problems, and figuring out the most effective and efficient way to address them. Once you've identified a problem, you can also assess its complexity: Is it a straightforward challenge that you and other experts on your staff can solve fairly quickly with your current skill set or the support of technical experts, such as creating a system for collecting data on student achievement or behavioral incidents? Or is it a more complex problem, such as improving reading proficiency for struggling readers, that will require experimentation and ongoing learning by you and a range of stakeholders in your building? Overcoming a challenge like this requires staff to change practices, and sometimes beliefs, and to work together to identify, test out, and learn from new approaches. Leadership expert Ronald Heifetz of Harvard University calls these challenges technical and adaptive, respectively.[11]

Too often leaders overly rely on making technical fixes and avoid tackling adaptive challenges that may require major shifts in practice and perspective. If changes do not get at the root of a problem, the improvements likely will not last long. For example, buying a new literacy intervention program will do little to raise reading scores long term if you haven't done a thorough diagnosis of other school practices to determine what other actions are missing that might help improve students' reading skills.

To make long-term improvements at your school, you have to treat adaptive challenges as the complex problems that they are. The work of addressing such complex challenges should not rest squarely on a principal's shoulders. As Heifetz and his colleagues at Harvard University have aptly written, "An organization that depends solely on its senior managers to deal with the challenges risks failure."[12] When staff members help identify the root causes of a problem and determine the appropriate steps to address it, they are not only more likely to embrace the changes, but also more likely to generate better and different solutions than any one individual. A leader with strong adaptive leadership skills views challenges as an opportunity to mobilize staff to improve the school as a team.

Managing Change

Once you have identified a complex problem at your school, how can you manage the emotions involved in making change? Even if the intentions of those driving the change (school leaders or district/state leaders) are good and the changes will likely improve the school, they might be uncomfortable for affected staff. Such changes might require veteran teachers to rethink how they have been teaching math for years or create new responsibilities or expectations for teachers around how they support struggling students. Changes can require altering values, beliefs, assumptions, and habits of behavior. Teachers will want to know why the change is needed, how they will be affected, what new or additional work will be required, and how the effect of the change will be assessed. As Ken Blanchard has noted in his research on managing change, people go through several steps as they react to changes.[13] We have seen principals more effectively alter practices at their schools by being aware of the feelings their staff are experiencing as they wrestle with the changes and supporting them as they implement the work.

As the school leader, you are in a strong position to address and manage the anxiety and anger that deep change often prompts. You can do this by creating an environment in which people feel comfortable raising concerns, taking their concerns seriously, and addressing the concerns directly.

We have also seen effective leaders minimize concern and resistance and maximize success by making staff an integral part of the change process from the beginning.

Consider how you can mobilize your staff by being transparent about what the changes will mean for the individuals in your school and the school as a whole. It is likely your staff will want to know what they will lose when particular changes are made. If you work to understand these real or perceived losses, you can develop pacing strategies to help staff deal with the change without feeling overwhelmed. An overwhelmed teacher might opt to continue business as usual, undermining the changes you are trying to make.

Your staff will need support to be able to make the changes you expect of them, and to make them well. Principals with strong adaptive leadership skills show their staff empathy and regularly take the temperature of their teachers to see how they are handling the work. And they do not make the change process personal by focusing on individuals; they maintain focus on issues.[14] Undoubtedly, there will be confusion, disagreements, and hard conversations. If you show your staff that you understand their concerns and questions and that you want to work with them to implement solutions that will work for staff and students alike, the change process is more likely to be successful.

 TAKING A RISK ON A NEW TEACHING MODEL TO IMPROVE INSTRUCTION

Ranson IB Middle School, Charlotte, North Carolina

As a first-year principal, Alison Harris walked into a challenging situation at Ranson. Only half the students had met expected growth the previous year, and only 21 percent were performing at or above grade level in math and 25 percent in reading. On top of that, with just a month until school was starting, she needed to hire twenty-eight teachers.

"When I was asked to take the position, my boss asked if I could do structure and order," she recalled. "So that was what I did. With over a thousand students, any day could feel like an amusement park until there were clear expectations."

She called that first year "a whirlwind." In addition to managing students, she realized the adult culture needed just as much attention. She first had to address her staff's belief of what made for good teaching. "There was a sentiment that you were a good teacher if kids were quiet and sitting in class," she said of what she identified as one of the root causes of the academic struggles at Ranson. "I really had to help staff understand that that is not the definition of a good teacher. Great teaching is determined by what kids learn."

She recognized later that she made a lot of mistakes, particularly around the teachers she hired. Some teachers, including those on the instructional leadership team, did not support the changes she was trying to make: "They did not believe in what I believed in—that we had to have high expectations for all of our scholars and that adults were responsible for modeling that belief."

Having diagnosed these significant issues around staff mind-sets and the lack of shared agreement on what good teaching looked like, Harris knew she had to take some risks. She would have to help her staff experiment with new ideas and approaches if she was going to lead the school to improve. Staff members would have to change not only how they planned and delivered instruction, but also some of their core approaches to students and learning. She knew from her own hiring experience how hard it was to find high-quality instructors. At the same time, Harris heard data that resonated with her: only the top 25 percent of teachers nationwide produce the dramatic learning gains needed to close achievement gaps.

As a historically low-performing school on the west side of Charlotte, Ranson became part of Project L.I.F.T., a public-private partnership focused on improving the city's schools. The partnership gave participating schools the opportunity to implement an innovative instructional approach intended to extend the reach of high-impact teachers by expanding their roles as coaches throughout the building and increasing the number of students they teach in a day, all for additional compensation. Called Public Impact's Opportunity Culture initiative, the program introduced a variety of teaching models very different from the traditional classroom structure. One of the models had teachers identified as highly effective divide their time among teaching small groups of students, coteaching in classrooms, coaching, and reviewing data and planning with other teachers.

Among other things, Harris hoped Opportunity Culture would help strengthen the professional learning community at the school. When she arrived at Ranson, grade-level and content-specific teacher teams typically met only once a week, and there was rarely any follow-up collaboration between meetings. There was no system in place to ensure that teachers who needed support were benefiting from the skills of the school's stronger teachers. Opportunity Culture could change that.

Implementing this new teaching model was not without its challenges. It presented a range of technical challenges related to school schedule, classroom assignments, technology, and budgeting. Harris also had to address the adaptive challenges of changing long-held practices and deeply held assumptions. She knew that for this new structure to succeed in elevating the quality of instruction across classrooms, teachers needed to change their perception of their own work and that of their colleagues. Because some teachers would be given more leadership responsibility within classrooms, all teachers needed to develop trust and respect for one another. Harris also knew she would have to work closely with the new teacher leaders to consistently model and reinforce higher expectations for student learning and student capacity to persist and overcome challenges. The new teacher leaders had to learn how to lead other adults.

To manage the process and emotions of change, Harris started planning with her staff one year before the program was slated to officially start. "We asked the staff, 'What if you could expand your reach and move up the career ladder?' That provided a lot of energy and discussion." Harris made her staff an integral part of the change process. A planning committee of Ranson teachers and administrators discussed the different program models offered through Opportunity Culture to determine which best fit their school's needs and their goal of having excellent teachers reach at least 80 percent of students by the third year of the program. They looked for the root causes of low reading achievement at the school by analyzing detailed data about student performance and teacher effectiveness. The committee chose models that they hoped would take advantage of and expand on Ranson's existing pool of great teachers and use technology that was already available at the school. They decided to designate multiclassroom leaders who, in exchange for higher compensation, would lead a team of teachers, conduct small group instruction, and take accountability for their students' outcomes. In addition, they used technology in a way that addressed the learning needs of all students.

Harris led an unfunded pilot year to test out the program, appointing one of the school's strong teachers, a math coach, to try out new ideas around the use of technology in the classroom, observations, and feedback. The next year, that same math coach became the school's first multiclassroom leader. He led small-group instruction and oversaw four teachers, two paraprofessionals, a special education instructor, and two blended learning teachers. He was accountable for outcomes of the seven hundred students in those teachers' classes.

While that first year proved to stretch the capacity of the multiclassroom leader, Harris noted, "The instructional dynamic of our school was forever changed. We had proof that we could take excellent teachers and elevate them to roles where they could coach other teachers and provide small group instruction, coteach, and provide training. They are compensated. They own all of the data that they work with."

By the end of the first few months in the pilot, teachers for the most part were enthusiastic about making the changes more permanent. They wanted the ongoing, intensive support they would get from the expert teachers. Some of the more experienced teachers, however, expressed some concern that they would lose ownership over their classrooms. To address this concern, Harris and her expert teachers assured the rest of the staff that they were there to support their work but that all teachers would continue to take responsibility and ownership for improving instruction through their work in teacher teams.

After that first year of implementation, Harris expanded the model from one multiclassroom leader just for seventh-grade math to seven leaders covering every tested subject. Through this model, Harris said, her staff got stronger, teacher attendance increased, and teachers seemed more committed to the school. Student suspensions also fell, and student attendance and academic performance improved. In Harris's fourth year at the school, Ranson landed in the top ten for the district's average growth index.

By effectively managing the rollout of Opportunity Culture and taking a huge risk, she said, the culture of teaching and learning changed at Ranson. "We did not have a lot of push-back on the coaching piece," she said. "People were hungry for feedback. It became something people felt was good for [them] and good for our kids."

Principal's Tool 7.4: Identifying Adaptive Challenges

LEVER 5: RESILIENT LEADERSHIP

As Jim Collins explains in *Good to Great*, an effective leader confronts the "brutal facts" head-on while maintaining the confidence to take action.[15] The personal leadership actions related to resilient leadership reinforce this crucial balance. They call on leaders to seek out feedback, to reflect on where they and their schools need to improve, and to recognize where reality is falling short of their vision. But more important, they describe leaders who never give up on reaching that vision, and never stop believing that they themselves, their teachers, and their students can figure out how to succeed even when faced with tough challenges. These actions include the following:

- Demonstrate personal resolve and maintain core confidence and belief in self and the school even in the face of adversity.

- Continuously reflect on performance, seek feedback, and actively pursue opportunities to improve personal leadership and the school.

- Take initiative and remain solutions oriented at all times to move the work of the school forward.

- Build professional and personal supports, including adequate personal time, necessary for sustaining school leadership over time.

A resilient principal needs to feel comfortable honestly reflecting on his own work and being open to questions and challenges from his staff. We recommend that you regularly seek out feedback from your staff and peers. One principal in Brooklyn exemplifies this kind of resilient leadership in which he takes seriously the concerns his teachers raise.

David O'Hara, principal of Expeditionary Learning School for Community Leaders, whom we met in chapter 3, recognized that he had recently failed to communicate his expectations of a teacher in a timely manner. He has high expectations of everyone, he said, but in this case, he was not clear enough. He heard from other teachers that this instructor felt she had been reprimanded unfairly, that O'Hara had not made his expectations clear. So O'Hara approached her and suggested that to facilitate a thorough discussion of O'Hara's actions and the situation, they do what the staff does for its students: hold a restorative circle in which O'Hara, the teacher, and a few other instructors chosen by that teacher would discuss the incident and come up with ways to prevent incidents like this in the future.

O'Hara never shies away from analyzing his own work: "I think there could be better check points for myself to communicate to people earlier and often about how people can improve." As for the circle, he said it would not only facilitate communication between himself and the teacher. "I will be vulnerable as well," which he hoped would model for teachers how to turn the vulnerability of making a mistake into a learning opportunity.

O'Hara also has managed to stay focused on long-term success and remain solutions oriented even when faced with substantial challenges. During his first year at the school, the district rated the school a low D on its progress report, just two points away from failing and being considered for closure. Only 38 percent of seniors were on schedule to graduate that year. "To stand in front of the entire staff, half of whom were new, and say we are going to get through this and make some really awesome things happen at our school was tough to do," he said. When breaking the news, O'Hara was sure to recognize teachers for the great work they had already done, noting that students had made some improvement in proficiency. "I said, 'Let's continue the journey, we are making great progress. . . . We are not quite there, but we are on our way.'" Congratulating staff for their accomplishments made a big difference, he said. All of the teachers returned the next year. And four years later, the school received the highest grade from the district, an A.

Resiliency also means creating conditions that make your own job sustainable. Because the principalship is not an easy job, it is critical that you put systems in place to make it possible for you to stay in the job. Half of principals nationally leave their jobs within three years, and those numbers are higher in high-need schools.[16] There is no question that school leader turnover hurts our kids.[17] Strong leaders need strong teams to carry the work forward. Research has found that principals need mentors for at least their first two years on the job, if not more.[18] Mentors from outside the school can be particularly helpful for their impartial guidance. While securing a coach or mentor typically takes some investment, they have been found to be particularly effective when they are carefully matched to meet the principal's own growth needs and leadership style and are an integral part of a leader's work in the school.[19] After the KIPP charter school network significantly increased its investment in principal development, principal retention rose by 41 percent.[20] Some schools have also found it effective to support work-life balance by having principals share their personal goals with mentors and supervisors, whether they aim to go to yoga twice a week or cook a healthy meal for their families.[21]

> Principal's Tool 7.5: Reflection Questions on Resilient Leadership

> Principal's Tool 7.6: Personal Leadership Self-Assessment

NEXT STEPS

We hope this chapter has shown you what key personal leadership skills and actions look like in practice and how they can influence all the work you do at your school across all categories of the TLF. With the guides we have given you—the stories of principals putting these leadership actions to work, and the personal leadership tool we offer in the Principal's Tool Kit in the appendix—we hope you now feel equipped to reflect deeply on how you lead your school. Consider how you address change and how you inspire your staff to work toward the urgent mission of giving all students a great education, even under the toughest of circumstances. This chapter is designed for you to use over and over again, both on your own and in consultation with your trusted advisors, mentors, and colleagues. The better you understand how others perceive your work and how your own background and biases influence your work, the more effectively you will be able to lead your school in helping students make sustained improvements in their learning.

 WATCH PERSONAL LEADERSHIP VIDEO: In this chapter's companion video, you'll learn about great work being done at schools across the country in the category of personal leadership. To access the video, go to www.wiley.com/go/newleaders.

 Principal's Tools for Personal Leadership

Principal's Tool 7.1: Reflection Questions on Belief-Based and Goal-Driven Leadership
Principal's Tool 7.2: Reflection Questions for Considering Your Own Biases, and Those of Your Staff, Related to Diversity at Your School
Principal's Tool 7.3: Reflection Questions on Interpersonal Leadership
Principal's Tool 7.4: Identifying Adaptive Challenges
Principal's Tool 7.5: Reflection Questions on Resilient Leadership
Principal's Tool 7.6: Personal Leadership Self-Assessment

PART THREE
A ROLE FOR PRINCIPAL
SUPERVISORS AND COACHES

Chapter Eight
Principal Coaching Using the TLF

Principal Coaching Using the TLF

IF YOU ARE NO LONGER IN THE PRINCIPAL ROLE BUT WORK EVERY DAY TO SUPPORT and develop principals, then you likely see their daily struggles, celebrate their successes, and are always seeking new ways to improve principal practice and school results in the limited time you have with each principal. Whether you serve as a principal supervisor, principal coach, or principal mentor, you may be wondering how best to use the Transformational Leadership Framework (TLF) and this book in your work with principals.

Although the TLF is not a framework for evaluating principals, it does provide strong guidance to you and your principals in identifying their higher-priority areas for focus. In all of our work with principals, especially early-tenure principals, we have found that one of the greatest challenges for them is narrowing their focus to a few priorities and maintaining that focus through the inevitable challenges, excitements, and distractions that come at them every day. In this chapter, we suggest some ways that you can use the TLF in your supervision or coaching work with principals as you help them narrow and maintain that crucial focus.

Principal coaches and supervisors play a critical role in the development of school leaders and in the successful and sustained transformation of schools. Many of the New Leaders alumni who have been promoted to supervise or coach principals entered their new roles with little direct guidance. Often for these newly minted principal supervisors, training consisted of a map of schools, a list of principals, and the charge to improve schools over the next school year. Although each of these alumni had been a successful principal, most of them initially felt underprepared to coach principals and support the needs of multiple schools. This chapter lays out how to use the TLF as a guide in this work. The TLF offers a road map to the entire terrain of a principal's work, and it can provide the information needed to decide where your leaders and their schools should devote time and energy. You can also use the TLF to build a common approach to school transformation within your district. Whether you are new to the principal supervisor role or continuing to grow in your expertise, the tools in this chapter can support your thinking and approach.

The chapter walks through a school year of principal support outlining essential activities including diagnosis, action planning, ongoing coaching, and evaluation. At the conclusion of the chapter, we also identify some ways that other members of the central office can use the TLF to support schools and principals.

BUILDING ALIGNMENT ACROSS THE DISTRICT

When districts have multiple principal supervisors, we have found it important to build common language and implement a consistent approach to coaching. To develop shared practices, we begin by exploring the TLF. Using case studies, we practice diagnosing schools to see what challenges and solutions are generated by the group. We also participate in shared learning walks at schools to collect data and discuss practices we observe. Once we share our observations, we match specific practices to the appropriate TLF stage. Over time this practice helps us to develop a shared understanding of the framework and a consistent approach to diagnosis. We have found that these calibration conversations strengthen the skills of the principal supervisors while helping to ensure that there is a shared vision of school improvement and priorities across networks of schools.

ALIGNMENT CHECK

- Do all of the principal supervisors in your district have a common definition for what effective learning and teaching look like in practice?

- Do all of the principal supervisors have a common definition for what is included in an effective culture?

- Do all of the principal supervisors have common approaches to talent management and coaching?

- Do all of the principal supervisors understand the ways in which operations affects student learning?

- When principal supervisors observe school actions together, do they consistently identify them in the same stage of development?

Principal Coaching Tool 8.1: Calibrating and Aligning Practice

Prior to the Start of the Year: Supporting an Effective School Diagnosis

In chapter 2, we walked through the school diagnostic process. In this chapter, we focus on how you can participate in the diagnosis to support your school leaders. Taking part in the school's diagnosis can help you develop a deep understanding of each school's context, strengths, and needs, which can make you a more effective coach. When you are familiar with the school's diagnosis and action plan, you will be able to focus on the key priorities in your coaching practice. In addition, by helping school leaders complete a diagnosis, you can ensure that the principal's goals begin with and align to the plan to improve the school. The questions you pose and the perspective you bring to the diagnosis can help push the thinking of principals, especially newer principals who may not have the pattern recognition for this kind of analysis. We have seen the diagnosis and action planning process be especially important for first-year principals—and therefore for the coaches and supervisors supporting them—as they enter a new school and read the quality of school actions.

As you work with all of your principals, you can also aggregate the diagnostic results across schools to identify trends in your caseload of schools. The trend data can help you plan supports for your leaders. You can also help inform the strategies that the district employs by bringing school-level needs to conversations about district strategies.

DIAGNOSTIC TREND REFLECTION QUESTIONS

- What are the best possible supports for schools given these shared needs?
- How can you organize principals into relevant communities of practice based on their particular priorities for improvement?

As a principal supervisor or coach, you play a unique role in connecting district-wide strategies to the specific school context needs and action plans. Your work with the principals can build alignment and coherence between school and district strategies and plans. And you will also have insight into the district initiatives that may not fit the school's current needs and support adjustments to how or when the district strategy is implemented.

As we noted already, the diagnostic and the TLF are not tools for evaluating principals; they are tools to help you support principals in diagnosing and action planning.

Most important, the TLF can help you and your principals maintain focus through the challenges and daily distractions on the few focus areas that will drive school improvement.

Questions to Ask Principals during Diagnosis

- What evidence have you used? What have been your sources? How many stakeholders have you included in your assessment of the school? How did you select which stakeholders to include in the diagnostic process?
- What is your rating of the school by stage in each key lever? What are the greatest strengths and the greatest areas for improvement?
- How do those actions relate to your areas for student outcome improvement? Where do you see natural connections? Where do you assume the lower-stage school actions are a root cause for any student outcome challenges?

Once the diagnosis has been completed, you can play a similar role in reviewing and testing the school's action plan.

Questions to Review the Action Plan

- Has the leader determined the right priorities?
- Does the plan have strategies that are detailed enough to help guide the leader's practice?
- Does the plan have strategies that are detailed enough to help guide teacher practice?
- Do the goals set at the beginning of the school year address the areas where student achievement has been weak?
- Is it clear how goals will be achieved? Does the plan have clear strategies associated with it?
- Is it clear how progress will be monitored?

Setting Principal Goals

Once leaders have established their priorities and developed action plans, they need to set their individual goals. These goals should demonstrate how the leader will support the implementation of their plan. As the principal supervisor, one of your roles will be to assess that alignment and make sure that progress to the goal can be assessed using your district's evaluation tool.

We have used evaluation tools to evaluate the principal on the quality and the impact of their actions over time. For example, in the New Leaders principal evaluation rubric, our standards are listed as:

- Shared Vision, School Culture, and Family Engagement
- Learning and Teaching
- Talent Management
- Strategic Planning and Systems
- Personal Leadership and Growth

The evaluation rubric describes each of these standards across levels of performance and is used as a summative assessment of practice. Although your district's principal evaluation standards may not align as closely with the TLF categories, there is likely to be a high level of conceptual overlap. As a principal supervisor, we recommend you begin your support by focusing on the needs of the schools.

By focusing on the principal's actions, you can create an ongoing cycle of reflection with your leaders to assess how their actions are supporting the goals and strategies they have set for the year. Since the TLF connects principal actions with specific content areas, we have used the TLF in conjunction with principal evaluation tools that assess the overall effectiveness of the leader's practice. For example, the TLF helps us to describe how leaders can affect culture and learning and teaching.

Planning Your Coaching Time

From the school's plan, you can create a school visit focus and structure that will allow you to observe and provide feedback on the school's priorities. On your visits, you can spend time beyond talking with the principal observing for these school actions and looking at direct evidence of progress against the milestones outlined by the principal. In the Principal Coaching section of the Tool Kit in the appendix, you will find some detailed recommendations for site visits and debriefing that can support your visits and coaching.

As you plan, it might also help to recognize the varying needs of your schools and leaders. For example, principals new to their role may need more frequent touch points than those with longer tenure. By planning for the school context, you can avoid one-size-fits-all policies.

You will also have to balance the priority areas with getting an overall sense of the school. When you are building your plan, think about reserving 20 percent of your time for reviewing nonpriority areas so that you have a complete picture of the school.

Targeted Visits and Walk-Throughs

As Paul Bambrick-Santoyo describes in *Leverage Leadership*, walk-throughs are most effective when they are targeted and focused.[1] The four walk-throughs in the Principal

Coaching section of the Tool Kit suggest the range of ways to use this strategy in coaching principals. Focusing on the purpose of the walk-through will help you determine which questions to incorporate into your visit. Each of the suggested walk-throughs follows a similar structure:

- Preparation outlines the work before the walk-through including:
  - Gathering specific and relevant data
  - Reflecting on guiding questions for analyzing the data
  - Answering questions to help organize the team prior to the visit
- Guidance for conducting the walk-through
- Debriefing following a walk-through including:
  - Visit-specific debriefing questions
  - Guiding questions for analyzing collected evidence
  - Reflection questions for individual members of the school visit team

Walk-through I will help you support your principal's work around identifying priorities, setting goals, monitoring movement toward goals, and making adjustments as needed. Walk-Through II will help you support principals in evaluating teachers' work in ways that will support their growth. In walk-through III, you will help the principal determine whether she is making the most effective use of her time and budget. And with the guide in walk-through IV, you can support the principal in considering the kind of culture the school has and identifying where it could be strengthened to better align with the school vision and values.

Principal Coaching Tool 8.2: Sample School Walk-Through I: Focus on Action Plan Implementation

Principal Coaching Tool 8.3: Sample School Walk-Through II: Focus on Teacher Coaching

Principal Coaching Tool 8.4: Sample School Walk-Through III: Focus on Operations

Principal Coaching Tool 8.5: Sample School Walk-Through IV: Focus on School Culture

---

Mid- and End-of-Year Reviews

While we encourage you to have regular conversations with your principals about goals and progress toward them, both the middle and the end of the school year are good times to reflect on goals and assess progress. Early in the school year, review with your principals the diagnostic you will use for their reviews. The questions in Tool 8.6 in the Principal Coaching section of the Tool Kit are particularly important to ask of principals who are new to the school because initial impressions can sometimes be inaccurate. Were the priorities they identified at the beginning of the year the right ones? Do the initial judgments they made still seem accurate in terms of the stages of school actions? Are there important factors that were not considered in the original diagnostic that need to be built into the action plan? Many principals do great planning early on but struggle to stick to those plans for a variety of reasons. You can support your principals in maintaining their focus and progress toward goals and adjusting them as needed.

Principal Coaching Tool 8.6: Mid- and End-of-Year Review and Preliminary Planning

Personal Leadership

As a principal coach, you can help make sure that your principals are thinking about their personal leadership approach as they work to improve student outcomes. Your focus on personal leadership is especially important if the personal leadership levers are not included in your evaluation rubric. You might make the assumption that you have hired principals who have strong skill sets in personal leadership, but your role allows you to observe how they are approaching and addressing leadership challenges. Are principals taking the actions identified in the personal leadership levers? If not, the lack of these actions can often hold back a principal from succeeding in improving school actions in the other sections of the TLF. Some of the deepest transformational coaching and improvement in leadership comes from helping principals with these actions in the personal leadership section

Tool 7.6 in the Principal's Tool Kit is a personal leadership self-assessment tool. This assessment will be most useful to principals if they have a thought partner to help them consider the leadership skills they have and lack and what they can do to develop them. As someone who is familiar with a principal's work and her school, you could be an ideal thought partner.

DISTRICT-LEVEL STRATEGIES

While the principal job can feel too big for one individual, we have found ways to sustain effective leaders in their roles. In *Great Principals at Scale*, we outlined some of the ways that central offices can support and sustain effective leaders.[2] These practices can help you to retain your strongest leaders in their roles longer.

One way that districts can support effective leadership is by creating a collaborative culture in which principals are asked to openly share their needs. To create this type of environment, the district has to demonstrate that the principals can affect district decisions and influence services provided to schools. Principal supervisors can help to frame school needs and ensure that the principal's perspective is considered when district strategies are being determined or revised. When districts are collaborative, they are able to be strategic about which practices are decided centrally and which are decided at the school level, and they set up structures that allow support of school-based structures and flexibility in district-level decisions.

Learning and Teaching

Districts can provide high-quality curricula, instructional materials, and assessments to free up more time for principals to work on implementation. Although there can be a lot of benefit to creating curriculum at the school level, designing curriculum is hard work and time-consuming and may prove to be distracting. When schools begin with a common curriculum, they can focus their teachers' time on individualizing the curriculum and materials to student needs using the district curriculum as a starting point. When a common curriculum exists, instructional materials are aligned from grade to grade and across schools. This creates continuity for students who might switch schools and also helps with the use of common assessments in the district.

As a principal supervisor, you can ensure that your principals are using and building on centrally provided resources and tools to move toward stage 2 and 3 practices. As a coach or supervisor you can support the use of district-created or -endorsed curriculum. You can help principals dig into district curriculum and resources with their staffs to ensure consistent implementation of the curriculum, as well as a shared definition of rigor. When necessary, you can also share gaps in the curriculum with the central team tasked with managing curriculum and help your principals identify supplemental content. You can help your schools use the district-created data and analysis tools to support corrective instruction practices that engage teachers, students, and families in the data process.

Districts can invest in data infrastructure to support schools to ensure that multiple data points are easy to access. For example, districts with data in one place facilitate the use of these data by school-based teams. Spreading data across multiple websites, platforms, or drives can create barriers to regular use and make it hard for school teams to see the types of connections between data points that pinpoint interventions (e.g., a student's attendance rate compared to performance on assessments).

Operations

When districts create high-quality strategic plans that set clear goals and strategies, organizational structures, staffing plans, and budgets, principals begin their diagnosis and planning on the school level with clarity. Districts that have not yet created a clear strategic plan to guide their work will find chapter 2 in this book to be helpful.

When it is possible, including principals in planning to build school-level perspective into the district-level plan can be helpful. Once plans are developed, it is also helpful to link the district goals to individual school goals. Many goals may lend themselves to translation at the school level; for example, if the district is focused on improving the graduation rate, even a school well below the district average graduation rate can have a positive impact on the district rate by improving its own graduation rate. However, not all goals always translate neatly from the district level to the school level. For these goals, districts can support implementation by helping schools understand their role in implementing the goal.

Talent Management

Performance management systems for principals and teachers can help to create consistent expectations across a district. "Principals can be more effective when districts implement holistic performance management systems that systematically develop, support, motivate and retain quality leadership talent."[3] Common systems can also support the calibration of principal supervisors discussed earlier in the chapter and send the message to principals that expectations are consistent across the district. We have also seen districts focus the work of all central office teams more explicitly by creating performance management systems that are focused on consistent service to schools, student outcomes, and effective leadership practices.

Districts can provide important support to school leaders by giving principals authority over staffing. When they have more autonomy over staffing, they are able to broaden their searches for effective teachers and distribute their leadership across the school. Human resource teams at the district level can support school teams by creating district-wide pipelines of effective teachers, teacher leaders, and other personnel.

By observing practices and providing ongoing feedback, coaches can help principals improve their leadership skills and support school improvements. As you match your coaching steps to the needs of each leader, ask yourself, "How is my work developing the capacity of the principal? How am I supporting the school's goals?" For some leaders, your work may require that you help them improve their feedback; others might need help delegating to members of their team and still others with maintaining high expectations. In your visits, you get brief snapshots of a principal's work over time, and each snapshot can then be woven together to create a tapestry of the leader and the school. Using that tapestry, your work can help leaders reflect on their practice to improve their impact.

 Principal's Tools for Principal Coaching Using the TLF

Principal's Tool 8.1: Calibrating and Aligning Practice
Principal's Tool 8.2: Sample School Walk-Through I: Focus on Action Plan Implementation
Principal's Tool 8.3: Sample School Walk-Through II: Focus on Teacher Coaching
Principal's Tool 8.4: Sample School Walk-Through III: Focus on Operations
Principal's Tool 8.5: Sample School Walk-Through IV: Focus on School Culture
Principal's Tool 8.6: Mid- and End-of-Year Review and Preliminary Planning

CONCLUSION

AFTER SIX YEARS OF HARD WORK WITH HER STAFF TO SUCCESSFULLY TRANSFORM
Powell Elementary in Washington, DC, from a failing school to a thriving one, Janeece
Docal left the school to live closer to family in Spain. Her departure inspired an article in the local newspaper noting her many accomplishments at Powell.[1] In the article,
an instructional coach credited her with building systems and programs that allowed
teachers to work collaboratively, and the PTA vice president praised her for creating
a school that was not only excellent academically but also a vibrant and welcoming
community. In her introductory letter to parents, Powell's new principal O'Kiyyah
Lyons-Lucas (also New Leaders–trained) declared that she was honored to follow in
Docal's footsteps: "She is an amazing leader, which is evident in the numerous programs and strong culture among staff, students, parents, and community members."

If after reading Docal's story, you concluded, "Docal is an extraordinary person; I can't
do all that," think again. The accomplishments of the principals featured in this book
did not result from *who* they are. Being a transformational leader is not about creating a cult of personality. Rather, their success derives from *what* they did, the central
lesson of this book. The Transformational Leadership Framework (TLF) gives you a
system for enacting practices that allow everyone around you to excel, take ownership
for the school vision and mission, and participate in creating a school that prepares all
students for success in college, careers, and life.

If you reread the stories in this book, you will notice certain patterns. Principals who
follow the framework lead with openness and humility; they look to a range of data,
from assessment results to classroom observations, for guidance on where and how
to make changes; they build a team of colleagues who do this work together, regularly
reflecting on their own efforts and those of their colleagues and adjusting practices as
needed. They establish an ambitious long-term vision for their schools and achieve it
through incremental goals that are manageable and attainable. And they celebrate each
accomplishment along the way, building confidence in staff, students, and families to
tackle the next stage of the work.

Since you are reading this book, you are clearly committed to improving your
school. You recognize that you do not have all the answers and are open to trying a

different approach. This is a strong indication that you have what it takes to transform your school.

If you're unsure where to begin, go back to the introduction for guidance. It's easy to feel overwhelmed when you consider all the school improvement strategies you might adopt, but Docal approached this work as a step-by-step process, and you can too. The data you need to set priorities and begin taking action are all around you: assessment results, discussions between teachers and students during class, lesson plans, team meetings, conversations with parents, classroom material, and student work samples.

As you dig into this effort, it is essential to remember that you cannot do this work on your own. By definition, great leaders bring out the best in their teams. You almost certainly have teachers who want the best for your students, just as you do. They are ready to join you in this challenging, vital work; they simply need a seat at the table and your help identifying the most important areas for focus. Together you will make mistakes, learn from them, and ultimately turn those lessons into success for you, your students, and your broader community. And as you begin applying the TLF, you will quickly begin to see improvements in your students' learning, reinforcing your community's optimism as you continuously prove what's possible when this work is approached strategically and with high expectations for adults and students alike.

You can take heart in the fact that you are joining a movement of schools doing similar work: New Leader principals across the country have achieved inspiring results while using the TLF, and with the publication of this book, many more schools will benefit from the lessons of these great leaders. Consider passing a copy along to a colleague in your district. As more schools in your district use the TLF, your district as a whole will improve, creating new opportunities for you to collaborate, learn from one another, and build a network of schools where great teachers love to work and students get everything they need to excel in school and in life.

The Principal's Tool Kit

CHAPTER 2: DIAGNOSIS AND ACTION PLANNING

TOOL 2.1 POSSIBLE DATA SOURCES FOR YOUR SCHOOL DIAGNOSIS

School Culture	Learning and Teaching	Talent Management	Operations
• Discipline data	• Lesson plans	• Teacher evaluations	• Master schedules
• Attendance data	• Student work	• Feedback on lesson plans	• School priorities
• Tardiness data	• Teacher-created assessments	• Teacher retention rates	• Short- and long-term milestones and goals
• Behavioral expectations	• Data analysis protocol	• Teacher roster	• Community partnerships
• Safety and emergency plans	• Teacher team meeting protocol	• Teacher feedback	• Budget
• Schedule of parent activities	• Grading systems	• Instructional leadership team feedback	• Annual calendar
• School newsletter	• Assessment rubrics		• Professional development calendar
• Core vision and mission			

(continued)

School Culture	Learning and Teaching	Talent Management	Operations
• Student surveys • Student groups • Posters and newsletters • School and grade-level goals • College visits, community partnerships, job shadowing, internship opportunities, field trips, career day • Family college and career awareness programming, career programs • Student goal sheet • Assemblies and recognition programs, community service programs, teacher observation and walk-throughs data, student recognition for effort	• Daily/weekly intervention schedules create adequate time • Assessment calendar • Grade and content curriculum guide • Course descriptions include literacy expectations • Courses are well supported with a variety of teaching texts • Daily/weekly schedule reflects times for teachers to meet and discuss the successes and challenges of literacy strategy implementation • Response to intervention data and meeting minutes	• Classroom observations, observation records, teacher goal-setting worksheets and written feedback • Schedule of teacher observation and feedback meetings, written teacher evaluations, and teacher goal-setting worksheets • Team meeting minutes • Staff development plans and improvement plans for underperforming staff • School retention data, new staff supports, staff climate survey, and exit interview data	• Attendance systems • School building maintenance • Status of basic facilities (bathrooms, windows, sinks, locks are in working order)

CHAPTER 3: LEARNING AND TEACHING

Lever 1: Aligned Curriculum

TOOL 3.1 REFLECTION QUESTIONS FOR OBSERVING AND ASSESSING THE RIGOR OF INSTRUCTION

Question Type

- What kinds of questions is the teacher asking? Capture the teacher's wording by scripting notes as you observe.
- Once questions are captured, use Hess's rigor matrix as a guide to assess the level of complexity. Are the majority of questions asking students to recall or recite facts? Is there one correct answer?

Lesson Design

- Are teachers creating opportunities for students to make real-world applications of skills and standards?
- Are lessons designed so students are given differentiated supports or until the student is able to demonstrate learning independently?
- Are students expected to apply new concepts in several different contexts and to innovate?
- Are lessons designed to ensure that the students have many opportunities to defend their arguments by citing evidence from the text and making comparisons and connections across text content and real-life experiences?
- Is student dialogue an expected part of lessons? Are students expected to collaborate with one another? Are students asked to give one another feedback?

Formative Assessments

- Are teachers checking for student understanding in a way that requires students to think critically and defend their answers in writing or orally?
- How are assessments developed?
- Are assessments aligned to the standards taught?

Demonstration of Knowledge

- Does the learning activity connect to skills described in the standards? How do you know? How could the teacher assess student growth following this activity?
- Will the learning activity increase students' skill level? How do you know? How could the teacher assess student growth following this activity?

- Will completing the activity help students to master a skill or concept?
- Does the learning activity increase the students' conceptual knowledge? For example, in a math lesson does the activity give students an opportunity to demonstrate not just proficiency using a formula but a clear understanding about why the formula is being used?
  - How will (or how did) the teacher assess baseline conceptual knowledge of the skill being taught?
  - If students currently lack a conceptual framework on which to build how will the teacher scaffold the lesson?
  - How do you know if conceptual knowledge is growing? How will progress be measured?
- Are students challenged to process and synthesize new information and prior knowledge to solve problems?
- How are students asked to demonstrate their knowledge?
- How could the teacher assess student growth following the activity?

TOOL 3.2 SAMPLE UNIT PLAN FOR FOURTH-GRADE ELA

EL Education
Focus: Sharing Opinions
Title: The Most Helpful Simple Machine
In this unit, students will use their research on simple machines to form an opinion and write an editorial. This editorial will state the student's opinion on which simple machine he or she believes helps people the most. Students will read and analyze two editorials as mentor texts in order to study author's craft, specifically how to identify opinions in writing and how authors use reasons with evidence to support their opinions. Students will then plan for their editorials by revisiting their notes in their Simple Machine science journals and the central text, *Simple Machines: Forces in Action*, by Buffy Silverman, to develop reasons for their opinions and gather evidence to support these reasons. Students will then draft their editorials and revise their work based on a series of lessons in which students examine the characteristics of opinion writing.

- How do simple machines affect our lives?
- How do readers and writers form and support opinions?

Simple machines affect force, effort, and work.

Assessments

Reading and Answering Questions about Editorials This assessment centers on standards NYSP12 ELA CCLS RI.4.8 and RI.4.4. Learning targets are: "I can explain how an author uses reasons and evidence to support particular points in a text," and, "I can determine the meaning of academic words or phrases in an informational text." Students will read and answer questions about an opinion piece—an editorial—with a particular focus on author's craft. They will then answer text-dependent multiple choice and short answer questions.

Part I, Planning and Drafting an Editorial, and Part II, Revising to Create a Polished Editorial This two-part assessment centers on standard NYSP12 ELA CCLS W.4.1: "I can write an opinion piece that supports a point of view with reasons and information." In this on-demand assessment, students will select another simple machine (different from that on their performance task) to write an editorial about why this new simple machine could be the most helpful in daily life. In part I, students will select their new simple machine and plan for their writing by rereading the text, *Simple Machines: Forces in Action*, by Buffy Silverman, and revisiting notes in their Simple Machines science journals to develop reasons for their opinion and gather evidence to support these reasons. Then they will complete a draft of their editorial. In part II, students will revise to create a polished editorial based on the Simple Machine Editorial rubric created in this module.

This module is designed to address English language arts standards. However, the module intentionally incorporates science content that many teachers may be teaching during other parts of the day. These intentional connections are described below.

NYS Science Core Curriculum

- Science Learning Standard 4: The Physical Setting
  - Students will understand and apply scientific concepts, principles, and theories pertaining to the physical setting and living environment and recognize the historical development of ideas in science.
- Key Idea 5: Energy and matter interact through forces that result in changes in motion.

Readings

1. Buffy Silverman, *Simple Machines: Forces in Action* (New York: Heinemann, 2009).
2. EL Education, "No More Junk in Our Schools," written for instructional purposes.
3. EL Education, "Who Cares about Polar Bears?" written for instructional purposes.

This unit is approximately 3 to 4 weeks, or 17 to 19 sessions of instruction. Here we give a few sample lessons.

	Lesson Title	Skill/I Can Statements Directly Related to ELA Standards	Skill/I Can Statements Beyond the Standards	Assessments	Materials
Lesson 1	Reading Editorials, Part I: Determining Authors' Opinions	• I can write an editorial stating my opinion about which simple machine benefits people the most in their everyday lives. (W.4.1) • I can explain how an author uses reasons and evidence to support particular points in a text. (RI.4.8)	• I can determine an author's opinion in a text. • I can write a gist statement about an editorial. • I can form an opinion about simple machines for my editorial.	• Exploring Opinions as Readers and Writers anchor chart	• Exploring Opinions as Readers and Writers anchor chart • Simple Machines Chalk Talk charts • Chalk Talk protocol
Lesson 4	Mid-Unit Assessment: Reading and Answering Questions about Editorials	• I can determine the meaning of academic words or phrases in an informational text. (RI.4.4) • I can explain how an author uses reasons and evidence to support particular points in a text. (RI.4.8)	• I can explain how an author uses reasons and evidence to support an opinion.	• Mid-Unit 3 Assessment: Reading and Answering Questions about Editorials • Tracking My Progress, Mid-Unit recording form	• Concentric Circles

| Lesson 9 | Revising for Word Choice: Scientifically Accurate Vocabulary | • I can express ideas using carefully chosen words. (L.4.3)
• I can write an opinion piece that supports a point of view with reasons and information. (W.4.1)
• I can use the writing process to produce clear and coherent writing (with support). (W.4.5) | • I can use vocabulary from my research on simple machines to write scientifically accurate descriptions in my editorial. | • List of key vocabulary words
• Revised draft
• Exit ticket | • Simple Machines Editorial rubric chart |
| Lesson 16 | End of Unit Assessment Part II: Revising to Create a Polished Editorial and Author's Chair Celebration | • I can write an opinion piece that supports a point of view with reasons and information. (W.4.1)
• I can produce writing that is appropriate to task, purpose, and audience. (W.4.4)
• I can effectively engage in discussions with diverse partners about fourth-grade topics and texts. (SL.4.1) | • I can write an editorial stating my opinion on which simple machine benefits people the most in their everyday lives.
• I can plan, draft, and revise an editorial in the course of two lessons.
• I can listen as my peers share their writing and give specific praise for their work. | • End of Unit Assessment Part II: Revising to Create a Polished Editorial
Tracking My Progress, End of Unit recording form | • Author's Chair Celebration |

TOOL 3.3 REFLECTION QUESTIONS FOR ALIGNED CURRICULUM

- How well do your teachers know the standards? How do you know?
- Are your teachers able to distill the skills embedded within each standard? How do you know?
- How familiar are the teachers with the curriculum? How do you know?
- How close is the alignment between unit plans and lesson plans?
- How do teachers use the standards in planning units? Do teacher team planning sessions begin with a discussion of a specific standard that will be taught? If not, why not? Do completed unit plans align to the standards? Do units consistently connect to specific standards? How do you know?
- How well do your teachers know the scope and sequence? How do you know?
- Do observed lessons clearly connect to specific standards?
- When lessons are not connected to specific standards what do you do?
- If you find teachers are not planning lessons grounded in the standards, how are teachers determining appropriate learning targets? Why aren't they using the standards?

TOOL 3.4 DIAGNOSTIC TOOL FOR LEVER 1, ALIGNED CURRICULUM

Focus Areas	Stage 0	Stage 1	Stage 2	Stage 3	Score
Planning aligned to rigorous standards	• Less than 25% of teachers have unit plans that they follow. • Daily lesson plans lack alignment to standards.	• 40% of teachers have unit plans that link standards, assessments, and materials.	• 75% of teachers have unit plans that link standards, assessments, and materials.	• 100% of teachers have unit plans that link standards, assessments, and materials.	• Stage 0 • Evidence of Stage 1 practices • Evidence of Stage 2 practices

Focus Areas	Stage 0	Stage 1	Stage 2	Stage 3	Score
	• Some teachers have no evidence of daily lesson planning based on standards.	• Unit plans show a progression of objectives but are sometimes disconnected from current data and lack clear assessments of objectives. • A majority of daily lesson plans have mastery objectives, but assessment and differentiation efforts are often poor or not well linked to objectives.	• There is a clear link between standards, assessments, and materials in all unit plans; alignment with college-ready standards is apparent. • Unit plans show a clear progression of objectives over time, are linked with student data, and have assessments matching the level of expected rigor. • Daily planning always includes mastery objectives, differentiation, and assessment.	• Unit plans are clearly aimed at students meeting standards in alignment with the rigor level of college-ready standards. • All planning documents have strong evidence of differentiation based on recent student data. • A system for checking, supporting, and critiquing planning is implemented by teacher leaders throughout the school.	• Evidence of Stage 3 practices

Lever 2: Classroom Practices and Instruction

TOOL 3.5 QUESTIONS TO CONSIDER WHEN ESTABLISHING COMMON ROUTINES

1. How do students enter the classroom?

2. What are students expected to do when entering the classroom?

3. How is attendance taken?

4. What happens when a student arrives late?

5. How are school- or class-related announcements made?

6. What is the procedure for students to ask questions? What is the process for students to get clarification? What is the procedure for students to ask for help?

7. How do students get supplies? What happens when a student is missing a necessary supply, tool, or book?

8. What are the procedures for groups? Do students have specific roles in groups? If so, how do they know their roles?

9. How do students submit completed homework?

10. How do students submit completed class work?

11. If there are multiple centers, how do students move from center to center? How is the length of each center determined?

12. What are the cleanup or wrap-up procedures at the end of the class period?

13. How do students know what work, if any, is expected between classes?

14. How do students leave the classroom? What is the dismissal procedure?

15. How do students move through hallways?

TOOL 3.6 ACTIVITY: IDENTIFYING COMMON ROUTINES

Outcomes

By the end of the session we will:

- Share classroom routines and procedures that we currently use in our classrooms
- Explore what makes an effective classroom routine or procedure
- Identify three to five common routines and procedures we agree to implement in our classrooms

Note: *If your staff is large you may want to do this activity in smaller groups rather than have the entire staff together. If you are bringing multiple groups together you can use your instructional leadership team to determine the three to five routines you will be monitoring.*
Around the room, label chart papers with the following headings:

- Classroom entry
- Attendance
- Student questions
- Supplies

- Centers
- Classroom dismissal
- Blank sheet (ask participants to add a category or add a routine that your school has previously identified as an area that needs to improve)

Ask participants to briefly write on sticky notes the current routine or procedure in their classrooms for each category listed on the chart paper. Ask the participants to star any routines that work well in their classrooms.

Once everyone has added a sticky to each chart have the group divide so that there are three to four people assigned to each topic and chart (feel free to add or modify categories depending on the size and needs of your team).

Divide the group into small groups and assign them to one of the charts. Tell them that they will be working on that chart to review and synthesize the sticky notes attached to the chart. Prior to their review of each chart, ask each group to answer the following:

- How would you define *effectiveness* for this category? For example, how would you know that you had an effective dismissal routine?
- What would you be able to observe in a classroom where this practice or routine is effective? What would an effective procedure look like?

Have each group share out its definition of effectiveness. *Note: You may want to provide an exemplar to support participants that fits your school.* Allow other groups to ask clarifications or to offer suggestions to tighten the definitions.

As groups share, identify common ideas. Some ideas might include:

- "You would see it all the time."
- "The procedure would happen quickly so that time was focused on instruction."
- "Students would know what they were expected to do."

Once each group has shared, ask each small group to return to their category. Ask each category group to identify a beginning set of criteria to assess the effectiveness of a procedure and ask them to apply those criteria to the sticky notes that are on their chart paper. Specifically ask them to identify:

- Similarities and differences between the routines and procedures
- Themes that emerge from the stickies

Once each group has pulled out commonalities and differences, have the group synthesize the current routines into two or three recommended routines that would meet the effectiveness criteria for that category.

Once each small group has refined the procedures for each category ask each member of the group to vote with dot stickers on the routine that they think should be implemented schoolwide. (Participants should have at least enough dots that they are able to vote for one procedure in every category, but if you choose you can give them the freedom to vote for more than one procedure within a category and/or to vote more than once for a procedure they really like. You may find that if one category, e.g. dismissal, has been chaotic that chart may get more attention than a category where the procedures are seen to be moving smoothly.)

Once everyone has voted, share out the routines that received the most votes. Ask participants if they need any clarification on the procedure, if there are any that they cannot live with, and if there is anything they will need to implement the procedure effectively.

Ask for a few volunteers to offer ideas for how they will share the agreed change in routine or procedure with their students.

TOOL 3.7 STAGE 2 INSTRUCTIONAL STRATEGIES PRACTICE ACTIVITY

Part I

- Pair your teachers. Then give them a common list of outcomes and identify what strategies they would select to teach that outcome.
- Have each pair explain why they selected a specific strategy. Next have the group use the following instructional strategy assessment protocol questions to assess if that strategy will help to students to meet the outcome and ultimately the standard.

The goal of this protocol is for teachers to review a chosen instructional strategy:

- If you used this strategy, what would you [the teacher] be doing for the majority of the lesson?
- What would the students be doing for the majority of the lesson?
- Predict the percentage of teacher and student talk

	0%	25%	50%	75%	100%
Teacher talk					
Student talk					

- Will the strategy require most or all students to participate?
- Does the strategy differentiate the needs of different types of learners?
- Can students move at their own pace through the lesson?
- Will students get to practice the skill being taught?
- Will students work independently or in groups?
- How will students' learning be assessed

Part II

Next, ask teachers to look at a sample lesson plan focused on one skill and ask, "Will this lesson or this activity help a student to master this skill? Why or why not?" Then ask the group to identify a strategy that might be added to the plan. Ask that each recommendation include an explanation of how the strategy would lead to mastery of the skill.

This practice can help the team see areas of growth and begin to address them by keeping the focus on improving the lesson plan for mastery and rigor.

Part III

Begin part III by saying to the teachers, "Now that we have reflected on general strategies to inform and improve the effectiveness of instruction, we are going to look at an existing challenge. Using your existing student data, identify a particular student challenge or misconception." Share the data set and trend findings and ask your teachers to review a sample lesson plan from a textbook. Then ask, "Given the struggles students are having according to the data set, what instructional strategies would you add or refine to ensure that students master the skills in which they are struggling?"

TOOL 3.8 DIAGNOSTIC TOOL FOR LEVER 2, CLASSROOM ROUTINES AND INSTRUCTIONAL STRATEGIES

Focus Areas	Stage 0	Stage 1	Stage 2	Stage 3	Score
Routines to focus on learning and maximize time	• There are no consistent schoolwide classroom routines. • Students cannot describe classroom routines.	• There are consistent classroom routines in 40% of classrooms, but they may not be shared across classrooms.	• At least 3 to 5 daily routines are consistent across all classrooms.	• The majority of daily routines are consistent across all classrooms.	• Stage 0 • Evidence of Stage 1 practices • Evidence of Stage 2 practices • Evidence of Stage 3 practices

(continued)

Focus Areas	Stage 0	Stage 1	Stage 2	Stage 3	Score
	• Less than 25% of teachers practice bell-to-bell teaching, and students regularly have unstructured time at the start and end of a lesson. • In most lessons, 10% to 15% of instructional time is lost due to inefficient routines.	• Teachers appear to have routines, but less than 50% of students can describe them. • 50% of students are engaged with learning within 1 minute of the start of class. • In most lessons, at least 15% of instructional time is lost due to inefficient routines.	• All students can describe classroom routines and expectations (entry, exit, transitions within the class, material distribution and collection, and homework). • 70% of students are engaged with learning within 1 minute of the start of class through the end of class. • In most lessons, less than 10% of instructional time is lost due to inefficient routines.	• All students can describe classroom routines/ expectations (entry, exit, transitions within the class, material distribution/ collection, and homework), and students have leadership roles for executing daily school and classroom routines. • 90% of students are engaged with learning within 1 minute of the start of class, through the end of class. • Routines are efficient and prevent time from being wasted.	
Instructional strategies	• Instructional strategies are superficially and inconsistently implemented.	• 3 to 5 consistent instructional strategies are implemented by 40% of teachers.	• 3 to 5 consistent instructional strategies are implemented by 100% of teachers.	• 100% of teachers implement nonnegotiable strategies with quality.	• Stage 0 • Evidence of Stage 1 practices • Evidence of Stage 2 practices • Evidence of Stage 3 practices

Focus Areas	Stage 0	Stage 1	Stage 2	Stage 3	Score
	• The majority of teachers express that they do not have the support they need to implement requested instructional practices. • Efforts to differentiate are inconsistent and rarely effective.	• The majority of teachers can describe schoolwide instructional strategies, but teachers may not always implement them. • 50% of teachers differentiate content, but they are only sometimes effective.	• 80% of teachers can implement the strategies proficiently. • 80% of teachers state that they have the knowledge, skills, and supplies needed to implement nonnegotiable strategies. • 80% of teachers proficiently implement the strategies with evidence of meaningful differentiation for students.	• During meetings, teachers and leaders are frequently questioning the rigor of their practices with the goal of constantly pushing students academically. • 75% of teachers demonstrate high-quality differentiation of strategies based on the needs of the students.	

Lever 3: Data

TOOL 3.9 REFLECTION QUESTIONS FOR IDENTIFYING DATA SOURCES AND ASSESSMENTS

Assessing Student Progress

1. What are the ways teachers assess student progress?
2. How frequently are students assessed?
3. How do you monitor frequency?
4. Are the assessments aligned to the standards?
5. How do you monitor alignment to standards?

6. Are students in the same grade and courses evaluated using the same criteria?
7. How are evaluation data analyzed by teams?
8. How are assessment data used to improve instruction?

Interim Assessments

9. Are interim common interim assessments available at the start of the year?
10. Are interim assessments implemented four to six times per year at every grade level?
11. Do you have common assessments that go beyond math and literacy?

TOOL 3.10 CORRECTIVE INSTRUCTION ACTION PLANNING TEMPLATE

Data Analysis/Misconception to Address

What is the misconception? (Identify standard or skill)

What data support this conclusion?

Summary of Previous Instructional Approach

Is this a previously taught concept? Yes _____ No _____

If yes, please provide a brief summary of the strategies previously used to teach the standard or skill in which students demonstrated the misconception in bulleted form below.

High-Impact Instructional Strategies and Opportunities for Practice:
What high-impact instructional strategies will you use to address the misconception you identified?

Why did you select these strategies?

How do they align to the misconception?

How will each strategy be implemented? What opportunities will students have to practice the standard/skill?

Whole Group: If you choose whole group instruction, explain why, and provide data that support the lack of differentiation.	**Small Group:** Which students need a deeper level of support than whole group? Why, and what data support this?	**Individual:** Which students need an individual level of support to reach proficiency? Why, and what data support this?

Assessment: How will the skill/standard be reassessed formally or informally to check for mastery? Why? Why did you choose these assessment types? How will they be used?

(*continued*)

| Supports for Student Efficacy | | |

Supports for Student Efficacy		
How will the students be engaged so that they understand what standard/skill still needs to be learned?	How are students involved in setting goals or next steps? What strategies are you using to motivate students to reach certain goals (e.g., motivational language, written work/feedback, exit tickets)?	How will they know when they've reached their goal (opportunities for reflection)?
Accountability: What Evidence Will Be Collected and Reported Back to the Team?		
What are the next steps for team members?	What are the due dates?	Who is responsible: one person or a group of people? This can be distributed.

TOOL 3.11 REFLECTION QUESTIONS FOR PROVIDING STUDENT FEEDBACK

1. In your school, how often are students given feedback on their progress? How do you know?

2. How is feedback given? How do you know?

3. What is the quality of the feedback? How do you know?

4. How are students asked to respond to the feedback? Are teachers using the same feedback process across all classrooms?

5. How is feedback given to families?

6. How often is feedback given to families?

TOOL 3.12 DIAGNOSTIC TOOL FOR LEVER 3, DATA

Focus Areas	Stage 0	Stage 1	Stage 2	Stage 3	Score
Continuum of assessments and data collection	• Teachers are confused about the expectations for DDI implementation. • If a DDI calendar exists, it is missing critical pieces and/or not followed throughout the year. • Data reports are available, but the turnaround of reports is inconsistent.	• 40% of teachers are clear about the expectations for DDI implementation. • There is a DDI calendar, but the teachers are unaware of it and/or it is not followed throughout the year. • Data reports are rarely available within a week; reports are often comprehensive, but are rarely concise.	• 75% of teachers are clear about the expectations for DDI implementation. • All teachers have a copy of the DDI calendar and follow it throughout the year. • Data reports are timely and presented concisely.	• 100% of teachers are clear about the expectations for DDI implementation • All teachers have a copy of the DDI calendar and it is followed through the year. • Data reports are available with a 24 hour turnaround; they are concise and easy to interpret	☐ Stage 0 ☐ Evidence of Stage 1 practices ☐ Evidence of Stage 2 practices ☐ Evidence of Stage 3 practice
Analysis and action planning	• Teachers rarely take initiative to analyze assessment results, and any analysis rarely results in a change to practice. • Professional development (PD) is often misaligned with the needs as indicated by interim assessment results.	• Teachers may take the initiative to analyze assessment results, but less than 50% are able to accurately analyze the data. • PD is rarely based on the needs indicated by the interim assessment results.	• 75% of teachers engage in deep analysis of assessment results. • PD is "real time" but may lack follow-through with expectations in the classroom for implementation.	• 100% of teachers engage in deep analysis of assessment results. • PD is "real time" based on student needs, and the PD is often led by leadership team members.	☐ Stage 0 ☐ Evidence of Stage 1 practices ☐ Evidence of Stage 2 practices ☐ Evidence of Stage 3 practice

Focus Areas	Stage 0	Stage 1	Stage 2	Stage 3	Score
	• Leadership team members have not been trained in leading DDI, and when they are involved, they show poor skills. • Teacher team data analysis is superficial. • Less than 25% of students know their assessment results and areas of weakness.	• Some leadership team members have been trained and have clear responsibilities for DDI. • Teacher team data analyses use a consistent protocol and attempt to identify reasons behind misconceptions. • 50% of students know their assessment results and areas of weakness.	• Leadership team members have been trained in all areas of DDI and have clear responsibilities for analysis and planning with teachers. • Teachers and leaders regularly analyze results in teacher team meetings and collaboratively develop strategies to address misconceptions. • 75% of students know their assessment results and areas of weakness.	• When leading analysis and planning meetings, leadership team members demonstrate strong skills in prompting teachers to do the cognitive work. • Leadership team members hold teachers accountable for action plan implementation. • During weekly teacher team data meetings, all leaders and teachers engage in item analysis; for every assessment cycle, teachers and leaders collaboratively develop corrective instruction plans based on deep analysis. • All students know their assessment results and their specific areas of weakness.	

TOOL 3.13 DIAGNOSTIC TOOL FOR LEVER 4, STUDENT-CENTERED DIFFERENTIATION

Focus Areas	Stage 0	Stage 1	Stage 2	Stage 3	Score
Interventions	• Students rarely receive necessary interventions. • Struggling students are rarely identified in a consistent process; processes are rudimentary and/or not in place. • Schedules are rigid and do not allow additional instructional time for students who have not mastered content during the class period.	• 50% of students receive necessary interventions in a timely manner. • Processes are in place to identify students in danger of failing to create plans to support them. • The school schedule supports intervention blocks that allow additional instructional time for students who have not yet mastered content; intervention blocks may be planned to overlap with electives.	• 75% of students receive necessary interventions in a timely manner. • Processes are in place to identify all struggling students and to create individual support plans that facilitate their learning. • The school schedule includes intervention blocks that allow additional instructional time for students who have not yet mastered content.	• 100% of students receive necessary interventions in a timely manner. • Processes are in place to create individual support plans for each student that supports their learning and ensures that interventions are matched to students. • The school schedule is designed to support fluid intervention groups; intervention assignments and schedules are frequently updated to reflect student needs and progress.	☐ Stage 0 ☐ Evidence of Stage 1 practices ☐ Evidence of Stage 2 practices ☐ Evidence of Stage 3 practices

(continued)

Focus Areas	Stage 0	Stage 1	Stage 2	Stage 3	Score
Accelerations	• Teachers rarely plan for acceleration or enrichment opportunities for students who mastered content. • Students who master content are often asked to complete additional tasks or to support other students.	• 50% of teachers include acceleration opportunities for all students in most lessons. • Students who master content are sometimes asked to support other students, but also have opportunities to take on additional challenges.	• 75% of teachers include acceleration opportunities for all students in most lessons. • Students who master content and complete work quickly are given learning extensions or enrichment activities.	• 100% of teachers include acceleration opportunities for all students in most lessons. • Students who master content and complete work quickly are able to accelerate their exploration of concept and are given opportunities to pursue independent projects based on their individual interests.	☐ Stage 0 ☐ Evidence of Stage 1 practices ☐ Evidence of Stage 2 practices ☐ Evidence of Stage 3 practice

CHAPTER 4: SCHOOL CULTURE

Lever 1: Shared Mission and Values

TOOL 4.1 ACTIVITY: CREATING AND SHARING A SCHOOL VISION

Outcomes

- To create a shared vision of success.
- To determine how the vision will be shared with others in the school.
- To discuss how the vision will be integrated into the school over time, and determine specific touch points where the vision will be reinforced for the school community.

Time	Activity
5–7 minutes	**SHARE OUTCOMES** • To create a shared vision of success. • To determine how the vision will be shared with others in the school. • To discuss how the vision will be integrated into the school over time and determine specific touch points where the vision will be reinforced for the school community. Share the structure for the session (options described below). *Note: This should include multiple community members, but should be structured in a way that will support the improvement of goals. There are a few ways to structure the activity:* Option 1: Hold a preliminary session with leadership team members, and then have a session with the staff to add details and refine some of the initial ideas. Option 2: Hold a staff-wide session with leadership team members as table facilitators. Option 3: Hold a preliminary session with leadership team members, and then have department meetings to add details and refine some of the initial ideas.
50 minutes	**CHARTING A VISION FOR THE NEXT FIVE TO TEN YEARS** When planning units or lessons, we often start with the end in mind, and we will begin this reflection in a similar way. Independently reflect on the following questions: In five to ten years: • What do you hope your current students will be doing? • What do you want learning to look like at your school? What will your future students be learning? Share your reflections with a partner or a small group. Where are your visions similar? Where do they differ? Together reflect and chart: • How do you want your school be known in your community? • Where will your current vision lead your school in five to ten years?
60 minutes	**CHECK YOUR VISION** • Does your current vision statement speak to the ideals you just charted? • Does it reflect the future you just mapped out? If not, how does it differ from the future you just imagined? Make side-by-side lists of the values expressed in your vision statement and the ideals of your school community. Look for areas of alignment, areas of contradiction, and any ideals that do not appear in the vision.

TOOL 4.2 HOW VISIBLE IS THE SCHOOL VISION AT YOUR SCHOOL?

Here is a diagnostic to help you determine how well you have rolled out and communicated the vision at your school and some strategies to make your vision more effective. For each question, check the appropriate column: "Not at All," "Somewhat," "Quite a Bit," or "A Lot."

	Not at All	Somewhat	Quite a Bit	A Lot
1. How accurately is your administrative staff able to describe the school's vision?				
2. How visible is your vision in the school building?				
3. How often do school administrators have an opportunity to reinforce the vision?				
4. How often do teachers have an opportunity to reinforce the vision?				
5. Does the school have structures that reinforce the vision?				
6. Are values aligned to the vision?				
7. Are values known and present to members of the school community?				
8. How well are the goals aligned to the vision?				
9. Is the vision reviewed to make decisions?				

If you answered "not at all" to more than a few questions, reflect on the following questions:

- Is the vision statement clear as written?
- If you answered "not at all" or "somewhat" to question 1, how does the staff's description of the vision statement differ from the actual vision statement?
- Has the vision been communicated to all school stakeholders? How has it been communicated?
- How are stakeholders expected to interact with the vision?
- Are there opportunities to make the vision more visible? What are they?

TOOL 4.3 REFLECTION QUESTIONS ON BEHAVIORAL EXPECTATIONS

1. Does your school have a clear set of behavioral expectations that teachers and students know across the school? How do you know?

2. Are the behavioral expectations connected to the school's values?

3. How do teachers teach and reinforce the behavioral expectations as a regular part of the school day? How do you know? What is your evidence that supports your assessment?

4. How consistently are the behavioral expectations implemented in each classroom?

5. Do students have a common experience in every classroom and for every student?

6. Are teachers and students clear about how infractions are addressed?

7. Is there consistency about which responses are handled at the classroom level versus those that are referred to school leadership? How well do teachers follow the response guidelines?

TOOL 4.4 BEHAVIORAL EXPECTATIONS SELF-STUDY

Thinking about school safety and discipline, review the following statements with your instructional leadership team (ILT) or similar schoolwide committee. For each statement, put a + if your group's response is a resounding YES, an X if it's not present in your school at this time, or a check mark if it's an important priority for improvement.

Student Actions	Your Team's Assessment
Students know that almost all adults will intervene in incidents of bullying.	
Students and staff know that the school will do everything it can to make the physical environment safe.	
Students know that consequences will be clear, fair, and consistent.	
Students are asked to take specific actions to correct or repair a situation or a relationship when they engage in unwanted behaviors.	
Students perceive most adults as respectful and caring.	
Students participate in service learning.	

(continued)

Adult Actions	Your Team's Assessment

Adults meet and greet students at the entrance of school during arrival and at the door as students arrive to class.

Adults are visible in the hallways during transitions.

Faculty receive and review discipline data for their classrooms to improve their effectiveness.

All teachers are expected to help plan and participate in at least one schoolwide initiative that supports a positive school culture.

Teachers take time on a regular basis to recognize and reward effort that contributes to the school community.

All teachers are expected to attend student events and activities.

All adults take responsibility for implementing positive or negative consequences for all students (even those not in their classes).

School Policies

The school has interventions and supports for students who have chronic behavior problems.

The school has established structures for students to raise concerns and generate solutions to challenges.

The school establishes and supports a culture of quality and student's academic success.

TOOL 4.5 REFLECTION QUESTIONS ON STUDENT EFFICACY

- How do teachers demonstrate belief that all students can grow and improve through effort and support?

- Do most or all students believe that they can improve their results through effective effort? How do you know? How do they demonstrate their belief?

- Are there consistent messages, themes, and activities that reinforce that belief throughout the school? Is so, what are some examples? How do you know that those examples are internalized by teachers, students, and families?

- How are students encouraged to prepare for their future? How are they encouraged to pursue higher education opportunities?

- How are students supported in planning for their future? How are they given feedback on their plans for the future?

- Do students set goals for themselves?

- How do students track their goals, and how often? Are those goals shared with their classmates? If so, how, and why?

- Do teachers make connections for students between their school work, college, career, and financial future? How do you know? How do they make the connections?

- What kind of information are students and their families given about the college application process? When is that information distributed? How well is it understood? How do you know?

Lever 2: Relationships

TOOL 4.6 ACTIVITIES TO DIAGNOSE AND SUPPORT THE INCLUSIONS OF STUDENT VOICE

To actively work to include student voice into your school consider the following steps:

Step 1: Access student perception. Using either the survey items below or another survey supported by your district, get a baseline anonymous data set of how your students perceive their ability to influence and have an impact on the school.

Step 2: Conduct student and teacher discussion groups. Using the protocol questions below, conduct informal discussion groups for a representative set of teachers and then for a representative group of students.

Step 3: Identify opportunities for improvement. From your survey responses and student and teacher discussion groups, identify areas where students could help to lead initiatives (discussion groups are less formal focus group sessions).

Step 4: Move students toward action. Mobilize students to take leadership to brainstorm and provide solutions for the priority areas.

ACCESSING STUDENT PERCEPTIONS

	Always	Often	Sometimes	Never
My opinion matters to teachers in my school.				
My opinion matters to the principal in my school.				
Adults in my school ask for my thoughts and opinions before making changes.				
Adults take my opinions into account when changing a policy or structure.				
I feel like adults in my school listen to my concerns.				
I feel like the school appreciates my individual needs.				
When I share a problem, the adults in my school help me to solve it.				
I feel like I can talk about challenges with adults at my school.				
There are opportunities for student to improve the school.				

Discussion Group Questions

Goal: The goal of this conversation is to explore ways that students at our school can share their thoughts and feelings about the school with the administration on a regular basis. We want to make sure that every student has a chance to share his or her experiences (good and bad), and we wanted to ask you as current student/teachers some examples of times you feel it is important to include students' voices.

Student Questions

- What do you like about being a student at this school?
- What would make it better? How could you share that idea with the principal?
- What opportunities do you have as a student here to make recommendations to teachers or principal?

Teacher Questions

- What do you like about being a student/teacher at this school?
- How do students lead in the school?
- How are students included in decision-making processes?
- What are some ways that including student voices would improve the school?

Moving toward Action

Given what you learned about student and teacher perceptions:

- Are there places where students do not feel like their voices have been heard?
- Are there places where you can include student voices more? How?
- If you took this survey again in six months, what would you like to be different?

Lever 3: Family and Community Engagement

TOOL 4.7 GUIDE FOR FAMILY ENGAGEMENT: REFLECTION ON THE CURRENT STATE

- How do you engage families?
- How do you ensure that families are aware of their student's academic progress?

REFLECTING ON FAMILY OUTREACH

	Always	Often	Sometimes	Never
Are academic goals for the year shared with parents?				
Are behavior expectations shared with parents?				
Are attendance goals for the year shared with parents?				
Do parents receive phone calls to give them regular updates about academic performance, not just for concerns but for all students?				
Do parents receive phone calls to give them regular updates about behavior?				
Are parents called when a student is in danger of failing?				

- What percentage of your families are engaged in a school activity every other month? Once a month? Once a week?
- Does your school serve a geographic region? If not, how do you help families to reach events?
- Did you survey parents to see what day and times work best for them?

DATA COLLECTION AND ANALYSIS SHEET

	Number of Parent Conferences	Conference Percent to Total Students	Number of Parent Events	Event Percent to Total Students	Frequency of Parent Events	Type of Event (Academic, Sporting Events, Celebration, Arts Event, Training)
Grade _____						
Grade _____						
Grade _____						
Grade _____						
Grade _____						
Grade _____						
Grade _____						
Grade _____						
Grade _____						
Grade _____						
Grade _____						
Grade _____						
School totals						

- What are your key messages about the role of families in the school?
  - How are teachers expected to interact with families?
  - How do you share those expectations?
  - Do teachers demonstrate a commitment to working with parents? How do you know?
- Does your leadership team view parents as critical partners in their students' education all the time? How do you know?
- How do you involve students in family outreach?
- Do you have per session dollars set aside to compensate any teacher time outside of contracted time?

CHAPTER 5: TALENT MANAGEMENT

Lever 1: Recruitment and Onboarding

TOOL 5.1 REFLECTION QUESTIONS AND TOOLS FOR STAFF HIRING

Prior to beginning teacher recruitment and hiring consider who is currently on your team.

Teacher Name	Tenure in Profession	Tenure in School	Grade Level Currently Teaching	Certifi-cation	Previous Year's Summative Rating	Practice Ratings	Student Growth Rating	Areas of Strength	Areas of Growth

- Are there content gaps on your team?
- Are there skill gaps on your team?
- Is there diversity of skill on your team?
- Is there diversity of experience on your team?
- Is there racial and ethnic diversity on your team?

Recruiting and Hiring

- How are candidates identified for openings at your school?
- Where did you find your most successful hires? Do the most successful hires have anything in common with one another?
- What is your current hiring process?
- If this practice has been in place for several years, have the teachers you have hired remained at the school? Have they been successful members of staff (based on evaluation ratings and/or improvement)?
- How do you include current members of your team in the hiring process?

- What are the criteria on which you screen candidates? In addition to pedagogical skills, do you also assess for:
  - belief in every student's ability to achieve at high levels?
  - alignment to the school's vision?
  - personal dispositions, such as a growth mind-set, willingness to work in teams, and resilience?
- How do you assess the candidates you see?
- How are final hiring decisions made?

Induction

- What are your expectations for teachers?
- How do new teachers learn about those expectations?
- How do you differentiate induction for new and returning teachers?
- How do you monitor and reinforce your expectations throughout the year?

Lever 3: Performance Monitoring and Evaluation

TOOL 5.2 IDENTIFYING TEACHER SKILL AND WILL TO DEVELOP

After observing each teacher briefly, divide your teaching staff into these three categories to determine your frequency and type of support. First separate teachers by their instructional skill using this table:

Skilled Instruction	Developing Instruction	Ineffective Instruction
1.	1.	1.
2.	2.	2.
3.	3.	3.
4.	4.	4.
5.	5.	5.
6.	6.	6.
7.	7.	7.

Next, rank these teachers in "will to develop" using the ways they take and implement feedback, support the school vision, and demonstrate a belief in all students:

	Skilled Instruction	Developing Instruction	Ineffective Instruction
High will to develop			
Low will to develop			
Need additional evidence			

With your instructional leadership team (ILT), create a schedule to observe teachers using their tier as a guide for frequency. High-risk teachers may need more support, while teachers who have demonstrated effectiveness may need less frequent touch points.

- How will you collect direct evidence of teacher practice?
- How and when will teachers receive feedback?
- Does the feedback you are giving or have given make it clear to teachers what about their lessons is successful and what needs to change to improve their lessons?
- How will you monitor how teachers implement your feedback?
- How will you use evidence collected over the year to come to a comprehensive evaluation of a teacher's practice? What evidence is included?

TOOL 5.3 INSTRUCTIONAL LEADERSHIP TEAM REFLECTION QUESTIONS ON TEACHER OBSERVATION AND SUPERVISION

Observation and Feedback (for all ILT members)

- What training and support will you provide to help ILT members collect direct evidence of teacher practice?
- How will you help develop ILT members to give actionable feedback?
- How will you monitor their observation and feedback of teachers?

Evaluation (for ILT members who will be formally evaluating teachers)

- How will you norm and calibrate members of our team who will be conducting teacher evaluations to ensure that you are rating teachers similarly?
- How will you divide teacher evaluations among your ILT members?

Lever 4: Professional Learning and Collaboration

TOOL 5.4 REFLECTION QUESTIONS ON PROFESSIONAL LEARNING

Professional Learning Structures

- How do you connect new initiatives with your year-long goals?
- Who leads professional learning?
- How do you monitor professional learning you are not leading?
- How are schoolwide topics identified?
- Are topics linked to school goals?
- Are the whole school improvement priorities clear to teachers?
- How do you track and align the whole school improvement priorities with teacher team development goals/needs and individual teacher development needs?
- How are teachers held accountable for implementing practices shared during professional learning structures?
- How do you introduce your teachers to new initiatives? How do you assess if teachers are implementing the content of trainings?
- Over time, how do you assess that professional learning sessions are improving teacher practice and student outcomes?

Teacher Teams

- How are teachers expected to work together?
- How are teacher teams structured?
- How do new teachers learn about your team structures?
- How are teams expected to align with and to support school goals and schoolwide focus areas for instructional improvement?

- If you have teacher teams in place:

  - How do teams function?

  - How frequently do they meet?

  - How are meetings structured?

  - What are the outcomes and outputs of meetings?

  - How do you monitor each team?

  - Do teachers know the focus areas of their grade or content-level team?

Individual Teacher Development

- Do teachers know their individual growth areas?

- How are growth areas identified?

- How do teachers track their progress toward growth?

- How are teachers supported in their practice?

- What does teacher coaching currently consist of?

- How do you currently introduce your teachers to new content?

CHAPTER 6: PLANNING AND OPERATIONS

Lever 2: Time Management

TOOL 6.1 A PROCESS FOR ANALYZING AND OPTIMIZING YOUR OWN TIME

An accurate account of where you spend (and waste) time can help you sidestep time-wasting activities. Getting an accurate assessment of time can take some effort, so we suggest you start by auditing one or two recent months of your current calendar to assess how you spend your *recorded* time. Of course, since we know we deviate from our schedules sometimes, we also recommend that you choose a few days for a real-time calendar analysis (this process will help you to identify gaps between what you planned to do and what you actually do).

It's helpful to repeat this review process on a regular basis to see how you're improving. You can also enlist the help of office staff to help you maintain an accurate calendar. Also, if there is an area you want to improve (for example, increasing time observing teachers), tracking your time can be helpful in attaining your goal.

Calendar Audit

Look back at the last month of your calendar. This may not be a completely perfect record of your time, but no matter how imperfect, it can tell you how you are planning to use your time and roughly where you are spending your time.

Reviewing your calendar, define categories that describe the various ways you spent your time, and for each category count up your total number of hours. Here are some categories you might want to use (create other categories as needed to match your own activities and priorities).

Time spent in classrooms

Time providing teacher feedback

Time in teacher team meetings

Time with leadership team

Time in lunchroom/yard/greeting students

Time meeting with families

Time in family/community events

Time in district-level meetings

Time spent on paperwork

Time in individualized education plan meetings

Time on student discipline issues

Use your monthly totals to determine the percentage of time spent on each activity. Consider these questions to help you analyze your findings:

- Were you surprised by where and how you spent your time?
- Are there any scheduled activities that you found you never got to? Are there any other activities that always seem to take longer than the time you allotted?
- Are there activities you have been doing that you could delegate to others? Identify the activities and the members of the staff who could assume this responsibility.

Real-Time Daily Analysis

The calendar audit asked you to complete a retrospective analysis. To add to your data, we recommend you complete real-time data collection for one day to assess how your plan may differ from the reality of your day.

Chose a day when you are planning to observe teachers. At the end of that day, annotate your calendar so it reflects how you actually spent your time that day. Then answer these questions:

- Were you able to keep to your planned schedule? If not, why not?
- If you deviated from your plan, what would allow you to follow your planned calendar? What systems could you put in place to prevent being sidetracked?
- If you were called to attend to other needs in your school, who on your team could help you manage that work?
- Where did you spend your time? Does this distribution of time match your priorities?

Lever 3: Budget

TOOL 6.2 REFLECTION QUESTIONS ON BUDGETING

- What members of your staff can you partner with in developing and revising your budgets? Whose input will you collect, and why?
- What percentage of your budget is staffing? Professional development? Materials? Consultants? Technology?
- What portion of your budget are you able to control at the school level?
- Break down your staff budget. Are staff assignments aligned with school priorities (i.e., is the proportion of money spent on math instructors, including coaches, aligned to the priority level given to math in your action plan)?
- Break down your materials budget. Is your school's spending on each subject area's materials in proportion to that subject's importance in your school's action plan?

Lever 4: Community and District Relations

TOOL 6.3 REFLECTION QUESTIONS ON EXTERNAL PARTNER ALIGNMENT

- Does the mission of the organization support the goals of the school?
- How will the organization help the school move toward its goals?
  - Will (or does) the work of the organization support student learning? How?

- Will (or does) the work of the organization support student social-emotional growth? How?
- Will the work of the organization support positive school culture? How?
- Is the organizational staff well qualified to supplement student learning?
- Does the staff reinforce the values of the school? How?
- What population of the school is the organization serving?
- Do you have systems in place for regular coordination between school staff and partner staff?
- How will you monitor the impact of the partner's work? Have you and the partner agreed on clear goals for their work and metrics to track progress? Has their work to date demonstrated the expected impact?
- Do the benefits of the partnership for students outweigh the costs (in money or staff time) of the partnership?

CHAPTER 7: PERSONAL LEADERSHIP

Lever 1: Belief-Based Goal-Driven Leadership

TOOL 7.1 REFLECTION QUESTIONS ON BELIEF-BASED AND GOAL-DRIVEN LEADERSHIP

- Describe the expectations you have for the adults in your school and for the students. What do those expectations look like in practice?
- How do you convey those expectations to adults?
- How are those expectations shared with students and families?
- How do you know when a staff member is not maintaining or reinforcing those expectations? What are some indicators you have seen or might see?
- When a staff member does not maintain the level of expectations important to the school community, what happens?
- How can you help staff to focus on student needs rather than the needs of adults?
- How can you create and maintain schoolwide urgency to improve school outcomes?
- How do you express urgency in attaining goals?
- What systems do you have in place for maintaining urgency?

Lever 2: Equity-Focused Leadership

TOOL 7.2 REFLECTION QUESTIONS FOR CONSIDERING YOUR OWN BIASES, AND THOSE OF YOUR STAFF, RELATED TO DIVERSITY AT YOUR SCHOOL

We all view situations through a lens made up of our past experiences and through the prism of race, class, sexual orientation, and gender. Part of leading with an equity lens is closely examining how your experiences have shaped your perception and adjusting your assumptions as needed.

Here are two sets of questions: one for you to consider as you explore your own personal biases and another that can help you think through issues of power and privilege within your school community.

School Leader

Personal Reflections

- How do you interact with groups different from your own?
- How would someone who currently works with you (or worked with you in the past) describe your interactions with individuals or groups different from your own?
- If you invited your close friends to a gathering, would the group be homogeneous?
- Do you regularly seek out evidence that will reveal your biases? If so, how? If not, why not, and what can you do to make that a part of your routine?
- How well do you listen to people with different points of view? When did you last learn something, or change an action, based on something from another point of view?

Reflections on the Staff and School

- Does the team you have hired share a similar cultural, race, and/or class background to yours?
- Do staff backgrounds reflect those of the students?
- Is your staff diverse? Does your staff bring a variety of perspectives and experiences to discussions? What influence do staff members have over decisions? Do you find that most decisions are led by a subset of your team? Does one group dominate decisions or have more influence?
- How often do you lead discussions about bias, equity, and diversity with your staff and school community?
- How often do staff members engage in discussions about bias, equity, and diversity with your staff and school community?
- How do power and privilege play out at your school?

- How can you become or remain aware of the power dynamics between you and your staff and families, particularly around areas of race and class?
- How can you shift power dynamics?
- Is the leadership team diverse and representative of the perspectives of the staff and students?
- Are there cliques among the staff? If so, are they based on race or other special populations?

Lever 3: Interpersonal Leadership

TOOL 7.3 REFLECTION QUESTIONS ON INTERPERSONAL LEADERSHIP

- Imagine you are joining a new group as its leader:
  - How would you introduce yourself?
  - What messages would you want to convey?
  - How would you expect a new group to respond to you?
  - What is different about introducing yourself as group or team leader than an introduction as a team member?
- Think about when you entered your current position:
  - How did you build rapport with your team?
  - Were there teachers or staff you struggled to build relationships with?
  - Why do you think you struggled to build a relationship with that (those) individual(s)?
  - What have you done to repair the relationship?
- How do you tailor your communication with staff, families, and other stakeholders?
- Think of one key message that you have to share (or recently shared) with your school community. How did you differentiate the message for the following groups:
  - Students
  - Families
  - Staff
  - Instructional leadership team
  - Other community members

Lever 4: Adaptive Leadership

TOOL 7.4 IDENTIFYING ADAPTIVE CHALLENGES

Think about a challenge you have identified or your staff has identified for you. What was the root of the problem?

- Was it something that could be solved by an expert who had additional skills or knowledge? Was there a "right answer" that already existed, but may not have been known by the team? [technical challenge]

  - Does the challenge require you to increase access to information? *For example, implement daily or weekly bulletin to share information.*

  - Could the challenge be alleviated by increasing communication or creating additional meetings? *For example, implement quarterly vertical team meetings.*

  - Does the challenge require you to change or modify a system? *For example, decrease the turnaround time to grade interim assessments.*

  - Could the challenge be solved by additional resources (time, materials, and personnel)? *For example, designate a staff member to support attendance initiatives.*

- Did it require staff members to change their practices and beliefs and/or the way they collaborate within a team? [adaptive challenges]

  - Does the challenge require you to rebuild fractured relationship or broken trust? *For example, debrief past incidents and create working norms to rebuild community.*

  - Could the challenge be alleviated by creating a shared vision for the school? *For example, beginning with a vision for the school that all team members participate in.*

  - Could the challenge be solved by setting common goals and creating role and responsibility clarity? *For example, cocreate goals where common strategies are identified and agreed on and where targets for specific roles are clear.*

In many cases, challenges have both adaptive and technical components you may need to address in your planning. Once you have reflected on the above questions, use the following table to plan your next steps:

Challenge:

(continued)

Risks if the issue is not resolved:						

Could this challenge put a schoolwide goal at risk of not being attained?	Yes	No	Could this challenge affect the way in which staff perceive their workplace?	Yes	No
If you answered no to one of the above questions, could this challenge wait to be addressed?				Yes	No
If the challenge can wait to be addressed, when will you come back to it?				Date:	

If the challenge should be addressed immediately, see below:

TECHNICAL:		ADAPTIVE:
Are there systems or processes you can put in place to help the problem? If yes, list them below. If not, move to the next question.		Are there trainings and support that staff will need to work together differently? Are there any issues that have been preventing a change in practice?

Yes	No	How will you help staff to share and manage their feelings if this requires a significant change in practice?
Systems and processes to be added:		
Why have they not been in place to date?		What resistance do you anticipate? How will you address that resistance?

Who will be responsible to taking the next steps?	Who will be responsible for taking the next steps?
By when:	By when:
How will you monitor implementation?	How will you monitor changes to practice?

Lever 5: Resilient Leadership

TOOL 7.5 REFLECTION QUESTIONS ON RESILIENT LEADERSHIP

- What activities do you take to reenergize yourself from the challenges of school leadership? How do you rejuvenate yourself?
- How often do you do these activities? When do you set aside time for yourself?
- Does time you have set aside for yourself get scheduled over?
- Think about a time when you were feeling discouraged. How did you refocus yourself? What allowed you to refocus?
- Could you replicate that experience when something else is challenging?
- What actions do you encourage your team to take to build and sustain the team in challenging moments?
- What actions do you encourage your team members to take to build and sustain themselves individually during challenging moments?
- What do you do when you recognize staff members are personally struggling with the work or something in their personal lives? What does your outreach look like? What kind of support do they receive?

TOOL 7.6 PERSONAL LEADERSHIP SELF-ASSESSMENT

TLF Key Levers					
Belief-based, goal-driven leadership: Leader consistently demonstrates belief in the potential of every student to achieve at high levels	As you assess your practice, consider the following: • How do you demonstrate belief in students? • How do you convey your belief in students? • How do your teachers know that you believe in students? • What happens when your belief is challenged? How do you handle those situations?				
	Indicators	**Rarely**	**Sometimes**	**Often**	**Always**
	Takes personal responsibility for the school's outcomes				
	Share hope and possibility about the future of the school with staff, parents, and students				
	Demonstrate the belief that all students can achieve at high levels, and reinforce the belief that effort can improve a student's outcomes				
	Demonstrate urgency and commitment to close the achievement gap by supporting all groups of students				
	Build a sense of urgency to achieve goals				
	Review and change policies or processes that place adult needs over student needs				
	Set goals that will push all students toward high levels of achievement				
TLF Key Levers					
Equity-focused leadership: Actively address statements of bias, cultural intolerance or prejudice; strive to create an equitable school that celebrates diversity and supports all students	As you assess your practice, consider the following: • How do you reflect on your biases, and how does your reflection change your practice? • How do you seek out and engage diverse perspectives? • How do you address the dynamics of power within your school community? • What are some examples of equitable practices that you have implemented? How do you know that they have been effective at dismantling inequitable practices?				

	Indicators	Rarely	Sometimes	Often	Always
	Explore how power and privilege affect your interactions with others				
	Seek out and incorporate diverse perspectives to build an effective organization				
	Confront culturally intolerant, biased, or racist statements				
	Assess biases and assumptions when making decisions and work to identify blind spots				
	Incorporate students', teachers', families', and communities' lives in the school				
	Address dynamics of power within the community to foster a pervasive ethos of equity				
	Initiate conversations about race, class, sexual orientation, and power				
	Use moments of conflict as opportunity to strengthen community				
TLF Key Levers					
Interpersonal leadership: Leader builds relationships and facilitates active communities of adults and students dedicated to reaching school goals	As you assess your practice, consider the following: • How do you develop community and relationships with your team? • How did you get your team to build into the vision and the school goals? • What is a relationship you have struggled to establish? How have you made progress on building the relationship?				
	Indicators	Rarely	Sometimes	Often	Always
	Maintain positive relationships with students, staff, and families				
	Create trusting relationships among staff, students, and families				
	Publicly share clear expectations				

(*continued*)

Indicators	Rarely	Sometimes	Often	Always
Deescalate and defuse challenging situations				
Use appropriate facilitation and communication strategies depending on the context or goal				
Facilitate active participation by multiple community members				
Honor all voices, and actively involve others in decisions that further the vision of the school				
Build teams that effectively collaborate				

TLF Key Levers

Adaptive leadership: Help staff, students, and families navigate changes to the school landscape while maintaining focus on the school vision; facilitate experiences that inspire changes in values, beliefs, assumptions, and habits of behavior that do not support success.

As you assess your practice, consider the following:

- How do you help your teachers and your team to manage changes?
- How do you help them prepare for changes they are facing?
- How do you identify the root cause of challenges?
- How do you keep your team inspired in the face of challenges?
- How do you challenge assumptions and habits that are not serving your team?

Indicators	Rarely	Sometimes	Often	Always
Recognize emotions including fear, loss, and resistance that accompany change				
Help and support staff to manage the emotions of change successfully while maintaining focus on the vision and school goals				
Identify root causes, especially those that require changes in beliefs, values, assumptions, and/or habits of behaviors				
Address deeper challenges involving changing beliefs; skillfully leverage existing strengths				

	Indicators	Rarely	Sometimes	Often	Always
	Take appropriate risks that will benefit the school, students, or district				
	Read group dynamics resulting from change and adapt approach accordingly				

TLF Key Levers

	As you assess your practice, consider the following:
Resilient leadership: Demonstrate resolve in the face of adversity and challenge, constantly looking for solutions that will move your school closer to its goals and reflecting on your own actions	• How are you resilient in the face of challenges? • What are moments when you model resiliency for your team? • How do you help your teachers and instructional leadership team develop resilient skills?

	Indicators	Rarely	Sometimes	Often	Always
	Remain focused on goals in the face of setbacks and challenges				
	Regulate stress appropriately				
	Demonstrate personal resolve and maintain core confidence				
	Maintain focus on solutions				
	Reflect on performance and seek feedback				
	Turn adversity and challenges into opportunities for progress				
	Pursue opportunities to improve personal leadership				
	Honors personal time to sustain school leadership over time				

CHAPTER 8: PRINCIPAL COACHING USING THE TLF

TOOL 8.1 CALIBRATING AND ALIGNING PRACTICE

Outcome: To gather data and evidence from a common setting to assess how each principal supervisor is rating similar school practices and to begin to calibrate ratings.

Time	Activity	Materials
10 minutes	**OUTCOMES** Introduce the outcomes and frame the goal of this activity as building a shared vision of effective principal practice. Use these talking points: • As principal developers, it is important that we are looking for similar practices and that when we observe practices, we are assessing them in similar ways. • We want to make sure that we have the same definition of what constitutes "good" and "effective" practice. • Today we will learn a little bit more about where each of us is currently assessing practices, but we will need more than one session to truly become normed and calibrated.	
15 minutes	**CURRENT PERCEPTIONS: ARE WE ALIGNED?** To get the group warmed up, have two signs posted on opposite walls of the group. Tell the group they are going to act as a human barometer to get a sense of how aligned they are. Ask everyone to stand and to stand near the sign that represents their perception of alignment; they can also stand between the two poles that the sign represents. Read out these statements (give at least one minute between transitions): • All of the principal supervisors in your district have a common definition for what effective learning and teaching looks like in practice. • All of the principal supervisors in your district have a common definition for what is included in an effective culture. • All of the principal supervisors have common approaches to talent management, including how they supervise principals and what they expect of effective talent management at the school level.	One sign that reads "completely" and the other "not at all"

Time	Activity	Materials
15 minutes	• All of the principal supervisors in your district understand the ways in which operations affects student learning. • When principal supervisors in your district observe school actions together, they consistently identify them in the same stage of development. Debriefing • What did you notice about how the group assessed your level of alignment? • Was the group in alignment with your perception? Talking points • [If your group thinks they are aligned] This is a good exercise for us to ensure that we maintain alignment, and it will give us a chance to test our alignment. • [If your group thinks they are misaligned] This will be a chance for us to build better alignment.	
60 minutes	VIDEO PRACTICE Directions We are going to select one category from the Transformational Leadership Framework to observe [you can also do this with a rubric from your district]. To gather evidence about a school, we will note low interference data and then we map what we saw to the framework. Take scripted notes observing what you see; please avoid making judgments. *Please note: with a video we will have some questions that we cannot answer, but we can pose wonderings that we would ask the school leader in person if this were a real case.*	Video of school or principal practice Data collection sheets

(*continued*)

Time	Activity	Materials

Play the clip twice for the group.

Action or category debriefing

- Debriefing question: What did you see in the video? *Chart out the evidence as a group.*
- What action does our evidence correspond to? *Select the portion of the framework together.*
- Look at the language in each stage and independently reflect: What stage does our evidence best fit into? *Have the group share their assessments to see where you all are:*
  - Is this action in stage 1, stage 2, or stage 3?
  - Identify outliers and ask them to *defend* their assessments using evidence.
  - Continue to discuss until the group can agree using the evidence at hand.

Time	Activity	Materials
20 minutes	DEBRIEFING	

What did you notice about how we collected evidence? (Probe: Did we all notice the same things?)
What was different about how we assessed the practices?
What positive or negative assumptions were we making?

TOOL 8.2 SAMPLE SCHOOL WALK-THROUGH I: FOCUS ON ACTION PLAN IMPLEMENTATION

Preparation

Prior to the visit, collect and review the principal's goals and school action plan based on the diagnosis, student achievement data for the previous school year, and any available interim assessment data or other student outcomes data (such as attendance or referral data).

Preparation for Conversation between the Visiting Team and Principal

- What do we expect to see given the strategies or goals that the school leader has identified as prioritized areas? What documents, such as action plans, school improvement plans, district improvement plans, or other plans, align to the goals?
- What are the areas where you need more information?
- What are the weak parts of the plan you want to probe?
- What are the milestones and measures of progress (identified in the plan) to follow up on?
- **Critical district strategies:** Which of the district focus strategies will the visit team focus on during this visit?

Ask Principals to:

- Gather evidence of progress toward their goals
- Prepare their reflections on school progress
- Bring observation and classroom visit data from two strong and two weak teachers

Visit

Ask the Principal to Share

- Reflections on progress toward her goals and the specific actions and strategies she is taking to reach her goals
- How she will know when she has attained her goals and what evidence will document that attainment
- How she is monitoring the district focus areas
- Any revisions to her original diagnosis based on ongoing observations of school actions

Debriefing

Following the first visit, the school visit team uses the following questions to frame the debriefing conversation:

- Did the principal's day-to-day work align to the goals she set at the beginning of the year? If not, why not? How have the goals been modified?
- How did the principal demonstrate progress toward goals?
- Are teachers receiving regular feedback? How is the principal implementing the teacher evaluation model?
- What did you see that raised questions? Why? What questions can you ask to gain insights into those areas and gain clarity to coach toward improvement?

TOOL 8.3 SAMPLE SCHOOL WALK-THROUGH II: FOCUS ON TEACHER COACHING

Preparation

Prior to the visit, collect and review informal and formal teacher observation data from at least one new teacher and one underperforming teacher, lesson and unit plans for the teachers whose classrooms you will be observing, and one professional development plan.

Preparation for Conversation between the Visiting Team and Principal

- What questions do you have about the supports being provided to teachers?
- What parts of the teacher evaluation rubric do you want to probe and explore through the classroom visits and/or principal debriefing?
- What are the areas where you need more information?
- How will you deploy team members to collect information on school culture?
- **Critical district strategies:** Which of the district focus strategies will the visit team focus on during this visit?

Ask Principals to Provide

- Year-long professional development calendar
- Observation data for all teachers who are underperforming
- Staff development plans and improvement plans for underperforming staff
- Schedule of classroom observations to assess frequency

Visit

Ask the Principal to Share

- How she is incorporating the teacher evaluation model into the support and assessment of practice
- The interventions and supports put in place (for average, underperforming, and high-performing teachers) that are supporting teacher development and the impact of supports and development activities
- Assessments of observed teachers

Observe

- How teachers are implementing strategies identified in the school goals or the professional development plan
- Culture practices you observe in classrooms and hallways

Debriefing

Following visit II, have a debriefing session with the visit team using the following questions to frame your conversation:

- What parts of the teacher evaluation model were successfully being implemented? Did the evaluation model seem to be part of ongoing formative conversations?
- Did the interventions, developments, and supports seem to have an impact on practice?
- What progress is the principal making in assessing teacher practice?
- What did you see that raised questions? Why? What questions can you ask to gain insights into those areas and gain clarity to coach toward improvement?
- What did you observe about the school culture in your visit?
- How did adults and students interact in and out of class time?

When you are trying to assess a principal's skill in giving feedback or if feedback is an area of growth, you can augment a coaching visit with the following practice.

To help principals remain focused on high-leverage strategies for feedback, we often focus a visit on one classroom with a teacher who falls into the developing category of practice and has been identified as coachable. Prior to observing the teacher, we meet with the principal to hear identified areas of growth for that teacher and to relate that teacher's growth area to any trends the leader is seeing across classrooms. We then observe the teacher for fifteen to twenty minutes and share the evidence you gathered with the principal. (Depending on the context, we may let the teacher know that we will be observing in advance of the visit.) What did we see? At this point, the goal is to remain low inference and not to draw conclusions based on what we see. Once all the evidence is shared, we then pull out the areas of improvement. These lists are often long and may include classroom management challenges, but to keep the leader focused, we whittle the larger list down to two or three areas for feedback.

If leaders begin to focus on feedback that will not affect instruction, you can refocus them using their schoolwide goals and the areas of growth initially identified for the teacher. Over time, principals become more familiar with this practice, and you will see shifts in their ability to provide targeted feedback.

TOOL 8.4 SAMPLE SCHOOL WALK-THROUGH III: FOCUS ON OPERATIONS

Preparation

Prior to the visit, collect and review the school schedule and budget.

The school visit team should convene and answer the following guiding questions prior to visit III:

- Based on the data you have collected how are the operations of the school supporting the school goals?

Preparation for Conversation between the Visiting Team and Principal

- How is the principal managing his time?
- How much time is spent focused on instruction?
- Are the principal's budgets aligned to the school needs and goals?
- Do the schedule and calendar maximize instructional time?
- What do we expect to see?
- **Critical district strategies:** Which of the district focus strategies will the visit team focus on during this visit?

Ask Principals to Gather

- School schedule and calendar
- Team meetings and agendas (including leadership teams, teacher team meeting, and faculty meeting)
- Budget to actuals

Visit

Ask the Principal to Share

- How and why he created the daily schedule
- How the schedule supports his goals
- Reflections on how he has adapted the schedule over the school year
- How he has been spending money in his budget and how he determines what to spend money on

Debriefing

Following the visit, have a debriefing session with the visit team using the following questions to frame your conversation:

- What data were included in the meeting or session you attended?
- Was there evidence that the data supported the goals of the school?
- Did the meeting conclude with clear next steps?
- How will the principal monitor the effectiveness of the operations?
- What did you see that raised questions? Why? What questions can you ask to gain insight into those areas and gain clarity to coach toward improvement?

PRINCIPAL COACHING TOOL 8.5 SAMPLE SCHOOL WALK-THROUGH IV: FOCUS ON SCHOOL CULTURE

Preparation

Prior to the visit collect and review student attendance data, culture survey data (if available), and school newsletters.

The school visit team should convene and answer the following guiding questions prior to visit IV:

- Based on the data you have collected, what indicators of a healthy culture will you look for?

Preparation for Conversation between the Visiting Team and Principal

- Prioritize what you would like to observe (see the list below of possible moments to observe)
- What do we expect to see?
- What questions do you have about the culture?
- How do staff, families, and students learn the school culture?
- **Critical district strategies:** Which of the district focus strategies will the visit team focus on during this visit?

Ask Principals to Gather

- Suspension data over time
- Records of implementation of any positive behavior or rewards system in place
- Records of referrals
- Student attendance reports
- Template of letters to parents of students with multiple absences
- Call logs to parents of students with multiple absences
- Flyers, newsletters, and school assembly agenda time celebrating students with perfect attendance or high attendance

Visit

Ask the Principal to Share

- What are the roles that every member of the team plays in maintaining the school's culture?
- What are the key messages that every student we talk to will know about going to school here?

- How do new members of the community learn the school culture?
- What are the touchstone moments to celebrate culture?
- Reflect on how they have adapted the culture over the school year

Observe

- *School opening:* How do the students enter the building? What adults are present, and how are they interacting with students?
- *Transition between classes:* What is happening in classrooms five minutes before a transition? What is the hallway like at transition points? What adults are present, and how are they interacting with students?
- *Lunchroom/recess:* What is the lunchroom like? How do students enter and leave the lunchroom? What is the level of noise of the lunchroom? What adults are present, and how are they interacting with students?
- *Dismissal:* What is happening in classrooms five minutes before dismissal? What is the hallway like at dismissal? What adults are present, and how are they interacting with students? What is happening outside of the school?

Debriefing

Following the visit, have a debriefing session with the visit team using the following questions to frame your conversation.

- What data were included in the meeting or session you attended?
- How consistent is the culture across the school?
- How are guests welcomed by office staff, teachers, and students?
- Are many students are out of class when class is in session?
- Are teachers representing high expectations in the classes you observed and incenting effort?
- Did the meeting conclude with clear next steps?
- How will the principal monitor the culture?
- What did you see that raised questions? Why? What questions can you ask to gain insights into those areas and gain clarity to coach toward improvement?

TOOL 8.6 MID- AND END-OF-YEAR REVIEW AND PRELIMINARY PLANNING

- Prior to your mid- and end-of-year conversations, complete the following chart based on your own indirect and direct observations.
- Ask the school leader to share her reflections on her practice using the same chart.
- Review her assessment of practice prior to meeting to ensure that you have identified areas where your assessments vary or where you have questions about their evidence.
- Plan to focus your conversation on areas where you have seen growth and areas where there has been a decline or you see cause for concern.
- Progress to date: What progress have you seen in:

Category	Progress	Evidence
Learning and teaching		
School culture		
Talent management		
Operations and planning		
Personal leadership		

- Given your evidence, what areas are you planning to prioritize?
- Given your evidence, where are you planning to focus your personal work next year?
- How will you tailor your work to support the priorities you have identified?

NOTES

Introduction

1. Lieberman, M. (2015, July 8). Powell principal departs after expanding enrollment, community engagement. *Northwest Current, 48.*
2. Gates, S., Hamilton, L., Martorell, P., Burkhauser, S., & Heaton, P. (2014). *Preparing principals to raise student achievement: Implementation and effects of the New Leaders program in ten districts.* Santa Monica, CA: RAND Corporation.
3. Seashore Louis, K., Leithwood, K., & Anderson, S. (2010). *Learning from Leadership Project: Investigating the links to improved student learning.* Minneapolis: Center for Applied Research and Educational Improvement, University of Minnesota.
4. National Conference of State Legislatures. (2012). *Preparing a pipeline of effective principals: A legislative approach.* Retrieved from http://www.ncsl.org/documents/educ/PreparingaPipelineofEffective PrincipalsFINAL.pdf
5. Seashore Louis et al. (2010).
6. Marzano, R. J., Waters, T., & McNulty, B. A. (2005). *School leadership that works: From research to results.* Alexandria, VA: Association for Supervision and Curriculum Development.
7. Bryk, A. S., Sebring, P. B., Allensworth, E., Luppescu, S., & Easton, J. Q. (2010). *Organizing schools for improvement: Lessons from Chicago.* Chicago: University of Chicago Press; Louis, K. S., Leithwood, K., Wahlstrom, K. L., & Anderson, S. E. (2010). *Investigating the links to improved student learning: Final report of research findings. Learning from Leadership Project.* Minneapolis: University of Minnesota; Aladjem, D. K., Birman, B. F., Orland, M., Harr-Robins, J., Heredia, A., Parrish, T. B., & Ruffini, S. J. (2010). *Achieving dramatic school improvement: An exploratory study.* Washington, DC: US Department of Education.
8. Scholastic Inc. (2012). *Primary sources: America's teachers on the teaching profession.* New York, NY: Scholastic and the Bill and Melinda Gates Foundation. Retrieved from http://www.scholastic .com/primarysources/pdfs/Gates2012_full.pdf
9. Hutchins, D., Epstein, J., & Sheldon, S. (2012). Effective Practice Incentive Community (EPIC). Data analysis for New Leaders. Center on School, Family, and Community Partnerships, Baltimore, MD: Johns Hopkins University.

Chapter 1: The Stages of School Development

1. Howard, J. Efficacy Institute. Waltham, MA.

Chapter 2: Diagnosis and Action Planning

1. Reeves, D. (2006). *The learning leader: How to focus school improvement for better results.* Alexandria, VA: ASCD; Fernandez, K. (2011). Evaluating school improvement plans and their effect on academic performance. *Educational Policy, 25*(2), 338–367; Reeves, D. (2008). Leading to change/making strategic planning work. *Educational Leadership, 65*(4), 86–87
2. Broadhead, P., Cuckle, P., Hodgson, J. & Dunford, J. (1996). Improving primary schools through school development planning. *Educational Management and Administration, 24*(3), 277–290.
3. Elmore, R., & McLaughlin, M. (1988). *Steady work: Policy, practice and the reform of American education.* Santa Monica, CA: RAND.
4. Collins, J. (2001). *Good to great.* New York: HarperCollins.
5. To paint a comprehensive picture of the effective principal and school actions we witnessed in our research in a broad range of schools across the country, we fictionalized Jones Elementary. This is the only school featured in the book that is fictional.

Chapter 3: Learning and Teaching

1. Bryk, A., Sebring, P., Allensworth, E., Easton, J., & Luppescu, S. (2010). *Organizing schools for improvement: Lessons from Chicago.* Chicago, IL: University of Chicago Press.
2. Bloom's Taxonomy; Webb's Depth of Knowledge; Hess Rigor Matrix; Strong, R., Silver, H., & Perini, M. (2001). *Teaching what matters most: Standards and strategies for raising student achievement.* Alexandria, VA: ASCD.
3. McTighe, J., & Wiggins, G. (2012). *Understanding by design framework.* Alexandria, VA: ASCD.
4. Marzano, R., & Toth, M. (2014). *Teaching for rigor: A call for a critical instructional shift.* West Palm Beach, FL: Learning Sciences Marzano Center.
5. Beck, I., McKeown, M., Hamilton, R., & Kucan, L. (1997). *Questioning the author: An approach to enhancing student engagement with text.* Newark, DE: International Reading Association.
6. Bambrick-Santoyo, P. (2010). *Driven by data: A practical guide to improve instruction.* San Francisco, CA: Jossey-Bass; Boudett, K., & City, E. (2005). *Data wise: A step by step guide to using assessment results to improve instruction.* Cambridge, MA: Harvard Education Press.
7. Allensworth, E., & Easton, J. (2007). *What matters for staying on track and graduating in Chicago Public Schools.* Chicago, IL: Consortium on Chicago School Research at the University of Chicago.
8. Fenton, B., & Murphy, M. (2009). *Data-driven instruction.* ASCD Express. Retrieved from http://www.ascd.org/ascd-express/vol5/508-fenton.aspx; Chappuis, J. (2009). *Seven strategies of assessment for learning.* Boston, MA: Allyn & Bacon: Pearson; Stiggins, R., Arter, J., Chappuis, J., & Chappuis, S. (2006). *Classroom assessment for student learning: Doing it right—using it well.* Portland, OR: Educational Testing Service; Black, P., & William, D. (1998). Inside the black box: Raising standards through classroom assessment. *Phi Delta Kappan, 80*(2), 139–148; Bambrick-Santoyo, P. (2010).

9. Sternberg, R. J. (1994). Allowing for thinking styles. *Educational Leadership, 52*(3), 36–40; Guskey, T. (2010). Lessons of mastery learning. *Educational Leadership, 68*(2), 52–57.
10. Bambrick-Santoyo, P. (2010).
11. Miller, J. (2013). A better grading system: Standards-based student-centered assessment. *English Journal, 103*(1), 111–118.
12. Miller, J. (2013).
13. Dweck, C. (2007). *Mindset: The new psychology of success*. New York, NY: Ballantine Books.
14. For references, see Hughes, C., & Dexter, D. D. (N.d.). *Response to intervention: A research review.* www.rtinetwork.org/learn/research/researchreview

Chapter 4: School Culture

1. Goddard, R. G., Hoy, W. K., & Woolfolk Hoy, A. (2004). Collective efficacy: Theoretical development, empirical evidence, and future directions. *Educational Researchers, 33,* 2–13.
2. Dweck, C. (2007). *Mindset: The new psychology of success*. New York, NY: Ballantine Books.
3. Dweck, C. (2007).
4. Nelson Laird, T. (2014). Reconsidering the inclusion of diversity in the curriculum. *Diversity and Democracy, 17*(4), 12–14. Association of American Colleges and Universities.
5. Mitra, D. L. (2008). Student voice in school reform. Albany, NY: SUNY Press.
6. Miedel, W. T., & Reynolds, A. J. (1999). Parent involvement in early intervention for disadvantaged children: Does it matter? *Journal of School Psychology, 37*(4), 379–402; Sanders, M. G., & Herting, J. R. (2000). Gender and the effects of school, family, and church support on the academic achievement of African-American urban adolescents. In M. G. Sanders (Ed.), *Schooling students placed at risk: Research, policy, and practice in the education of poor and minority adolescents* (pp. 141–161). Mahwah, NJ: Erlbaum.
7. Jordan, G. E., Snow, C. E., & Porche, M. V. (2000). Project EASE: The effect of a family literacy project on kindergarten students' early literacy skills. *Reading Research Quarterly, 35*(4), 524–546.
8. Bowen, G. L., Hopson, L. M., Rose, R. A., & Glennie, E. J. (2012). Students' perceived parental school behavior expectations and their academic performance: A longitudinal analysis. *Family Relations, 61,* 175–191.

Chapter 5: Talent Management

1. Chetty, R., Friedman, J., & Rockoff, J. (2012). *The long-term impacts of teachers: Teacher value-added and student outcomes in adulthood*. National Bureau of Economic Research working paper 17699.
2. Speech to New Leaders Aspiring Principals Program participants, Fall Foundations seminar, October 2008.
3. Metlife. (2013). *The MetLife Survey of the American Teacher: Challenges for School Leadership*. New York, NY: Metropolitan Life Insurance Company. Retrieved from https://www.metlife.com/assets/cao/foundation/MetLife-Teacher-Survey-2012.pdf
4. Marvel, J., Lyter, D., Peltola, P., Strizek, G., & Morton, B. (2006). *Teacher attrition and mobility: Results from the 2004–05 teacher follow-up survey*. (NCES 2007–307.) Washington, DC: U.S. Department of Education, Institute of Education Sciences, National Center for Education Statistics. Retrieved from http://nces.ed.gov/pubs2007/2007307.pdf

5. Fenton, B. (2009). Hiring an aligned instructional staff. *ASCD Express, 5*(5). Retrieved from http://www.ascd.org/ascd-express/vol5/505-fenton.aspx

6. TNTP. (2012). *The irreplaceables: Understanding the real retention crisis in America's urban schools.* Retrieved from http://tntp.org/assets/documents/TNTP_Irreplaceables_PrincipalGuide_Web.pdf

7. Wahlstrom, K., Seashore Louis, K., Leithwood, K., & Anderson, S. (2010). *Learning from Leadership Project: Investigating the links to improved student learning.* Minneapolis, MN: Center for Applied Research and Educational Improvement, University of Minnesota.

8. Manno, C., & Firestone, W. (2008). Content is the subject: How teacher leaders with different subject knowledge interact with teachers. In M. Mangin & S. T. Stoelinga (Eds.), *Effective teacher leadership: Using research to inform and reform* (pp. 36–54). New York, NY: Teachers College, Columbia University; Lord, B., Cress, K., & Miller, B. (2008). Teacher leadership in support of large-scale mathematics and science education reform. In M. Mangin & S. T. Stoelinga (Eds.), *Effective teacher leadership: Using research to inform and reform* (pp. 55–76). New York, NY: Teachers College, Columbia University.

9. Croft, A., Coggshall, J. G., Dolan, M. Powers, E., & Killion, J. (2010). *Job-embedded professional development: What it is, who is responsible, and how to get it done well.* Washington, DC: National Comprehensive Center for Teacher Quality. Retrieved from http://learningforward.org/docs/pdf/jobembeddedpdbrief.pdf?sfvrsn=0

10. Rabin, R. (2014). *Blended learning for leadership: The CCL approach.* Greensboro, NC: Center for Creative Leadership. Retrieved from http://www.ccl.org/Leadership/pdf/research/BlendedLearningLeadership.pdf

11. New Leaders. (2014). Emerging Leaders Program implementation study preliminary findings. Unpublished raw data and analyses.

12. Lord, B., Cress, K., & Miller, B. (2008). Teacher leadership in support of large-scale mathematics and science education reform. In M. M. Mangin & S. R. Stoelinga (Eds.), *Effective teacher leadership: Using research to inform and reform.* New York, NY: Teachers College Press.

13. Yoon, K. S., Duncan, T., Lee, S. W.-Y., Scarloss, B., & Shapley, K. (2007). *Reviewing the evidence on how teacher professional development affects student achievement.* Washington, DC: U.S. Department of Education, Institute of Education Sciences, National Center for Education Evaluation and Regional Assistance, Regional Educational Laboratory Southwest. Retrieved from http://ies.ed.gov/ncee/edlabs

14. Farkas, S., Johnson, J., and Duffet, A., with Syat, B., & Vine, J. (2003). *Rolling up their sleeves: Superintendents and principals talk about what's needed to fix public schools.* New York, NY: Public Agenda. Retrieved from http://www.publicagenda.org/files/rolling_up_their_sleeves.pdf

15. Marshall, K. (2009). *Rethinking teacher supervision and evaluation.* San Francisco, CA: Jossey-Bass; Platt, A., Tripp, C., Ogden, W., & Fraser, R. (2000). *The Skillful Leader: Confronting Mediocre Teaching.* Action, MA: Research for Better Teaching; Bambrick-Santoyo, P. (2012). *Leverage Leadership: A practical guide to building exceptional schools.* San Francisco, CA: Jossey-Bass.

16. Jackson, R. (2013). *Never underestimate your teachers: Instructional leadership for excellence in every classroom.* Alexandria, VA: ASCD.

17. Robinson, V. (2011). *Student-centered leadership.* San Francisco, CA: Jossey-Bass.

18. Leana, C. (2011). *The missing link in school reform.* Stanford, CA: Stanford Social Innovation Review; Bryk, A., S., Sebring, P. B., Allensworth, E. M., Luppescu, S., & Easton, J. Q. (2010). *Organizing schools for improvement: Lessons from Chicago.* Chicago, IL: University of Chicago Press.

19. Barber, M., Whelan, F., & Clark, M. (2012). *Capturing the leadership premium: How the world's top school systems are building leadership capacity for the future.* New York: McKinsey.

20. Fullan, M. (2014). *The principal: Three keys to maximizing impact.* San Francisco, CA: Jossey-Bass.

21. Brosnan, M. (Spring, 2015). Humility, will and level 5 leadership: An interview with Jim Collins. Independent School Magazine.

Chapter 6: Planning and Operations

1. Horng, E., Klasik, D., & Loeb, S. (2009). *Principal time-use and school effectiveness* (CALDER Working Paper 34). Washington, DC: Urban Institute.
2. Rice, J. K. (2010). *Principal effectiveness and leadership in an era of accountability: What research says.* Washington, DC: National Center for Analysis of Longitudinal Data in Educational Research. Retrieved from www.caldercenter.org/upload/CALDER-Research-and-Policy-Brief-8.pdf; Grissom, J. A., & Loeb, S. (2009). *Triangulating principal effectiveness: How perspectives of parents, teachers, and assistant principals identify the central importance of managerial skills* (CALDER Working Paper 35). Washington, DC: Urban Institute.
3. Hess, F. (2013). *Cage-busting leadership.* Cambridge, MA: Harvard Education Press.
4. Orr, M. T., King, C., & LaPointe, M. (2010). *Districts developing leaders: Lessons on consumer actions and program approaches from eight urban districts.* Waltham, MA: Education Development Center.
5. Covey, S. (1989). *The seven habits of highly effective people: Powerful lessons in personal change.* New York, NY: Simon & Schuster.
6. Lemov, D. (2010). *Teach like a champion: Forty-nine techniques that put students on the path to college.* San Francisco, CA: Jossey-Bass.
7. Lemov, D. (2010).
8. National SAM Innovation Project. Retrieved from www.samsconnect.com. The SAM approach teaches principals to identify other key staff who can serve as "first-responders" for regular, important school issues such as parent questions, student discipline issues, and district information requests.
9. Aronson, J., Zimmerman, J., & Carlos, L. (1998). *Improving student achievement by extending school: Is it just a matter of time?* PACE Media/Education Writers Seminar; Walberg, H. J. (1998). Uncompetitive American schools: Causes and cures. In D. Ravitch (Ed.), *Brookings Papers on Education Policy* (pp. 173–205). Washington, DC: Brookings Institution; Northeast and Islands Regional Educational Laboratory. (1998). *Block scheduling: Innovations with time.* Providence, RI: Northeast and Islands Regional Educational Laboratory; Harmston, M. T., Pliska, A. M., Ziomek, R. L., & Hackmann, D. G. (2003). *The relationship between schedule type and ACT assessment scores: A longitudinal study.* ACT, Inc.
10. Tennessee School Improvement Planning Process. Airways Middle School (2007–2008). Retrieved from www.mcsk12.net/schools/airways.ms/site/documents/AirwaysHybridSIP07Final.a68.doc
11. Tennessee School Improvement Planning Process. (2007–2008).
12. Leithwood, K., Louis, K. S., Anderson, S., & Wahlstrom, K. (2004). *How leadership influences student learning.* New York, NY: Wallace Foundation.

Chapter 7: Personal Leadership

1. Brown, S. L., Herron, S. Y., & King, G. (2008). Assessing dispositions of administrative intern candidates. *AASA Journal of Scholarship and Practice, 5*(1), 27–35.
2. Day, C., Sammons, P., Leithwood, K., Hopkins, D., Harris, A., Gu, Q., & Brown, E. (2010) *Ten strong claims about successful school leadership.* Nottingham: National College for Leadership of Schools and Children's Services.
3. Collins, J. (2001). *Good to great: Why some companies make the leap and others don't.* New York, NY: HarperCollins.
4. Dweck, C. (2007). *Mindset: The new psychology of success.* New York, NY: Ballantine Books.
5. Fullan, M. (2014). *The principal: Three keys to maximizing impact.* San Francisco, CA: Jossey-Bass.

6. Nelson Laird, T. (2014). Reconsidering the inclusion of diversity in the curriculum. *Diversity and Democracy, 17*(4), 12–14.

7. Bryk, A., Sebring, P., Allensworth, E., Easton, J., & Luppescu, S. (2010). *Organizing schools for improvement: Lessons from Chicago*. Chicago, IL: University of Chicago Press.

8. For more resources on this work, we recommend Stone, D., Patton, B., & Heen, S. (2010). *Difficult conversations: How to discuss what matters most*. New York, NY: Penguin Books; Scott, S. (2004). *Fierce conversations: Achieving success at work and in life one conversation at a time*. New York, NY: Berkley, particularly the chapter "Take Responsibility for Your Emotional Wake."

9. Bryk, A., & Schneider, B. (2003). Trust in schools: A core resource for school reform. Educational Leadeship. *60*(6), 40–45.

10. Covey, S. (2006). *The speed of trust*. New York, NY: Free Press.

11. Heifetz, R. (2014). *Can leadership be taught?* Lecture at Harvard Kennedy School. Retrieved from https://www.youtube.com/watch?v=xd72Us7tlQI

12. Heifetz, R., Grashow, A., & Linsky, M. (2009, July–August). Leadership in a (permanent) crisis. *Harvard Business Review. 87*(7–8); 62–9; 153. Retrieved from http://www.ocvets4pets.com/archive17/Leadership_in_a__Permanent__Crisis_-_HBR.org.pdf

13. Blanchard, K. (January, 2010). Mastering the art of change. Training Journal. Retrieved from www.kenblanchard.com/img/pub/blanchard_mastering_the_art_of_change.pdf

14. Heifetz, R. (1994). *Leadership without easy answers*. Cambridge: Harvard Business Press.

15. Collins, J. (2001).

16. School Leaders Network. (2014). *Churn: The high cost of principal turnover*. Retrieved from https://connectleadsucceed.org/sites/default/files/principal_turnover_cost.pdf

17. School Leaders Network. (2014).

18. Mitgang, L. (2007). *Getting principal mentoring right: Lessons from the field*. New York, NY: Wallace Foundation.

19. School Leaders Network. (2014).

20. School Leaders Network. (2014).

21. O'Connell, A. (2015, July 22). How a charter school giant revamped its culture to put a stop to burnout. *Fast Company*. Retrieved from http://www.Fastcompany.Com/3048498/Most-Creative-People/How-A-Charter-School-Giant-Revamped-Its-Culture-To-Put-A-Stop-To-Burnout

Chapter 8: Principal Coaching Using the TLF

1. Bambrick-Santoyo, P. (2012). *Leverage Leadership: A practical guide to building exceptional schools*. San Francisco, CA: Jossey-Bass.

2. Ikemoto, G., Taliaferro, L., Fenton, B., & Davis, J. (2014). *Great Principals at Scale*. George W. Bush Institute, Alliance to Reform Education Leadership, and New Leaders.

3. Ikemoto, G., Taliaferro, L., Fenton, B., & Davis, J. (2014).

Conclusion

1. Lieberman, M. (July 8, 2015). "Powell principal departs after expending enrollment, community engagement." *The Northwest Current*. Vol. XLVIII, No. 27.

INDEX

A

Academic success classes (ASC), 93–94
Accelerations, 55, 89, 95–96
Acorn Woodland Elementary School, Oakland, California, 132–136, 142–143, 238
Action plan: four key steps for, 29, 31; and goal setting, 29, 31, 40–47, 194, 196, 197; monitoring and adjusting, 29, 31, 47–48; questions to review, 260; sample, 43–45. *See also* School planning
Adams, C., 212–214
Adaptive leadership, 229, 231, 245–250
Adrianzén, M., 188, 189–190
Adult and student efficacy, 100, 114–120, 121
Adult-student relationships, supportive, 101, 125–127
Advisories and referrals, 124–127
Aguilar, C., 118
Aguirre, C., 145–146
Airways Middle School, Memphis, Tennessee, 219–221
Alfred Nobel Elementary School, Chicago, 188–190, 199
Aligned assessments, 52
Aligned curriculum, 53, 54, 56–67
Alignment across the district, 258
Assessments, interim, 76, 77, 78
Attendance rates by grade, 32, 39

B

Baity, L., 85, 86, 87
Bambrick-Santoyo, P., 82, 180, 261
Barber, M., 184
Behavioral expectations, 21, 22–24, 25, 100, 109–114
Belief based and goal driven leadership, 228, 230, 232–236
Benjamin, S., 20–21, 23, 24, 26, 27–28, 29, 111
Benjamin Banneker Academic High School, Washington, DC, 125–127
Berger, A., 125–127
Bladensburg High School, Prince George's County, Maryland, 202–206

Blanchard, K., 246
Bloom's taxonomy, 60
Boston Collegiate Charter School, Boston, Massachusetts, 161, 178–179, 191
Brooklyn Latin School, Brooklyn, New York, 153–155, 156, 157, 191
Brown, D., 225
Bruce Randolph School, Denver, Colorado, 111–114, 125
Bryk, T., 240
Budget: and external partnerships, 195, 217–218; and facilities, 195, 218–221; as part of planning and operations, 195; and resources, 195, 211–217
Bullying and diversity, 133

C

Callahan, E., 161, 179
Carbone, J., 233–236
Carmona, A., 215–217
Challenge 2010 plan, 112, 114
Change, managing, 246–247
Character and competence, 240–241
Classroom observers and meeting facilitators, supporting ILT members as, 167–168
Classroom practices and instruction, 53, 54, 68–75
Coaching principals: and alignment across the district, 258; and district-level strategies, 263–266; and goal setting, 260–261; mid- and end-of-year reviews, 262–263; and personal leadership approaches, 263; planning time for, 261; and school diagnosis, 259–260; targeted visits and walk-throughs for, 261–262, 266; tools for, 266; Transformational Leadership Framework (TLF) for, 257–258
Cognitive rigor matrix, Hess's, 60
Collaborative teacher team structures, 186–190
College and career aspirations, 115, 116, 119, 121
Collins, J., 228, 251
Community and district relations, 221–225
Cooper, T., 73, 74–75